In Those Days as Today

In Those Days as Today

Preaching Through the Book of Judges

James Ellis III

RESOURCE *Publications* · Eugene, Oregon

IN THOSE DAYS AS TODAY
Preaching Through the Book of Judges

Copyright © 2025 James Ellis III. All rights reserved. Except for brief quotations in critical publications or reviews, no part of this book may be reproduced in any manner without prior written permission from the publisher. Write: Permissions, Wipf and Stock Publishers, 199 W. 8th Ave., Suite 3, Eugene, OR 97401.

Resource Publications
An Imprint of Wipf and Stock Publishers
199 W. 8th Ave., Suite 3
Eugene, OR 97401

www.wipfandstock.com

PAPERBACK ISBN: 979-8-3852-4893-3
HARDCOVER ISBN: 979-8-3852-4894-0
EBOOK ISBN: 979-8-3852-4895-7
VERSION NUMBER 08/27/25

To the cadre of colleagues, mentors, and congregants who have journeyed with me—rubbing weary shoulders, slaying demons (mostly our own), holding energetic babies who drool, and discipling the people God sends our way. An unpopular truth of life and ministry is that *everybody ain't for everybody*. You can only genuinely do life with those who want to do it with you. The isolation is real. Hang in there.

To the late Dr. Harold T. Lewis—who I knew through his service at Calvary Episcopal Church in Pittsburgh, Pennsylvania; to longtime pastors Rock Dillaman (Allegheny Center Alliance Church) and Andy Davis (First Baptist Church of Belton); to retired pastor-scholar Dr. Emmanuel McCall; and to Dr. Stacy Minger of Asbury Theological Seminary: These saintly practitioners offered me accessible, exceptional, humble, and sober evidence as to why preaching passionately and accurately, and doing so within one's convictions and abilities, is vital. There is little worse than preaching nonsense, except perhaps preaching while trying to be someone you are not.

To Renata, my wife of 18 years. If people ever start buying these books I write in droves, maybe we will finally get that off-the-grid home on the East Coast, with the Atlantic Ocean in the backyard. Thanks for putting up with my vampire-like nighttime routines and my long-winded text messages.

To the small-but-mighty people of Maplewood Reformed Church: Thank you for helping me tame lawn-invading squirrels and navigate the drama of becoming a first-time homeowner of an old house—all while we journeyed together through the Book of Judges and the full counsel of God's Word. Whether God's plan keeps us together for nine more months, six more years, or some other stretch of time, please know of my deep affection for you. No matter what, my prayer for you remains: *May the Lord our God be your anchor, in joy and in pain, with you now and forever more, until the very end of the age.* Amen.

Contents

Acknowledgements | ix
Introduction | xiii
Setting the Scene | xix

In Those Days: Joshua 24:14–18, September 10, 2023 | 1
Matters of Loyalty: Judges 1—Judges 2:5, September 17, 2023 | 5
Trusting God with Another Generation: Judges
  2:6–15, September 24, 2023 | 9
Divine Compassion: Judges 2:16–23, October 1, 2023 | 13
Evaluations of Submission: Judges 3:1–11, October 8, 2023 | 17
An Unlikely, Likely Choice: Judges 3:12–31, October 15, 2023 | 23
Passing the Buck: Judges 4, October 22, 2023 | 30
Sometimes We Need to Sing: Judges 5, October 29, 2023 | 36
The Weight of Asking God to Wait:
  Judges 6:1–18, November 5, 2023 | 41
Fear's Familiar Tentacles: Judges 6:19–40, November 12, 2023 | 48
A Tale of Two Testimonies: Judges 7, November 19, 2023 | 54
Leadership Woes: Judges 8:1–21, January 7, 2024 | 60
Welcome to the Club: Judges 8:22–34, January 21, 2024 | 65
The Smokescreen of Sameness: Judges 9:1–29, January 28, 2024 | 70
The Company You Keep: Judges 9:30–57, February 11, 2024 | 75
Despicable Me: Judges 10, February 18, 2024 | 80
The Consequences of Rejection: Judges 11:1–11, April 7, 2024 | 85

A Desperate Pledge: Judges 11:12–33, April 14, 2024 | 90
No More Passing the Buck: Judges 11:34–40, April 21, 2024 | 95
Obituaries, Hypomnesia, and Eternity: Judges 12, April 28, 2024 | 99
The Calm Before the Storm: Judges 13, May 5, 2024 | 104
It Is Too Late to Say "Sorry" Now?: Judges 14:1–9, Mother's Day, May 12, 2024 | 109
Dumb, Dumb, and Dumber: Judges 14:10–20, May 19, 2024 | 114
A Popular Fool's Game: Judges 15, May 26, 2024 | 120
But You Know Better: Judges 16:1–14, June 2, 2024 | 125
The Tulip That Grew from Concrete: Judges 16:15–22, June 9, 2024 | 131
Appreciating the Sequel: Judges 16:23–31, Father's Day, June 16, 2024 | 136
The Midnight Train to Georgia: Judges 17, June 23, 2024 | 142
When the Clergy Become Compromised: Judges 18, June 30, 2024 | 148
There's a Flag on the Play: Judges 19:1–15, July 7, 2024 | 154
Wicked Men: Judges 19:16–30, July 28, 2024 | 159
When It Happens on Our Watch: Judges 20:1–23, August 4, 2024 | 166
But What Happens When? Judges 20:24–48, August 11, 2024 | 170
When Even Good is Bad: Judges 21:25, August 18, 2024 | 175

Bibliography | 181

Acknowledgements

I CANNOT SAY IF it makes me an old-school preacher or just a stubborn one, but none of these sermons was preached—let alone assembled into a collection—with the crafty aid of research assistants, ghostwriters, or technological chatbots. If you are too busy, or consider yourself too important, to exegete a passage and labor over how to boldly proclaim its truth, then perhaps you are not truly called to this work, I don't care how big of a following you have. My dearly departed mentor, Dr. James E. Massey, once remarked: "This digital culture has made more information so readily available. . . [it] has accustomed us all more to mechanics and movement, rather than to meanings. We are preoccupied with surface matters, not depth in sermons. And the scriptures are always 'deep calling to deep.'" My hat goes off to the preachers who have been faithfully proclaiming God's Word longer than I've been alive—most of them without the now-standard conveniences of instant access and effortless communication. I will gladly bodyslam any New Age preacher who suggests that all their gadgets and gizmos make them smarter—or better equipped—for this sacred work. Just give me their names. I'll take care of the rest.

Pastors' wives—and their children, if they have them—often carry a heavy burden because of their husband's vocation. I know ministry families today come in many forms, but this is the dynamic I know best. Subtly or overtly, some churches expect a two-for-one deal like they're ordering fast food: they draw on the gifts of both husband and wife, while only he receives a paycheck. And the opinions are endless. Whether you take vacation—or *when* you take it. Whether the wife attends VBS or leads the women's ministry—or not. Whether your kids participate in the Easter egg hunt—or don't. Everyone has something to say. And that's not even counting the preaching. Most Sundays, the husband is in the pulpit doing the hard work of proclaiming God's Word—while the "first lady" sits through it all, again and again, often under just as much scrutiny. She and her husband are unable to arbitrarily choose their church like those outside of the pastoral vocation can and that, if we're honest, is beautiful some days and really, really sucky other days. Shoutout to pastors' wives around the world who carry that title, but are not only—and certainly not primarily—defined by it.

Specifically, when it comes to my wife, I deeply value her support and affirmation—but I also make it clear where I am serving: she won't be at every happening. If you want me, then you need to adjust to that new normal. It is *my job* and even I will not be at every event, so she definitely will not. She loves God, loves the Church, and wants me to thrive wherever we're sent but part of honoring her means doing what I can to remove damaging expectations. Sometimes she needs—and frankly, deserves—a break. As much as she is a committed member of the congregation, her first ministry is to walk beside me as my helper. And she cannot do that well if she's stretched too thin trying to meet every varied thought of what a "pastor's wife" should be or do. So, I'm perfectly fine with that, whether others are or not. That's just how it's going to be.

Finally, none of this would be possible without the intimate, powerful hand of God—granting undeserved gifts, granting understanding, and opening doors that only He can close. I'll be honest: it's been hard at times to watch cut-rate, arrogant, biblically and theologically crooked preachers enjoy booming book sales and generous compensation, while those striving to do it the "right way" often struggle just to make a living. But this tense dance around the prosperity of the wicked is nothing new—it's ancient news. In the end, as Psalm 73:24 reminds us, our task is to seek the Lord's counsel and trust him to handle the rest. Still, *the struggle is real* and godly ministers often suffer in silence on these and related topics.

In his 1980 book *Biblical Preaching: The Development and Delivery of Expository Messages*, the great pulpiteer Haddon W. Robinson wrote:

> Those in the pulpit face the pressing temptation to deliver some message other than that of the Scriptures—a political system (either right-wing or left-wing), a theory of economics, a new religious philosophy, old religious slogans, or a trend in psychology. Ministers can proclaim anything in a stained-glass voice at 11:30 a.m. on Sunday morning following the singing of hymns.

Yet when they fail to preach the Scriptures, they abandon their authority. No longer do they confront their hearers with a word from God. That is why most modern preaching evokes little more than a wide yawn. God is not in it.[1]

I cannot preach like Haddon W. Robinson, James E. Massey, Peter J. Gomes, H. Beecher Hicks Jr. whatsoever, or anyone else for that matter—and I learned a long time ago that I am not supposed to. I suck at being them. But God, in His grace, has equipped me to cultivate the particular trailmix of traits He's given me, and to be the best version of myself I can be. So, that's where I keep my focus. Believe it or not, I am really good at being *James Ellis the Third—no middle name.* May the Spirit of the living God keep the flame burning brightly within me to preach like it matters—because it does.

—James
www.jamesellis3.com

---

1. Haddon W. Robinson, *Biblical Preaching: The Development and Delivery of Expository Messages* (Grand Rapids, MI: Baker Book House, 1980), 21.

Introduction

Though far from being a recluse, I am a private person. A proud introvert. Security-conscious. Cautious by instinct and conviction. I care deeply for people, but I do not assume that everyone means well. Moreover, I do not believe the average day comes, like a gift card, preloaded with divine insulation from harm or injustice purely because I love God. That's not how life works. That's make believe—not reality. Theologically speaking, humans are not merely just a little off kilter. We are bonkers!

Apart from Jesus Christ, we are all submerged in what Scripture calls sin. It shapes our motives, distorts our thoughts, and promotes actions that reflect the worst of humankind, whether it looks that way or not. Yes, we can still do good. Kindness and the pursuit of earthly justice are accessible. Smiles are free. Hugs are powerful. But left to ourselves, we lack the ability to truly "do no harm." God's standard is perfection and every single one of us fall short by default.

This truth is captured with raw beauty and sobriety by Cleophus LaRue, who once commented: "Humans, at their best, are some odd mixture of dust and divinity . . . some strange assemblage of treasure and trash. . .in all of us there is a healthy smattering of gold and garbage."[1] I believe that. I see it in myself. I see it in the world.

As quiet and insular as I am, God's leadership has obliged me to foster a commitment to obedience, imperfect though it is. I strive to listen and respond when the Spirit leads—no matter how uncomfortable it

---

1. Cleophus J. LaRue, Jr. retired from Princeton Theological Seminary in 2024 after 27 years of service, concluding his tenure as the Francis Landey Patton Professor of Homiletics. The quote comes from his sermon on Acts 17:16–23, titled "Why Bother?", delivered as a guest preacher at National Presbyterian Church in Washington, DC, on August 15, 2010.

may feel. And I can tell you that it is often just that: *uncomfortable*. This is how I came to be a pastor, preacher, and author. It is all upstream from my natural disposition. But it bespeaks what you sign up for in becoming a Christian. You surrender your will for what God says is best, for you individually and for humanity at-large.

This book is a collection of sermons preached to a local congregation—Maplewood Reformed Church, situated in a modest town by Lake Michigan called Holland. We are at 133 East 34th Street. Preaching there week after week, as their pastor, in a post-pandemic era that can fixate on performance, algorithms, analytics, and optics, sometimes felt like an act of futility. That is not a dig at my dear Maplewood crew, mind you; it just reflects today's dominant societal dynamics no matter where you are. There's no denying that attention spans have shrunk considerably. Many people are conditioned by seeker-sensitive, motivational talks devoid of biblical substance that impersonate sermons. They are fluffily engineered for fame, not spiritual transformation. Plagiarism is more prominent and acceptable than ever.

Complicating matters further, I'm a manuscript preacher. This means, at the very least, that I type my sermons out, which amount to somewhere between 2,000 and 3,000 words each time, each week. That's *a lot* of writing even if you enjoy writing. God bless those who can, but I am not gifted in the areas of improvisation. The Holy Spirit moves in advance during my days of research, writing, and preparation *and* during the specific instance of proclamation. As much as sermons were meant to be preached in real-time to real people, there is something special about revisiting what a preacher has said weeks, months, or years after the fact that is in writing. Thus, sermons should ultimately be written not for grammatical perfection, *per se*, or scholarly precision, but for God's life-changing Word to be explained. Nevertheless, with literacy waning these days, written sermons are not something many people are accustomed to anymore.

Beyond the literacy angle, disseminating a book of sermons is risky because it opens me up to irrational critique or misunderstanding. And we know, social media and the Internet have encouraged everybody to become armchair theologians. But even fellow, experienced preachers might legitimately take issue with my exegesis, illustrations, or application. This comes with the territory, but it can still be frustrating. Preaching reveals who you are and what you believe most, in a markedly vulnerable way that only preachers, especially those who pastor those they preach to, really understand. It wins some, offends others. And that's okay. I'm cool with that. *I said what I said.* I didn't preach these sermons in the first place to please Maplewood and certainly haven't assembled them here thinking everyone will agree with everything. My hope is to have honored God, and nudged people to take His Word seriously, to serve Him more fully.

This collection centers on the Book of Judges—my favorite in the Old Testament. Classified as a historical book of the Bible, it is routinely neglected by preachers; I'd say ranking just behind Leviticus and Numbers in what most of them avoid like the plague, other than an isolated sermon here or there. Yet, I find it tremendously relevant and by virtue of what is shared in 2 Timothy 3:16–17, it must always be timely since the Apostle Paul stated: "All Scripture is God-breathed and is useful for teaching, rebuking, correcting and training in righteousness, so that the servant of God may be thoroughly equipped for every good work." *Judges is in the Bible.* Consequently, we cannot dismiss it or childishly explain it away to make us feel better.

Judges is full of blood and guts. It is scandalous and disturbing—it reveals the worst in God's people and exemplifies God's abundant grace, time and time again, while acknowledging that a final day of divine reckoning fast approaches. It is a book about cycles: sin, consequence, deliverance, forgetfulness. *Repeat.* It is a mirror to human nature and a cry for holy intervention.

I preached these sermons to people who, like many churchgoers, were not super familiar with Judges. Some, in decades of faithful attendance at Maplewood, shared that they could count sermons on one hand from the book. Lots of preachers shy away from violence and chaos. And I understand the tendency, but I also believe that Judges is theologically rich, socially significant, and convicting. It shows what happens when we demand kings, reject God's covenant, and sabotage peace. If a preacher can't connect those dots to today's world, we have a huge problem. I have a hard time trusting preachers who conveniently mow around controversial passages and complex books of the Bible.

I write and preach as someone who didn't grow up in the church. I came of age in the DMV during the volatile '80s and '90s, surrounded by instability and exposed to some less than pleasant behavior in a *hood adjacent* life that necessitated toggling between safety at home and violence, and even gunplay, at school. Add to that my experience as an African American ministering mostly in predominantly White, and often non-Baptist spaces (being ordained in the Baptist tradition myself)—and it becomes clear that I've rarely been *comfortable* in ministry. I do, however, know a thing or two about being a fish out of water. But I also know the hand of God seeing fit to send me into spaces where my voice might not be expected or appreciated, but is still necessary.

And the thing is, I don't need anyone's confirmation of this. I have receipts and more importantly, a testimony. Wearing rose-colored glasses doesn't serve anyone well. I believe Christians are called to be salt and light—not to retreat from the world, but not to become advocates of how the world goes about its business either. We are ambassadors of a Kingdom that upends every human power structure. One day, sorrow and injustice will end. But for now, we live in the tension of a broken, beloved world. That is the *already but not yet*, and Judges speaks directly into that paradox.

Lastly, I say this with full humility and full confidence: I am not a special preacher. To view myself as elite is wrong for all sorts of reasons that it would take too long to explain here. In fact, I hope that I'm a better pastor than I am a preacher. Nonetheless, I'm not blind to the preaching gifts God has given me. I've been graced with a temperament and voice, a capacity to understand and explain Scripture, and a passion for it. I did not ask for it—but I've grown to love preaching. Respectfully, I am not a "three points and a poem" preacher. You might hear a reference to Shania Twain next to Buju Banton or MC Lyte. You could hear the retelling of a scene from *New Jack City* in the same breath as me referring to the wonderful film *Tortilla Soup* or a documentary I've watched. I'm a firm believer that if I want to help the Bible, and the application of its rich treasures, to come alive to people, in exegeting the text I must look for bold, relatable, contextual connections to life as we know it to be.

Also, I abhor preaching with low expectations of the hearers. Regardless of any perceived social background or education level, I believe the pulpit must speak in ways that are familiar to people while also raising the bar—whatever that looks like. Minds are meant to be stretched and sanctified. It should not be about impressing others; just faithfully reflecting the image of the God who created us, which means He created our minds and values them.

Preaching makes for a strange life. It is satisfying, but also highly differentiated. *If you know, you know*—and if you don't, that's fine, too, but maybe this book will help you understand a bit better. Preachers need

INTRODUCTION

to know this: You will never please everyone. Fixating on pleasing people turns applause into an idol and treats God as a spectator.

This book is not about applause. It is about faithfulness.

In *Preaching Through a Storm: Confirming the Power of Preaching in the Tempest of Church Conflict*, H. Beecher Hicks, Jr. captures one critical dynamic of preaching with piercing clarity:

> Authentic preaching is not the preacher's product. It is, at its highest and best, a response to the whisperings of the Almighty and a faithful recital of a Word which comes not *from* us, but *through* us. The preacher-pastor who is more concerned about what people think than how people live in response to the demands of the gospel is little more than a leaky vessel in search of a storm.[2]

I am nothing more than a lowly raggamuffin in need of bread, who was found, even sought out by the Bread of Life, to be fed, sealed, protected, equipped, and sent to help facilitate for others what was so graciously done for me.

In each sermon—the New International Version (NIV) Bible translation is referenced throughout—you will see this sentence from Judges mentioned as a refrain: "In those days Israel had no king; everyone did as they saw fit." May the Lord keep us tethered to him on this beautifully wacky journey called life.

Welcome to Judges!

—James Ellis III, DMin
Maplewood Reformed Church
Winebrenner Theological Seminary
Holland, Michigan

---

2. H. Beecher Hicks, Jr., *Preaching Through a Storm: Confirming the Power of Preaching in the Tempest of Church Conflict* (Grand Rapids: Zondervan, 1987), 102.

Setting the Scene

I AM NOT A fan of book introductions. Perhaps it's because they often feel so redundant or long-winded. When I don't skip them entirely, I sometimes find myself muttering, "Get on with it already" while reading them. Therefore, I hope the remarks you've just read felt worthwhile. If not, trust me, I understand. We can still be friends. I have included this section not to belabor the point, but because of the distinct nature of this collected work.

These sermons weren't preached to an online audience of strangers who, however sincerely though incorrectly, consider me their pastor. My congregation is what I call a highly manageable size. "Small but mighty," I often tell them. I know all our members by name. I love them. And I believe we are better for having journeyed through Judges together. Chances are, you don't know them—or me—from a can of paint. So, offering a bit of context about them, how we came together, and the church's story feels like the least I can do.

This is my second time sensing God's call to Holland, Michigan—an uncommon move for an African American, if you know anything about the area. In 2016, my wife and I left Washington, DC, when I accepted a chaplaincy role at Hope College. We stayed until 2019 before moving 2,350 miles northwest—more than two hours north of Seattle—to British Columbia. We weathered COVID-19 there, which hit just six months after our arrival, while I served as lead chaplain at a Canadian and overtly Christian university (which is a kind of anomaly in Canada), overseeing a team of full-time chaplains, part-time staff, and student leaders.

As 2022 approached and the pandemic began to ease, we felt drawn back to U.S. soil. My wife and I grew up as military brats and while our previous time in Holland was fine, we weren't desperate to return, although as the possibility was considered it felt more compelling on various fronts. What attracted me to Maplewood Reformed Church was their humility and honesty. From what I've gathered, they are, understandably, not the same church they once were, just in positive ways. Loss—of members, of momentum—has a way of repositioning people for deeper spiritual growth, if they desire it. The search committee was transparent. They shared past and present budgets and gave me their honest assessment of how the church arrived at this point.

During my first stint in Holland, I had never even heard of Maplewood. This is not surprising in a town of 35,000 with around 170 churches. Crazy, right? But what I appreciated most was that they didn't waste my time or theirs. They told me straight-up a range of what they could afford to pay me, even acknowledging that I could, rightfully so, make more at a larger church. I was honest that if I did become their pastor, I likely could not make it a long-term place of service outside of the compensation increasing, which they not only grasped but supported.

We worked through our differences, like baptism. I hold to believer's baptism by immersion (you gotta get dunked deep in the water!), whereas they practice infant baptism. It was a wonderfully God-honoring process. And by God's grace, it still is. If things changed tomorrow and our relationship soured, as sad as I'd be, I would still say: they've been good to me, and we've been good to each other. This has easily been the most fulfilling church assignment of my career. They are not perfect, but they have been the perfect church for me in this season. We trust God with whatever comes next.

Yet, ours is a precarious, though increasingly common situation, except that I'm African American and the congregation is predominantly White. In my experience, clergy in the U.S., regardless of background, rarely serve outside their denomination or racial group—*they can, of course*, but usually don't. We tend to favor familiar, easy, homogeneous spaces. I doubt that kind of tribal allegiance will serve the Church well in the days ahead, but, hey, I can only do my part.

I will say that I have little patience for people of *all backgrounds* who wax poetic about the importance of racial reconciliation for Christ, but do so from the perch of privilege. James 2:26 makes it clear that the Bible embraces the idea that talk is cheap. I'll leave that alone to marinate. If Maplewood had still been thriving when our paths crossed, they likely wouldn't have highly considered a non-RCA pastor who isn't Reformed and isn't planning to become so. And hiring a Black pastor? As some current members have candidly shared with me, appropriately at leadership meetings where we've often discussed all this, it probably would've never happened either—not necessarily out of malice, but as a reflection of the cultural silos many people were stuck in at that time.

For most of its 84 years, Maplewood averaged 300–400 in worship. It was a neighborhood church tucked away, just off East 32nd Street in the *Maplewood neighborhood*—then a suburban edge of the city with new subdivisions popping up like Pop-Tarts. Families walked to church, sent their kids to Maplewood Elementary School a few blocks away, and knew each other. Many members worked at Hope College or Western Theological Seminary, both proud RCA institutions at the time. Including interim pastors, I'm Maplewood's 18th pastor. I cannot say whether this is good or bad, but I do know there were conflicts along the way—typical of any organization and church. The church once brimmed with extended families, neighbors, and friends of friends. Growth came more from those organic ties than from evangelistic effort, I think. Yet they've also long been a generous church, often giving half their annual budget to global missions. Years ago, they sold the next-door parsonage to help pay for a new roof, so the church remains debt-free.

Around 25 years ago, I estimate, Maplewood began slowly declining, like many older congregations. Younger generations wanted something new. The neighborhood shifted. Founding members passed away, retired to the South or West, or transferred to nearby churches to be closer to grandkids. Christianity's privileged place in society faded as well—by a few notches, or maybe 15, or 40. During all of this, Maplewood struggled to adjust. There very well may be more to the story, but if there's any juicy tea, I don't know it. No scandal or singular blow that I'm aware of led them to today. The pandemic hit hard, as it did everywhere, however. The debates over masks and safety measures only added to the strain and attrition.

Today, Maplewood consists of a large, well-kept building with a spacious sanctuary and balcony—whose capacity is just short of 500—nursery, gym, commercial-grade kitchen, and around 20 offices and classrooms. Once bustling with Sunday school classes, Bible studies, and children's ministries, most of those rooms now sit quiet. The building is a blessing—but also a burden to heat, cool, provide insurance for, clean, and maintain. It remains our greatest material asset, however, and we strive to steward it well. Part of my pastoral charge has been to help discern whether it appears God's will is for us to keep pressing forward or to prepare, in time, for a dignified closure. Not all closures result from failure. Sometimes it's just the natural conclusion of a church's life cycle. People don't live forever, so why do we assume every Second Baptist, 18th Street Presbyterian, or Community Church will?

The verdict is still out on where God will lead us, but we've recently signed leasing agreements with local groups to partner in sharing the building. That passive income will help underwrite our budget, but we're aware that to survive, let alone thrive, we need younger members and a good number of them. Depending on the time of year—especially with snowbirds retreating every so often to Arizona and Florida—we have 25–30 people in worship. Most are in their 70s to 90s and have been retired for some time. Our eldest member is 101. We're talking about former teachers (one taught for 49 years), engineers, nurses, a family physician, business owners, factory workers, veterinarians, machinists, photographers, and homemakers. Several are widows or widowers. Some are married. Others never were. During my time here, our longest-married couple reached 67 years before the husband died last fall. From the pulpit, I get to see a lot, so I can tell you who tends to doze off and when, who listens with their eyes closed, who takes notes, who fiddles with their phone, and where everyone sits.

When I preach, I try to speak to Maplewood's most present generations—referencing their music, books, and history when and how I can—especially since many are lifelong residents of Holland and the West Michigan region, with a few who have been at the church virtually their entire lives. But I also incorporate contemporary culture, because if we truly want to welcome new and younger people, I must offer both comfort and challenge in what I say. None of it is an exact science. It takes discipline to proclaim the Word of God in ways that stretch across generations. This is the congregation I preached to each Sunday in this Judges collection over a year's time. They are great!

They laugh at some of my jokes and entertain my love for movies, music, and books, and even say, "*Amen*" now, which is a big, big deal! We have fun, we cry, and we grapple with serious questions from Scripture and what is happening in the world. Preaching in a local church, especially as a solo pastor, is hard—rewarding, but hard. Most of us don't have the luxury of *just preaching*. We're not sitting by a body of water reading in contemplative bliss. No, we research, write, and rehearse sermons while also making hospital visits, printing bulletins, leading Bible studies, resolving conflicts, attending events, sending e-mails, and sometimes taking out the trash. And still, someone will say, "Oh, I thought all pastors did was preach."

It's a grind not meant for the faint of heart.

I preach and pastor because God has called me—not because the pay matches my education and experience, or because I'm always pumped about doing it, to be honest. But I take it seriously. As seriously as a heart attack. Because the One who empowers me to do this work does so for His glory. As 1 Samuel 15:22 reminds us, "Obedience is better than sacrifice."

In Those Days
Joshua 24:14–18, September 10, 2023

IN JUDGES, YOU'LL FIND this haunting refrain: "In those days Israel had no king; everyone did as they saw fit." As we move through the book, we will begin to see just how much *those days* mirror *these days*. The people of ancient Israel are not so different from the people around us—or even the people within us. Ever since Adam threw his wife under the proverbial bus in the garden to deflect blame, humanity has been born into insurrection against God. Helpless but assertive, like infants we do not know better, but reject the idea that we do not know better. We reject His boundaries and question His intentions. We want what we want when we want it. Period. In 1986, the Beastie Boys shouted to the world with their popular song, "(You Gotta) Fight for Your Right (To Party!)."[1] It was obviously tongue-in-cheek rebellion, but spiritually, it speaks to a deeper posture of protest: one that accuses the God of heaven of being unfair, controlling, and callous—a cosmic killjoy. If we even believe He exists at all, we still behave as though He needs our help to get it right. But Scripture reminds us that this behavior is far from innocent. It represents an intimately evil posture that pays the high wage of death.

Sin is persistent, calculating, and completely unbiased. Beauty, money, intelligence, fame, or strength—none of it can save. Blood must be paid with blood. This is why, ever so mercifully, God sent Jesus, His one and only Son, into a world that hated him, a world He created and loved, to set free whoever would believe in Him *by grace through faith*. Still, the rhythmic indictment of Judges sounds its alarm: "In those days Israel had no king; everyone did what was right in their own eyes." To understand Judges rightly, we must start with Joshua. It only makes sense. In the final

---

1. Beastie Boys, "(You Gotta) Fight for Your Right (To Party!)," 1986.

chapter of that book (Joshua 24), we find God recounting to His people the love story He's written with them at the center. He reminds them: "I gave you a land you did not labor for, and cities you did not build. You live in them and eat from vineyards and olive groves you did not plant."[2]

Despite Israel's lengthy record of grumbling, infighting, idolatry, and spiritual adultery, God has remained faithful. He has been their covenant-keeping God. But now Joshua, their aging leader, is nearing death. He knows how quickly their loyalty evaporates. His words are not just firm, they are protective. He pleads with his people who are first of all God's people, not to be wooed away by the sweet-smelling incense of the surrounding cultures, not to adopt the seductive beliefs of nearby nations. If they are to remain faithful, they cannot be moral contortionists. Compromise is not an option. And yet—compromise isn't always a bad word. There is such a thing as godly compromise. Christian living requires deference and servanthood. In marriage, in parenting, in friendship, in the workplace—healthy compromise is crucial. It denotes the cost of doing business with other human beings. However, there are limits that we get weird talking about all of a sudden. Some values—and more of them than we're comfortable admitting—cannot be up for negotiation. This does not speak to a tactical game of survival. Rather, it is about Christian ethics.

The problem arises when tolerance mutates into spiritual erosion. Improper compromise is subtle. It whispers that peace is worth any price. It asks you to betray your values just enough to blend in. And too many Christians go along to get along. But I beg you: for the love of God Almighty, don't be one of them. We compromise when we date or marry someone who does not share our most dearly held biblical convictions about God, especially regarding salvation—whether they follow Rastafarianism, the Five-Percent Nation, are Jehovah's Witnesses, or belong to Hebrew Israelite or nationalist groups. Maybe they're agnostic or atheist. Maybe they practice ancestor worship or Islam, Hinduism, or Wicca. Or maybe the issue isn't spiritual so much at first glance: perhaps they're just dishonest, abusive, addicted, or a wildly immature jerk—and we know it, but we move forward anyway. We override wisdom and ignore holiness because we're infatuated with their looks, their paycheck, their potential, or their personality. That's compromise. We let negative influences invade

---

2. Josh 24:13.

our lives for fear of being excluded or else left alone. That's compromise. Insider trading. Academic dishonesty. Flirting at work. Infidelity in any form. All of this is compromise.

Joshua knew the dangers. In verses 14–18, he gives no gentle suggestions. His command is clear: "Now, therefore, fear the Lord and serve Him with all faithfulness. Throw away the gods your ancestors worshiped and serve the Lord." Then he raises the stakes: "But if serving the Lord seems undesirable to you, choose this day whom you will serve. But as for me and my house—we will serve the Lord." Joshua's bold stand wasn't shaped by public opinion but by divine memory. He knew what God had done, for the people and for himself. And to their credit, if only temporarily, the Israelites replied, "We too will serve the Lord, because He is our God." But one command in verse 14 is often skipped or softened: "Fear the Lord." Some of us read that and retreat into tribalism, building walls God never commanded. Others slide into unorthodox softness, following whatever crowd seems most spiritual. Both are errors. The problem is we have become far too casual about God. We treat His presence as a given, His voice as background noise. We act as though He owes us attention, as though His grace is obligatory. But reverence is not outdated—it is timeless. It's the soul's only right response to a holy God.

Reverence is the remedy to compromise. Your emotions are too volatile. Your logic is too limited. Your flesh is too persuasive. But the Word of God is true. It's the only foundation worth building on. That, however, takes resolve. Jesus said it plainly in Matthew 10:28: "Do not fear those who kill the body but cannot kill the soul. Rather, fear him who can destroy both soul and body in hell." If Jesus is who he says He is, and if you've chosen to follow him as Lord and Savior, what business do you have watering down his truth to gain acceptance? Now hear me: believing the truth about God does not give you license to bully people into agreement. That's not the Gospel either. Nor should it lead you to silence, muting your convictions to avoid ever offending someone. Some of the strongest Christians I know are unshakably rooted in their faith, yet insanely humble and personable. They don't argue with everyone, but they also don't hide. When the time comes to speak up, they do so with accuracy, grace, and courage.

Judges demonstrates that compromise that contradicts God's Word is dangerous. As Old Testament scholar Lawson Stone puts it:

"Compromise, by its very nature, never announces itself as sin, but in its subtle degrees and shades, it undercuts the entire mission and life of the community of faith."[3] I've seen that firsthand. Back in 2016, when my wife Renata and I lived in Holland, she once went to bed without removing her contact lenses. It would prove to be a horrible oversight. By the next morning, she was in serious pain. She can be a bit of a drama queen, which I think even she can admit on a good day, but this time around I knew something was going on. A visit to the ophthalmologist revealed a deep scratch on her cornea caused by a lens that had essentially fused to her eyeball. Ouch! What seemed like a small, innocent neglect became a serious issue. That's how sin often works.

What feels insignificant in the moment can cause serious damage when left unchecked.

Thank God for healing—and thank God for the spiritual healing Christ offers us when we confess that we've royally compromised and then ask for forgiveness. Jesus died to overcome your brokenness and mine. He offers an exit from the crooked roads of misguided sovereignty and invites you to rest with him on higher ground, in a land flowing with milk and honey. But that promise requires a pledge: Allegiance to Jesus and rejection of the old self. The Bible is not soteriologically varied, I need you to know. Heaven isn't a "choose your own adventure" amusement park ride. There is no back door. No loophole. No cheat code. No shortcut. You either receive the gift of adoption through Jesus, or you don't. No compromise. God will never adjust Himself to suit your preferences. No compromise. Christians are not called to be porous, leaking with every cultural fad or value. We are called to stand, to hold, to persevere. Yes, grace abounds. Yes, God loves you. But still—we are duty-bound to reject compromise. "If serving the Lord seems undesirable to you, then choose this day whom you will serve."[4]

---

3. Philip W. Comfort, ed., *Joshua, Judges, Ruth (Cornerstone Biblical Commentary)*, 227.

4. Josh 24:15.

Matters of Loyalty
Judges 1—Judges 2:5, September 17, 2023

It shows up when Jardani Jovonovich, the once-retired assassin in the *John Wick* film series, uses the word *fealty*[1] while calling in favors from old allies—friends, business associates, and the feared Ruska Roma, a group of Russian gypsies who took him in as an orphan in Belarus. We've seen it adjudicated under pressure in *A Few Good Men* and glorified in the classic 1960 western *The Magnificent Seven*. We cheer when Denzel Washington's Robert McCall character, by *The Equalizer* trilogy's end, finally lives by his own words: "You gotta be who you are in this world, no matter what."[2] Husbands and wives say vows about it when they promise to have and to hold one another, for better or worse, richer or poorer, in sickness and in health, to love and to cherish until death parts them. And back in 1974, Shirley Brown would shoot her shot on the subject in her R&B chart-topping song "Woman to Woman," a lyrical manifesto of allegiance professing just how much she would do to keep her man, directed to a fellow female rival.

What I'm talking about today is not limited to big screens and love songs. It's animated in *Lady and the Tramp*, *The Good Dinosaur*, even episodes of *Babar the Elephant*, *Teen Titans Go!*, and *The Powerpuff Girls*. It's what haunted Amir in Khaled Hosseini's *The Kite Runner*. Lucifer, Cain, and Pilate. It is what Judas failed at. And anyone familiar with *La Cosa Nostra*—the Mob—knows how it, this thing, is both prized and betrayed. Politicians invoke it, then violate it. Teams rely on it. Wars depend on it. Alma maters solicit it. Humanity has a lot to say about it. Kendrick Lamar summed it up best with his 2017 track whose title needs no explanation:

---

1. *John Wick*, 2014.
2. *The Equalizer*, 2014.

"LOYALTY."[3] Too often, we demand it from others while offering a half-hearted version ourselves. We minimize the loyalty God deserves from us and live like the old theme song from *The Addams Family*: "They do what they wanna do, say what they wanna say, live how they wanna live, play how they wanna play."[4] Apart from the macabre and the deadpan stares, we've got more in common with them than we think.

Judges Chapters 1 and 2 show a people falling apart after Joshua's death. The refrain that echoes through the book—"In those days Israel had no king; everyone did as they saw fit"—is already beginning to take hold. To their credit, the twelve tribes—Reuben, Simeon, Judah, Dan, Naphtali, Gad, Asher, Issachar, Zebulun, Benjamin, Ephraim, and Manasseh—do start off on a good foot. Hallelujah for good beginnings. There's camaraderie, cooperation, even generosity. Larger tribes assist smaller ones in battle. See verse 3. There's unity. See verses 12–15. And there's justice tempered with mercy. After defeating the Canaanites and Perizzites, they capture a cruel king, Adoni-Bezek. They cut off his thumbs and big toes—not out of sadism, but because that's what he had done to 70 other kings. "Now God has repaid me," he confesses. They could've tortured or killed him, but instead they imposed what they saw to be a fitting judgment, yet with restraint. But by the beginning of Chapter 2, something's gone wrong. An angel of the Lord arrives with a rebuke: "I brought you up out of Egypt and led you into the land I swore to give your ancestors. I said, 'I will never break my covenant with you, and you shall not make a covenant with the people of this land.' But you have disobeyed me. Why have you done this?"[5]

Why? Well, Kendrick tried to tell us. The Israelites compromised. They negotiated. They made deals. They didn't follow through. They were the opposite of loyal. Verse 19 tells us that some Canaanites got a pass because their chariots were "fitted with iron." Verse 22 details an alliance with a man from Luz—a name that in Hebrew means "separation" or "to turn aside," which seems eerily appropriate. Manasseh failed to drive out enemies, too. Instead of obeying God, they pressed the Canaanites into forced labor. The compromise spread, so the angel announces a consequence: "I will not drive them out before you; they will become traps

---

3. Kendrick Lamar, "LOYALTY," 2017.
4. "The Addams Family Goes to School," 1964.
5. Judg 2:1–2.

for you, and their gods will become snares to you."⁶ The people weep. They offer sacrifices. But they still miss the point. They thought loyalty could be replaced with ritual. That if they just said sorry and gathered together a burnt offering, all would be forgiven. But God wanted more than remorse—He wanted obedience. As Samuel would later say in 1 Samuel 15:22, "To obey is better than sacrifice." God wasn't calling them to xenophobia⁷—He loves all people, because He made all people. But He was calling His people to be distinct. He knew that if they mingled with those who worshipped other gods, they would end up confused, compromised, and distant from Him.

Paul David Tripp wrote, "Obedience is freedom. Better to follow the Master's plan than to do what you weren't wired to do—master yourself."⁸ Loyalty means submitting to the Spirit of God, who reshapes and retrains everything inside us to be faithful. As Craig Barnes notes, "We have far too many plans and not nearly enough dreams. We are never saved by our plans."⁹ Yet, many of us dare attempt to treat God's commands like fine print—terms to renegotiate, not sacred vows to uphold. But that's not how it works. Through Christ, the Law has been fulfilled. Jesus lived the perfect life, died a sacrificial death, and was raised to new life. In doing so, he became our substitute. If we renounce our old ways and submit to him—if we believe and confess that Jesus is who the Bible says he is—then God will not just *consider* giving us eternal life. He *will*. That's loyalty. And, no, perfection is not the aim in case you're asking. Jesus handled that. His righteousness is our covering. At judgment, God won't see your flaws—He'll see your Savior. Still, however, God calls believers

---

6. Judg 2:3.

7. This is an irrational fear or hatred of foreigners that is often paired with a nationalist superiority complex. When operating alongside American exceptionalism, for example, it can manifest as the belief that every policy, political structure, and product developed in the U.S. is superior to those elsewhere. In this mindset, immigrants—if they are permitted to enter at all—are seen with disdain, scorn, or suspicion, rather than respect or openness.

8. Paul David Tripp, *New Morning Mercies: A Daily Gospel Devotional*, 22.

9. M. Craig Barnes served as Senior Pastor of the National Presbyterian Church in Washington, DC, from 1992 to 2002. During that time, he delivered a sermon on December 14, 1997, titled "Straightening Out Christmas" (based on Luke 3:1–6), in which he shared these words. After leaving National Presbyterian, he held a dual appointment as the 10th Senior Pastor of Shadyside Presbyterian Church and the Robert Meneilly Professor of Pastoral Ministry at Pittsburgh Theological Seminary. I arrived in Pittsburgh for the 2009–10 academic year to complete my S.T.M.—a one-year, post-master's research degree—at Pittsburgh Theological Seminary, which enabled me to study under Dr. Barnes.

to a life of faithfulness. We should be, to reference Kendrick's song again, loyal.

Christianity is not the spiritual version of *Let's Make a Deal*. There will be moments when the path ahead isn't obvious. But loyalty is still possible. You and I can be faithful. God knows our minds are powerful, and He knows how easily we wander, so He gave us His Word—a shared vocabulary and way of life to keep us close and loyal to Him. That's why we tithe. Why we forgive. Why we serve in Jesus' name. Why we study Scripture, speak truth in love, bridle our tongues, and walk upright in a bent world. The Bible gives us rhythms, postures, and disciplines—things to do and things to avoid—to keep our loyalty alive. When we start leaning on our own understanding, however, as the Israelites did when facing iron chariots, we stop trusting the God who delivered us. That's how you end up claiming you're all-in for Nikon, but every photo you have has been shot with a Canon camera. You say you love Pepsi, but your fridge is full of Coke. You root for the Detroit Lions, but cheer when the Chicago Bears score. You once were a diehard Popeyes disciple, but now it's Chick-fil-A every week. That's not preference—that's defection. And when it comes to God, defection leads to unrest. It's like a parent saying to a defiant child: "I'm not interested in what you thought—I'm interested in what I told you to do." So, yes—use your mind. Use your gifts. Use your friends. Use the resources around you. But use them in service of God's will, not your own. Although God always does the heavy lifting, He expects our yes to be yes. Ask yourself: "How does what I want to do align with what God already said?" May it be said of us—not in shame, but in confidence—that we are guilty of loyalty.

Trusting God with Another Generation

Judges 2:6–15, September 24, 2023

As a nod to the 1960 Sam Cooke classic from which it takes its name, *Cadence* hit theaters in 1990. Charlie Sheen stars as the lone White inmate in an Army stockade, joined by four incarcerated African American soldiers. The film features powerful performances from Larry Fishburne, Michael Beach, and Sheen's real-life father, Martin Sheen. During their time together, these men learn—each in his own way—about hatred, brotherhood, truth, integrity, and compassion. Through the soul-stirring vocal paces they chant, they find a rhythm not just of survival, but of shared humanity. These calls become a rite of passage, a bond forged between men who come to understand that no matter what, they are far more than the large "P"—for "prisoner"—printed on the backs of their green uniform shirts.[1]

Fast-forward to *Black Panther*, the highest-grossing film ever to feature a predominantly Black cast, earning $1.3 billion globally. One of my favorite moments is the arrival of M'Baku, leader of the Jabari Tribe. Preceded by an intimidating procession of his warriors, he steps forward to challenge for the throne of Wakanda in ritual combat. As they enter, he loudly proclaims "Maafa," a Kiswahili term meaning "unspeakable disaster or calamity."[2] It refers to over five centuries of genocide, enslavement, and colonial oppression endured by African people—and

---

1. *Cadence*, 1990.
2. See Marimba Ani, *Let the Circle Be Unbroken: The Implications of African Spirituality in the New Diaspora* and Rhonda Wells-Wilbon, "Lessons From the Maafa: Rethinking the Legacy of Slain Hip-Hop Icon Tupac Shakur," *Journal of Black Studies*, March 2010.

the generational trauma still reverberating today. This single word, spoken with gravity, marks not only their arrival but also their identity. His tribe replies, "Yeah." Together they grunt, "Hoogh." It's a powerful and unforgettable scene that captures a commitment to tradition, resilience, and cultural pride. These scenes symbolize a shared value system: a deliberately cultivated, deeply rooted way of life passed down from person to person, family to family, and community to community.

Turning to Scripture, we find that God's people, too, faced a crisis of generational disconnect. A faithful generation had come and gone, but their children no longer saw life—or God—the same way. Worse still, rebellion became their default. Last week, we examined Israel's actions in the immediate aftermath of the Joshua era. The consequences of their poor choices arrived quickly, delivered by the judgment of an angel of the Lord. The writer of Judges then pauses the narrative, zooming out to recap Joshua's legacy before the spiritual collapse. Verses 6–7 tell us that the people "had seen all the great things the Lord had done for Israel." For many, these wonders occurred in their lifetime; for others, they were reinforced through storytelling so vivid and so persistent that the next generation understood them as real and essential. Still, as the saying goes, "When the cat's away, the mice will play." With leadership gone, the people went off the rails. Joshua, after decades of faithful service, died at 110 and was buried "in the hill country of Ephraim."

Philosopher George Santayana wrote in *The Life of Reason: Reason in Common Sense,* "Those who cannot remember the past are condemned to repeat it."[3] But what we see here is more severe. Forgetting the past is one thing. Rejecting the divine order that sustained your people is another. Shame, shame, shame—you know your name. God never insisted every detail of life fit into a rigid formula. Whether you prefer Lucky Charms or Cinnamon Toast Crunch, T-Mobile or Verizon, Cracker Barrel or The Wooden Shoe[4]—that's not what defines your faith. Some people (like me) absolutely despise raspberries because of their massive, alien-like seeds; others love fruitcake but can't stand couscous. God isn't micromanaging your grocery list. However, covenantal obedience is a different story. In matters where God has clearly spoken and His people have agreed to follow, mutinous conduct hurts His heart. As Psalm 103 reminds us, "He

---

3. George Santayana, *The Life of Reason: Reason in Common Sense,* 284.
4. This is a storied breakfast spot in Holland, MI.

does not treat us as our sins deserve," but He also won't overlook our intentional non-compliance. Before Joshua died, the people had the opportunity to renew their vows to God: to cast away idols, recommit their hearts, and serve the Lord alone. But they didn't. They failed to act until it was too late. Judges 2 offers a flashback to highlight how much leadership matters—but also that leadership alone isn't enough. "In those days Israel had no king; everyone did as they saw fit." The next generation, we are told, "knew neither the Lord nor what He had done for Israel." Verses 11–15 describe the fallout: they worshiped foreign gods and lost God's favor. "Whenever Israel went out to fight, the hand of the Lord was against them . . . They were in great distress."

It raises the question: is some of our present-day stress the result of insisting on our own way when God has already shown us a better one? Here, we witness the tragic consequences of rebellious children raised by faithful parents. The older generation was not perfect, but they were sincere, consistent, structured, and deeply invested in their children's spiritual formation. They told the stories of God's faithfulness, modeled Sabbath worship, and lived lives of prayer. But when those who had lived through slavery and the Exodus—the ones who knew oppression, who fought for what they loved—were gone, their children drifted. They knew better, but they chose compromise. A little Yahweh, a little Baal. Their parents had done their part. Now grown, they chose to go at it alone. In 1979, by way of their hit song The Buggles declared, "Video Killed the Radio Star,"[5] and if that is true, well, then the Internet age of today has slaughtered nearly everything imaginable. Much that was good is now gone. As Ecclesiastes 1:9 reminds us, "What has been will be again. . .there is nothing new under the sun." I won't say definitively that God has turned His hand against any particular generation, but this much is true: they must come to know God for themselves—or reject Him. Worrying won't change that. As the famously unattributed saying goes, "Worry is like a rocking chair—it gives you something to do, but gets you nowhere." If you're young, hear this from someone now middle-aged: I'm not afraid of your music, even if it sounds like mumbling to me. I'm not afraid of your principles or feelings, even when they shift every three minutes, confusing even you. And most importantly, I'm not afraid of you. My job is to love you right where you are. That means getting to

---

5. The Buggles, "Video Killed the Radio Star," 1980.

know you, walking beside you, listening deeply, and always—whether I seem cool or crazy—pointing you to Jesus.

And if you're older, know I need to tell you something: God's got this. *Do you hear me?* Anxiety, manipulation, and condemnation won't win the day. The same God who was with you when you were young and confused is with them, too. Today's young people are not a lost cause. God is not asleep, on vacation, or preoccupied running errands. One thing about the next generation is certain: they are next. God has a plan. Yes, some of their views on sex, marriage, and morality are foolish—but as wise elders we are here to love them anyway. And while ignorance or defiance plays a role in why they are how they are, so do the brokenness they've witnessed from adults like us in homes, churches, and society. Their view of faith may be warped, but God's grace is not. Therefore, from a place of love and empathy, show them your scars. Pull out the old photos. Tell the stories of how God carried you through. Be honest about your regrets and conceited calculations. Let them see that even in your doubts, you've chosen God again and again—only because He first chose you. That's what God does: He matures and disciplines His people. And He'll do the same with them.

Divine Compassion
Judges 2:16–23, October 1, 2023

MAYBE YOU'VE KNOWN SOMEONE—or have been someone—who imagined God as a distant, overbearing, big meanie figure in the sky, staring down at humanity with fiery contempt and disappointment. Influenced by poor biblical interpretation or secular misconceptions, this view portrays God as perpetually frowning, as though no act of faith or obedience could ever meet His standard. But if we give both the Old and New Testaments a fair reading, I believe a different image emerges. Jonathan Edwards, often considered the greatest theologian in American history, delivered his famous sermon "Sinners in the Hands of an Angry God" on July 8, 1741. Yes, we are sinners—I agree wholeheartedly. Scripture is clear: "All have sinned and fall short of the glory of God."[1] God's judgment is real, and rebellion against Him is not something to take lightly. However, God is not a cruel or insecure tyrant who delights in punishing His creation. On the contrary, He grieves. So, if anything, we are sinners in the hands of a *compassionate* God. Compassion does not negate justice—people can still be held accountable for their actions—but even amid judgment, God's mercy compels a response rooted in love. That is the beauty of this morning's text.

The Israelites, as recorded in Judges, "refused to listen to their judges" and "prostituted themselves to other gods," stubbornly clinging to evil practices. This non-compliance led to God withdrawing His protection. And yet, even in setting boundaries and consequences, God showed restraint through the judges He raised up. Judges 2:18 tells us, "The Lord relented because of their groaning under those who oppressed and afflicted them." Imagine that. God's people violate their covenant

---

1. Rom 3:23.

with Him in the most blatant ways—tearing it apart into 10,000 pieces, setting fire to the remnants, and living as though God were just one of many optional deities. They went from serving the Lord under Joshua to practically forgetting Him altogether upon his death. Still, despite their brazen idolatry, untrustworthiness, and immaturity—not misunderstanding, not honest wrestling, but deliberately rejecting God—God relents. He relents, and He does so repeatedly throughout Scripture. As the psalmist writes, "He does not treat us as our sins deserve or repay us according to our iniquities."[2] That is not something to take lightly—it's everything to be thankful for. What I find striking is that the Israelites did not even recognize their wrongdoing. There is no record of them repenting on their own volition or initiative. There was no apology, no heartfelt remorse. They weren't in counseling for spiritual rebellion. They were content doing what they were doing, and only became bothered when defeat and suffering interrupted their plans. Yet even then, God heard their groaning—not their repentance, not their reform—just their pain. And He cared. Even though the suffering was their own doing, God still cared. And He still cares today.

Given the severity of the covenant breach, God could've walked away. He could have wiped His hands clean. *Good riddance. Farewell. Ciao.* But He didn't. And He doesn't. Though their trouble was self-inflicted, God didn't begin a deep-throated laugh like a cartoon villain or rejoice in their destruction. Instead, in His righteousness and dependability, He chose mercy. That should move us to do likewise. We may not always have a clear blueprint for how and when to show undeserved compassion, but as Ephesians 5:1–2 exhorts: "Follow God's example, therefore, as dearly loved children and walk in the way of love, just as Christ loved us and gave himself up for us as a fragrant offering and sacrifice to God." According to Judges 2:16, "Then the Lord raised up judges." This was God offering the Israelites a lifeline—a temporary but tangible rescue from themselves. Permanent salvation, of course, comes through Jesus Christ, who came down from heaven, took on human flesh, and gave Himself "as a ransom for all."[3]

The book of Judges ends with the haunting line: "In those days Israel had no king; everyone did as they saw fit." That disobedience made

---

2. Ps 103:10–14.
3. 1 Tim 2:6.

God "very angry," as verse 20 states. And it wouldn't be the last time His people believed lies and followed destructive paths. The Old Testament—especially Judges—can seem like a bleak landscape filled with violence, betrayal, and chaos. There's blood, war, idolatry, sexual violence, greed, prophetic warnings, and betrayal—followed by even more blood. And when you think that maybe the bloody parts are over, here comes some guts and scandal for good measure. It may not make for a comforting devotional to read by the lake in some posh villa, but it is real. In his 1889 essay "The Decay of Lying," Oscar Wilde wrote, "Life imitates art far more than art imitates life."[4] Whether or not you agree, Scripture shows that people then were as complex and flawed as we are now—capable of both great faith and tragic failure.

God is the Father of a prodigal people—then and now—who struggle to be content with Him and what He lovingly provides. Throughout Judges, we will see that the Israelites, like us, often chase after anything that promises a more presumably autonomous or exciting life. But they're wrong every single time. So are we. It's a repeating cycle: God's people rebel, God confronts them, they offer shallow remorse, and God graciously provides another chance—knowing they will fail again. This is well captured in a nostalgic yet insightful way by a classic children's show from the '80s and '90s. Shari Lewis, the beloved and talented puppeteer who passed away at 65 from uterine cancer, had a program called *Lamb Chop's Sing-Along, Play-Along*. On that show, there was a song kids and adults alike would sing titled, "The Song That Doesn't End."[5] This brings to mind the idea that, without question, sin is humanity's best-selling song of all time. We have become experts at going around and around the mulberry bush, justifying thoughts and actions that only end up hurting ourselves and others.

I have always been a baby, toddler, and little kid person. When we lived in Holland before, I helped teach the 4-and-5-year-olds in children's church. Over the years, I have also helped with VBS and babysat many kids. And, admittedly uncharacteristic of most men, if there's a baby around, I am always eager to hold them. I mean, who in their right mind wouldn't jump at the opportunity to hold a baby, is what I think! I'll walk around with that little sucka, talk to them, make silly faces—whatever

---

4. Oscar Wilde, "The Decay of Lying," *The Nineteenth Century* 25, no. 147 (January 1889): 36–56.

5. Shari Lewis, "The Song That Doesn't End," 1992.

it takes. I'm committed. Even though my current work focuses more on shepherding adults through situations that are complex or no fun at all, I pray to the Lord God Almighty to always remain a kid at heart in the best of ways. One quirky skill I have, which either delights or terrifies children (whichever it is they are not shy about letting you know) is making an elephant sound. It's called *trumpeting*, and it is how elephants communicate across long distances. Elephants are believed to be one of the world's most empathetic species. You may have seen stories on *National Geographic* or similar programs where a single elephant or even an entire herd risks danger to help another animal in distress—not just other elephants, but different species. Elephants are compassionate. God is compassionate. And we are called to be compassionate as well.

The compassion we see here is significant. God is justifiably angry, yet also deeply troubled by the self-destructive choices of His beloved people. That tension matters.

As much as we're called to show compassion to others—however the Spirit leads us, which will vary from situation to situation—I'm convinced that our first step must be learning to receive God's compassion ourselves. We have all faced seasons where we've mixed Christianity with a little superstition, treated Bible study like just another podcast or TV show to nonchalantly digest, or gotten so enchanted with fiction that truth starts to feel like a distant cousin we are estranged from. The struggle to remain dedicated to God is real, so I don't say any of this with judgment—we're all in the same boat. Let's learn to receive God's compassion and reflect that compassion back to one another, living in community, walking in grace.

Evaluations of Submission
Judges 3:1–11, October 8, 2023

IF YOU DIDN'T KNOW—*I didn't until I looked it up*—the United Nations designated September 21 as the International Day of Peace back in 1981. The goal was to encourage global cooperation through a 24-hour, nonviolent cease-fire. It was never intended to solve all the world's problems overnight, but rather to promote and support gestures of friendship, reconciliation, and respect across lines of difference. Christians, of course, claim to know something about peace as well. We have a rich musical heritage of praising God by lifting our voices in song. Part of that tradition includes lyrics like:

> When peace like a river attendeth my way,
> When sorrows like sea billows roll;
> Whatever my lot Thou hast taught me to say,
> "It is well, it is well with my soul!"[1]

Bethel Music has a song titled "Peace." The Nashville-based worship collective The Belonging Co—which was born out of a church by the same name—released the track "Peace Be Still" in 2017, featuring Lauren Daigle. Back in 1992, Sandi Patty sang a song called "Child of Peace." As we begin today, I want to reflect on the idea of peace.

Though not exhaustively, I'd say that Christians come to know peace in two primary ways—both as nouns. Grammatically, a noun is a person, place, or thing. Spiritually, peace is both a posture and a person. It is accurate to say, "I have peace"—meaning tranquility, calm, or contentment. And it is also appropriate to say, "I have Peace"—meaning Jesus. For us, peace speaks both to a relationship and a reality. Aligning myself with

---

1. Horatio G. Spafford, "It Is Well with My Soul," 1873.

the blood-stained banner of God's one and only Son endows me—ennobles and enables me[2]—with a peace He lovingly provides. The world didn't invent, manufacture, or distribute this peace, so the world can't take it away. In some cultures, including among many Christians, the word *shalom*, meaning "peace," is used as a greeting. We serve the Prince of Peace—One who is never shaken or stirred, whose peace surpasses all understanding, and who calls his followers to be peacemakers. And yet, as children of God tasked with bearing witness to the supremacy of Christ in this untamed, chaotic, and charred world, we find ourselves both knowing peace and fighting for it. Peace is something to cultivate, sacrifice for, and defend. A staple in recovery communities, Reinhold Niebuhr's now-famous Serenity Prayer includes these words: "Living one day at a time, enjoying one moment at a time; accepting hardship as a pathway to peace."

Working backward through our text, notice what verse 11 tells us: "The land had peace for forty years, until Othniel son of Kenaz died." We see in verse 7 that Israel had once again—surprise, surprise—done what was evil in the sight of the Lord. As He warned, God allowed them to suffer defeat. But then, just as we saw last week, there then came that divine empathy we need so much—that *grace-wrapped interference*. When the people cried out for help, the Lord responded. He was under no obligation to act, but He did. He raised up Othniel, the first in a long line of judges, to deliver them. And that single act of compassion led to forty years of peace.

If you've ever experienced peace—for a short or long season—you need to know this: peace is a gift not to be taken for granted. The Israelites' behavior made it clear they didn't deserve peace at all. I'm not saying that's your story. Maybe, if we're honest, it's 50/50 in some situations. But it's also true that sometimes we're just minding our own holy business when chaos strikes from nowhere. In those moments, when the hardships feel the most unfair, peace matters even more. Whatever the case, when peace shows up—and you didn't rob, steal, or kill to try to make it happen—you have something to shout about. *I have something to shout about.* A professor of mine once wrote:

---

2. Rabbi Dr. Ari Berman, "To Ennoble and Enable: An Inaugural Vision," address delivered at Yeshiva University, 2017.

> ... if in fact you are engaged in the struggle God has called you to be engaged in, then the struggle is over before it begins. The struggle is God's struggle. In other words, you are not called to prevail in your conflicts. That's God's job. Your calling is to witness, to watch exactly how God does that.[3]

That's why four hours, four days, four months, or four years of peace is worth getting excited about. And if you've ever had the gift of forty years of peace—well, you just might lose your mind in gratitude. Now, peace doesn't necessarily mean you've hit the lottery, taken a six-month cruise around the world, or lived without a single health scare. What it *does* mean is that life is relatively undisturbed—in all the best ways. We're talking: That new supervisor—who's been on a tear hiring and firing, and who many think is making life needlessly difficult—has decided to leave you alone. The roof repair came in at a fraction of the original quote. The doctor says with steady physical therapy after the accident, you're going to be okay. The IRS? They're sending you a real, bonafide refund check. Your kids, your grandkids, your spouse or best friend, your walking buddy, your small group—the folks you've been doing life with since you moved here? They're all doing pretty well. That kind of peace isn't something to ever take for granted. It's not a given. When you recognize it, you ought to be grateful.

Now, let me be clear: this isn't the eternal, Jesus-kind-of-peace. That peace is fixed and unshakable. That's the peace the world can't give or take away. Remember the *Time* magazine cover from April 8, 1966? In bold red letters, it asked, "Is God Dead?" He is not. The tomb is empty. Jesus is alive, seated at the right hand of God the Father, interceding for all who dare to believe. Therefore, if God is alive—and He is—and if He gives peace through Himself, through the Holy Spirit—and He does—and if He is never-ending—then *His* peace is also without end.

But what I'm talking about here is that other kind of peace—the earthly, provisional peace. The kind you know is good while it lasts, but you also know it won't last forever. And here's the hard part—something I know you don't want to hear any more than I want to say it: To truly value peace—especially when it shows up in the middle of a storm—you must get familiar with conflict. That's why when the bell rings for a "recess period" in your life—protecting you from flashing sirens like mental or physical anguish, relational breakdowns, another move, another loss,

---

3. M. Craig Barnes, *Hustling God: Why We Work So Hard for What God Wants to Give*, 92.

another betrayal, another relapse, another diaper blowout at the worst time, another appointment, another argument, another pill, another 10 pounds, another bill—it's *wise*, *true*, and *rational* to give thanks. Give thanks for peace *and* for the One who provides it—whether in big or small doses—even as He *is* the final, ironclad embodiment of peace. The Psalmist says: "Turn from evil and do good; seek peace and pursue it."[4] Thank God that Othniel did his part, giving the Israelites peace they hadn't even asked for. And with that, let me transition by quoting the legend himself, Forrest Gump: "That's all I have to say about that."[5]

What's intriguing throughout Judges 3:1–11 is the underlying theme of evaluation. Verse 3 tells us that God left certain nations in the land "to test all those Israelites who had not experienced any of the wars in Canaan." In essence, the Israelites were cohabiting—what in one lexicon we might call "shacking up"—with the very people God had clearly told them to avoid. They were, quite literally, sleeping with the enemy. And they knew it. And they didn't care, so they did it anyway. *Just like us.* Yes, God allowed this because of their rebellion. But He also allowed it to play out as a test, to see whether they would eventually wake up, get off the struggle bus, and choose to obey Him. That was a real option. Still, as the passage reminds us, "In those days Israel had no king; everyone did as they saw fit." God's testing wasn't only about obedience, though. The Israelites also needed the combat experience—and the cultural tension. They were forced to grapple with foreign ways of living and loving that clashed with the ways that honored "the Lord their God." Sadly, we modern believers aren't built as Ford-tough as we think we are. Here's the core of my point: we often take offense at the idea that God would dare to evaluate us—that He would test us to reveal where our true allegiances lie, or to prepare us for what's ahead. "Who does God think He is," we wonder, "to use difficult circumstances to determine where I am and where I need to go, according to His loving wisdom?"

But the truth is, sometimes we need adversity to know if what we claim to believe is what we actually believe. As the boxing legend Mike Tyson once said, "Everyone has a plan until they get punched in the mouth."[6] If you've ever been punched in the mouth—if you've ever received devastating news that you cannot change or been disillusioned

---

4. Ps 34:14.
5. *Forrest Gump*, 1994.
6. Mike Tyson, interview by John Saraceno, *USA Today*, 2004.

beyond belief, you know that feeling deep in your gut. We like to think we'll stay strong. That if our children stray far from what we taught them, we'll respond with faith and not fire. That if we lose the job we love—or even the job we hate—we won't unravel. That when mocked or isolated for our faith, we'll stand strong and keep our hands on the gospel plow. But talk is cheap. Our God is not. Even under grace, not the Law—and far from works righteousness, which is a trap—God still needs to measure if our faith is genuine or just noise. The old saying goes, "If at first you don't succeed, try, try again."[7] And that's true. God loves us. He never gives up on us. He is our Advocate. But the hard truth is, most of us are terrible test-takers.

One lazy activity I've been known to indulge in, especially on a rainy or boring day, is watching episode after episode after episode (my wife can confirm this) of *Family Feud*. Each round begins and ends with Steve Harvey announcing something like, "The top seven answers are on the board. We asked 100 women. . ." or "We asked 100 men. . ." Then comes the fill-in-the-blank prompt: "Name a place a man has a good time until his wife shows up," or "Name a word you might hear a director shout on a movie set." The contestants yell out their guesses, and with his big, larger-than-life mustache and a suit that's custom-made—though, let's be honest, often way too shiny—Steve announces the results. What I hope we understand from this section of Judges is that, at its core, the Christian life is an open-book test. Teachers, professors, and students alike should appreciate the significance of that. God, in His grace, gives us the most important answers to life's most important questions. He does this chiefly by revealing Himself—His character, His essence, His jealous and steadfast *hesed*, that Old Testament word for covenantal lovingkindness—through Scripture. In advance, God has plainly and intelligibly laid out who He is—"I am that I am"[8]—who we are—"In the image of God, He created them; male and female"[9]—and how we're supposed to respond to who He is, given who we are: "Love the Lord your God, walk in obedience to Him, keep His commands, hold fast to Him, and serve Him with all your heart and with all your soul."[10]

7. Thomas H. Palmer, *The Teacher's Manual*, 1840.
8. Exod 3:14.
9. Gen 1:27.
10. Deut 6:5.

Christianity is not some secret society with hidden codes and handshakes. It's all out in the open. Sure, there in the course of life, unanswered questions and unfulfilled longings remain. We don't know why the good die young, or why terrible things sometimes happen to the most devout, compassionate people. But if we know the One who knows everything, maybe that should be enough for us—as the incredibly *finite*, *fragile* human beings that we are. You might be frustrated with certain parts of your life. That's real. It happens. However, even in the midst of uncertainty, what you *do* know is that the answer to your situation is not infidelity, theft, resentment, violence, or idolatry. We're still called to study—to show ourselves approved—and not to think or behave like pleasure-seeking fools. Witchcraft, selfish ambition, drunkenness, sexual immorality, hatred—none of these lead to passing the open-book test. The fact that the test *is* open book speaks to God's generosity. In evaluating us, He gives us a clear way out: "so that you can endure it."[11] That way out is called submission. The answers are not in your lust or your flesh. With the Holy Spirit as your tutor, you need to know that the most critical answers are in the book, the Word of God, that reveals Jesus. "In the beginning was the Word, and the Word was with God, and the Word was God."[12] You and I don't need to know everything. We never will, yet we *do* need to know the God of the Bible. Through the stories of the Israelites and others, Scripture teaches us that, ultimately, what God desires most is submission.

---

11. 1 Cor 10:13.
12. 1 John 1:1

An Unlikely, Likely Choice
Judges 3:12–31, October 15, 2023

"There's more than one way to skin a cat." Now, if the cat lovers among us—whoever they are—can momentarily set aside their affection for Garfield, Oliver, Tom, Sylvester, Chloe, Felix, Figaro, or Snowball, we'll see that *The Cat in the Hat*, perhaps the most iconic feline of them all, was onto something when he said, "I know it is wet and the sun is not sunny, but we can have lots of good fun that is funny."[1] Of course, we're not talking about literal taxidermy or animal cruelty here. The phrase simply means that accomplishing a task is rarely limited to a single method. To that end, consider the NBC sitcom *Punky Brewster*, which originally aired on September 16, 1984, and was briefly rebooted in recent years—only to be quietly canceled. Set in Chicago, the show followed young Penelope "Punky" Brewster, who had been abandoned by her parents and was navigating the harsh realities of the foster care system. Through repeated attempts to run away and then finally being adopted, Punky—always clad in bright colors and mismatched outfits—became a symbol of resilience for a generation of girls who grew into women that related to her defiant charm. Her tomboy style, sharp wit, and big personality proved that femininity could encompass a wide spectrum of strengths and quirks. It reminded us that being different isn't just tolerable—it's worth celebrating.

On a different note, I recently finished reading *African Samurai: The True Story of Yasuke, a Legendary Black Warrior in Feudal Japan* by Thomas Lockley and Geoffrey Girard.[2] Narrated as a historical biogra-

---

1. Dr. Seuss, *The Cat In the Hat*, 7.
2. See Thomas Lockley and Geoffrey Giard, *African Samurai: The True Story of Yasuke, a Legendary Black Warrior in Feudal Japan*.

phy, it's a gripping account full of adventure, corruption, and the chaotic glory of feudal monarchies—definitely not PG-13 material. Yasuke, kidnapped as a child from Africa after the slaughter of his village, ended up in Asia with Jesuits. He later became a mercenary and bodyguard. Along his journey, readers are introduced to the wide world of samurai, sumo wrestlers, warrior monks, and ninjas, learning that martial arts are not only about size or brute strength, but about discipline, precision, stealth, dexterity, and honor. One of the key lessons: never underestimate an opponent's heart. The relentless will to survive or outwit is formidable. In fighting, as in life, one size does not fit all.

That's why it's fitting that while the official motto of the U.S. Marine Corps is *Semper Fidelis*—Latin for "Always Faithful"—its unofficial one is "Improvise, Adapt, and Overcome." The military is known for cultivating creative problem-solvers, capable of expecting the unexpected and preparing for the worst, most unforeseen situations. Another example of nontraditional thinking comes from sports. As you may know, professional athletes tend to hire agents—often lawyers—to handle the negotiation of contracts, endorsements, and sponsorships. They can earn commissions ranging anywhere from 3 to 20%, depending on league rules and the type of deal. But earlier this year, in a move that surprised many, Baltimore Ravens star quarterback Lamar Jackson negotiated a landmark five-year, $260 million deal entirely on his own. It pays him $52 million per year. On a smaller, yet still impressive scale, offensive lineman Laremy Tunsil of the Houston Texans signed a three-year, $75 million contract extension, also without an agent. By doing so, he saved roughly $3 million—enough to buy his mother a house, which he proudly did. The lesson? Wisdom is sometimes conventional, but it's not *only* conventional. God is not limited by categories. He can do much with little, little with much, or much with much. More often than not, He operates in ways that disrupt our assumptions about what is possible or best.

Today's text introduces several unconventional dynamics. Once again, the Israelites have fallen under foreign rule—this time under King Eglon of Moab—for eighteen years. "Why?" you might ask. The answer, as the book of Judges frequently reminds us, is: "In those days Israel had no king; everyone did as they saw fit." In response to the desperate cries of His people, God appoints Ehud as a judge to deliver them. He's the second judge; Othniel was the first—whom we discussed last week—and you'll recall he defeated Cushan-Rishathaim, king of Aram, ushering in forty years of peace. As the old Mighty Mouse theme song from 1958 famously declares, "Here I come to save the day!"[3] That's essentially Ehud's calling. A Benjamite by birth, Ehud's mission was to ignite a revolution against the Moabites, beginning with their king.

To do that, he had to take out the head of the snake, as the traditional Arabic proverb says: "If you cut off the head, the body will die." Killing Eglon was the necessary first step, but it required unusual cunning. Ehud couldn't exactly stroll up to the palace, ring the bell, announce his intentions, and expect to survive. He had to be strategic—quiet, clever, and unexpected. Most of us can relate: sometimes there's something we want to do—good or bad—but we know it can't be done out in the open. So, like Ehud, we find another way.

Ehud initially gained access to Eglon under the pretense of delivering a tribute—likely a customary annual payment. He dropped off the goods, offered the appropriate pleasantries (something like "Long live the king"), and began his journey home. But verse 19 tells us he turned back and said, "Your Majesty, I have a secret message for you." We believe this movement—arriving, leaving, then returning—was a calculated tactic. With the guards and even the king now somewhat familiar with him, his return wouldn't raise alarms. And it worked. Eglon dismissed his attendants, allowing Ehud to speak with him privately. To increase the sense of urgency and perhaps lure the king from his seat, Ehud added, "I have a message from God for you." Importantly, he used the general Hebrew term Elohim—more universally accepted—rather than Yahweh, which might have provoked suspicion or hostility. After all, hearing that the God of a conquered people had a message for their oppressor might not sit well. Ehud, from the tribe of Benjamin—renowned for its elite left-handed warriors—seized the moment.

As Eglon stood, verses 20–21 tell us that Ehud pulled out a double-edged sword he had concealed under his clothing and plunged it into the king's large belly. He locked the doors behind him and slipped away undetected. The guards, assuming the king was indisposed, delayed their entry. Eventually, when they checked on him, they found Eglon "fallen to the floor, dead." Once safely away, Ehud rallied his fellow Israelites. Empowered by this bold act of deliverance, they attacked and defeated the Moabites. According to verse 29, "At that time they struck down about ten thousand Moabites, all vigorous and strong; not one escaped." With

---

3. *The Mighty Mouse Playhouse*, 1955–67.

their oppressors overthrown, Israel reclaimed control of the land and enjoyed eighty years of peace. Briefly, verse 31 introduces the next judge: "After Ehud came Shamgar son of Anath, who struck down six hundred Philistines with an oxgoad. He too saved Israel."

"You plus God equals a majority,"[4] as the saying goes. It's meant to highlight a profound truth: God can accomplish anything through anyone, regardless of their limitations. Seemingly insurmountable obstacles do not faze Him one bit. Time yields to His authority, so He's never in a rush. Enemies don't intimidate Him, and human inadequacies or a lack of resources don't keep Him up at night. God makes choices that make perfect sense to Him but routinely appear, from our finite and frail human perspective, improbable or illogical. And yet, because of Christ Jesus, we are not just survivors—we are overachievers, overcomers. As Paul writes, we are "more than conquerors."[5] In the book of Romans, he asks rhetorically, "If God is for us, who can be against us?"[6] Whether we find our backs against the wall or we are in a season of plenty and visible advantage, it's vital that we trust in God: in His limitless provision, in His unmatched ability to execute His good, perfect, and necessary plan. This isn't simply a feel-good underdog story. It's not the same as cheering on the quintessential little guy, like Walter Matthau's portrayal of a washed-up alcoholic coaching a rowdy team of misfits in the 1976 film *The Bad News Bears*. Sure, we all know and love stories of surprising victories—Cinderella, Rocky Balboa, Shrek, or Elle Woods in *Legally Blonde*. We admire Sigourney Weaver's Lieutenant Ellen Ripley in *Alien* (1979), or the brave kids of the Losers' Club in Stephen King's *It*, who dared to confront the nightmare that was Pennywise. Or perhaps you recall Captain Ahab's obsessive quest in Melville's *Moby-Dick*, trying to conquer the legendary white whale.

But here's the thing: starting from a low place doesn't automatically mean someone is on the right side of history—or God's side. It's more complex than that. The truth is, God's thoughts are not our thoughts, and His ways are not our ways. He's not like us. He frequently works miraculously through situations that, to us, seem hopeless—but they are only impossible by human standards. God operates both overtly and subversively. In His kingdom, the last are first and the first are last. As Jesus said:

4. Billy Graham, *The Reason for My Hope: Salvation*, 152.
5. Rom 8:27.
6. Rom 8:31.

> Blessed are you who are poor,
> for yours is the kingdom of God.
> Blessed are you who hunger now,
> for you will be satisfied.
> Blessed are you who weep now,
> for you will laugh.
> Blessed are you when people hate you,
> when they exclude you and insult you
> and reject your name as evil,
> because of the Son of Man.[7]

God is not confined by human systems of power or prestige. In fact, He uses the very marred confines of humanity to showcase His glory. Consider Moses, who doubted himself and struggled with speech. Or Joseph, hated by his brothers, sold into slavery, falsely accused, and imprisoned before becoming second-in-command in Egypt. Hadassah, an unremarkable orphan, became Queen Esther and saved her people. Sarah bore a child in her old age; Abraham was a hundred years old, and she wasn't far behind. And Joseph and Mary? They became parents to Jesus in the middle of scandal, raising a child conceived by the Holy Spirit—not by the conventional way, with the lights off and Luther Vandross playing in the background.

God made Ehud's left-handedness an asset in taking down Eglon. Believe it or not, but once upon a time, I was also left-handed—or at least was well on my way. My dad has hesitantly recounted this story, though my mom has happily filled in the details. When I was a toddler, evidently it was obvious that I tried to hold and pick up things with my left hand. My dad, who is right-handed, figured life was hard enough already. People, especially kids, can be cruel and unforgiving. When you stick out, accommodations have to be made (or not), and adjustment is never easy, no matter how you slice it. He didn't want that for me if it could be avoided. So, with his heart in the right place—though I don't recommend this—he began his intervention. If I picked something up with my left hand, he'd take it and put it in my right. If I waddled around the house carrying toys in my left hand, he'd transfer them to my right. And wouldn't you know it? Before long, I stopped favoring my left hand. Only God knows what might have been, but to this day, I am right-hand dominant. In this passage, it's easy to fixate on the dramatic details of a

---

7. Luke 6:20–22.

left-handed warrior, almost as if God expects you and me to maneuver around like Ehud—ready to ambush anyone who dares disrespect Him or harm us. But that's not the point. What we find in Judges 3:12–31 is a picture of asset-based[8] theology—an understanding that, depending on the mission or context, strengths can become weaknesses, and weaknesses can become strengths. Discerning which is which takes spiritual insight. It takes maturity. As Christians, we can't afford to be afraid of the unlikely, whatever or whoever that may be.

Ehud wasn't a superhero. He didn't wear tights, shoot laser beams, or stop locomotives with one hand. He was a regular Joe—or Jane—just like us. And just like us, God called him to service, to play a small role in a vast, ever-unfolding reality. Ehud obeyed God, and in doing so, he didn't use what he had to get what he wanted. There was no "shake what your momma gave you" attitude, no "if you've got it, flaunt it" outlook. He wasn't a narcissist, constantly calculating how others could serve him or how to exploit their gifts. Instead, he laid down his ego and anxiety and simply obeyed—boldly, faithfully stewarding how he was made to make a difference. He was a left-handed soldier. Odds are, most of us here this morning are neither soldiers nor left-handed. But we are retirees, aunts and uncles, moms and grandfathers, friends and professors. We are deacons, elders, ordained ministers, and laypeople—yet all of us are ministers in some capacity. We are gardeners, bakers, Kids Hope volunteers, handymen, and photographers. We sing, serve, pray, tithe, count money, and troubleshoot microphones when they give us trouble. We sew, quilt, and make blankets and brownies. We are police officers, business owners, engineers, avid readers and walkers, teachers, coaches, and career advisors.

Each of us excels in certain areas while lagging in others. And while it's good to know our strengths and weaknesses, we must never let them become an excuse for avoiding what God wants to do through us—however He chooses to do it. On May 30, 1792, in a sermon to pastors in Nottingham, England, William Carey said: "Expect great things from God! Attempt great things for God!"[9] Roughly four months later, he and his

---

8. For the foundational principles, minus the theology, see Gary Paul Green and Anna L. Haines, *Asset Building & Community Development*, Kathryn J. O'Day and John P. Kretzmann, *Change the Way You See Everything: Through Asset-Based Thinking*, or John P. Kretzmann and John L. McKnight, *Discovering the Other: Asset-Based Approaches for Building Community Together*.

9. See William Carey, *An Enquiry into the Obligations of Christians to Use Means for the Conversion of the Heathens*.

family were sent to India by the newly formed Baptist Missionary Society. That kind of encouragement is not restricted to those God summons to global missions. It's at the heart of Ehud's example, and it applies without exception to everyone who says they trust Christ.

Passing the Buck
Judges 4, October 22, 2023

God hath not promised skies of always blue
Flower-strewn pathways all our lives through;
God hath not promised sun without rain,
Joy without sorrow, peace without pain.

God hath not promised we shall not know
Toil and temptation, trouble and woe;
He hath not told us we shall not bear
Many a burden, many a care.

God hath not promised smooth roads and wide,
Swift, easy travel, needing no guide;
Never a mountain, rocky and steep,
Never a river, turbid and deep.

But God hath promised strength for the day,
Rest for the labor, light for the way,
Grace for the trials, help from above,
Unfailing sympathy, undying love.[1]

ANNIE JOHNSON FLINT WENT to be with the Lord in 1932 at the age of 66. Born in New Jersey, she lost her mother as a toddler and her father by the time she was six. She and her younger sister were then adopted by a childless couple, the Flints. Like many women of her time, Annie began a teaching career after graduating from high school. Within a few years, however, and within mere months of each other, her adoptive parents also passed away. Around that same time, Annie began experiencing

---

1. See Annie Johnson Flint, *What God Hath Promised*.

severe arthritis, a condition that soon made the stable career of teaching virtually impossible. At a sanitarium in Clifton Springs, New York, a place where many sought healing or answers, Annie received the devastating diagnosis that she would likely remain an invalid for the rest of her life. Yet even amid these trials, she turned to what had always been a refuge for her: poetry. Having given her heart to Jesus as a child, she now leaned into her gift as a writer not only as an emotional outlet but to support herself.

Her deeply honest, faith-filled compositions gained the attention of Christian publishers, magazines, and newspapers across the nation. Two days after her passing, *The New York Times* published a brief obituary titled: "Annie Johnson Flint, Dead; Widely Known Poet; Bedridden for 30 Years."[2] Whether due to circumstances beyond our control, personal missteps, or a mix of both, we all know what it feels like to wrestle with the demands of life. Decisions must be made, and one thing we all share is that we *do* make them. In Judges 4, we observe three people much like us. Two women chose not to pass the buck. Despite their flaws, they stepped into God's will with full courage and meekness. They had fears and misgivings, as we all do, but those didn't take center stage. As Edwin Friedman writes in *A Failure of Nerve: Leadership in the Age of the Quick Fix*, "Whenever a 'family' is driven by anxiety, what will also always be present is a failure of nerve among its leaders."[3] These ladies stepped up to the plate.

Until we die or Christ returns, the call for followers of Jesus is a life of ongoing deference. Our emotions and our logic can be helpful companions, *if* they move us toward God's will, revealed through Scripture and guided by the Holy Spirit—not toward justifying our disobedience. Deborah and Jael exemplify such bold obedience. Barak, on the other hand, well, not so much. So here's your homework: Take time this week to remember specific times when you did what was right—when you responded exactly as God was calling you to. Thank Him for the strength He provided and for His loving presence. But also reflect on the times when you failed miserably like Barak. And while you're there in honest reflection, let Psalm 145:8–9 wash over you: "The Lord is gracious and compassionate, slow to anger and rich in love. The Lord is good to all; He has compassion on all He has made." To borrow the words of Sidney

---

2. "Annie Johnson Flint, Dead; Widely Known Poet: Bedridden for 30 Years," *The New York Times*, 1932.

3. Edwin H. Friedman, *A Failure of Nerve: Leadership in the Age of the Quick Fix*, 2.

Lanier, a fellow poet who died 51 years before Annie: "We live in an age of half faith and half doubt; standing at the temple doors, head in, heart out."[4] Even so, God meets us in our incompleteness. He knows that we "know in part, and prophesy in part."[5] He is not a hardened taskmaster or slumlord. He's not an absent partner. He's not keeping a clipboard full of merits and demerits. He is holy, yes, and perfect, but also relational and sacrificial—the only One who, in Christ Jesus, "died for all, that those who live should no longer live for themselves but for Him who died for them and was raised again."[6]

By the time our story picks up, Ehud, the last judge, had already taken his eternal dirt nap. And, unsurprisingly, the Israelites were once again doing evil in the eyes of the Lord. Like someone at a club, house party, wedding reception, or family reunion who always pulls out the same tried-and-true dance move, annoying everyone, disobedience was Israel's default setting—and if we're honest, it's often ours, too. Fed up with God and His provision, they consistently reverted to their destructive habits, despite those habits *never* ending well. Barak was the military commander of Israel, while Deborah—like many women both then and now—was multitasking with grace. She was both a judge and a prophet. The Israelites had been "cruelly oppressed" for 20 years by Jabin, king of Canaan. When they finally cried out to the Lord for help (as they tended to do once their mess caught up with them), Deborah received God's command to tell Barak it was time to go to war. As we read in Judges 4:6–7, God promised him victory—*if* he obeyed. In verse 8, however, Barak claps back with a conditional response: "If you go with me, I'll go; but if you don't go, I won't go." At the very least, this reveals his shaky trust in God—and highlights just how steady and courageous Deborah was. Her reply? "Certainly I will go with you. But because of the course you are taking, the honor will not be yours, for the Lord will deliver Sisera into the hands of a woman."

I think of Deborah as the spiritual equivalent of Shaft. In the iconic 1971 Blaxploitation film *Shaft*, Isaac Hayes scored the soundtrack, and Richard Roundtree played the rule-breaking, womanizing private detective hero, John Shaft. Folks would say, "That John Shaft, he's a bad—" only to be interrupted with, "Shut your mouth!" Then came the reply, "I'm only

---

4. Sidney Lanier, *The Poems of Sidney Lanier*, 77.
5. 1 Cor 13:9–12.
6. 2 Cor 5:15.

talking about Shaft."[7] Well, Deborah was cut from the same cloth. You could almost hear someone say, "That Deborah, she's a bad—" and another voice jumping in, "Shut your mouth!" *"I'm only talking about Deborah."* She's the leader you want. She's the leader we should aspire to be.

And everything unfolded just as she said it would. With Jael's help, the very woman Deborah foretold would bring down Sisera, the Israelites triumphed over their captors. Notice how Deborah handled all of this. She didn't emasculate Barak or humiliate him for his reluctance or fear. She didn't say he was weak or worthless, even though that kind of treatment is common today. Instead, she chose compassion and cooperation, while also plainly telling the truth. Essentially, she said, "I'll go with you, no problem. But let's be clear—by altering what God told you, you're changing the outcome. He said *you* were to go. Your adjustment means the honor won't be yours." Sometimes, we know the cost of compromising upfront. Other times, we only find out later. But in every case, we shouldn't twist God's instructions to suit our comfort. We should move whatever needs moving to prioritize conformity to whatever God says. But if we're honest, we don't always do that. We doubt. We talk ourselves out of devotion, out of sanctification, because the odds look grim, or our weapons appear inadequate. Still, as our charismatic brothers and sisters often say, "Holiness is still right." Anything less than full obedience grieves God. Yet in His mercy, He continues to work through us—and in spite of us—for His good, perfect, and pleasing will.

Then there's Jael—another woman worth imitating within reason. While his army was being defeated, Sisera, commander of Jabin's forces, ran for his life like a fugitive on an episode of *Cops* or *Law & Order*. He ended up at the tent of Heber the Kenite, an ally, whose wife Jael was home. Being a good hostess according to the customs of the time, she welcomed the frantic general, gave him milk, covered him with a blanket, and offered him rest. Before dozing off, he told her to lie if anyone came asking if he was inside. Not exactly the way you'd expect a guest to behave, especially a desperate one—but that's what he did. And whether or not Jael fully understood the broader picture, God was at work. As Sisera slept, she seized her moment. Grabbing a tent peg and a hammer, she drove it through his temple, into the ground. As verse 21 concludes, "and he died." Yeah—*I bet he did.* A peg through your skull will do that. Nevertheless, Jael didn't pass the buck. She didn't wait for someone else. She played her part and we should commit to playing ours.

7. *Shaft*, 1971.

"In those days Israel had no king; everyone did as they saw fit." That's remains true for us in certain ways. Even though we believers have King Jesus—who is far better than any earthly politician—we still find ourselves out of alignment: passionately protesting, cursing, denying Him, and generally struggling, as is common to humanity, to know our place. On June 15, 1946, the year after her husband completed his fourth and final presidential term, First Lady Eleanor Roosevelt declared, "It is not fair to ask of others what you are not willing to do yourself."[8] In that spirit, let me join the assignment I gave to you. One of my "Deborah and Jael" moments was answering the call to pastoral ministry. To spend one's vocation depending on the faithful giving of others to, in a sense, sustain a large portion of your livelihood is, let's just say, a unique position to be in. I never expected that saying "yes" to God would lead to fame or fortune, but this life is not easy. Nevertheless, from the beginning I have tried to lean on the simple conviction that God would guide and sustain me—and He has; just not without trials.

Let me be candid with you, and Maplewood, this is a testament to my affection for you. Our church is what it is, and we're fervently praying for growth sooner rather than later, but the way you've treated me, my wife, one another, and our community has refreshed my faith. That said, if I were preaching a false gospel of health, wealth, and happiness; or some hollow version of progressivism that tears out parts of Scripture I don't like; or a vitriolic conservative theology that demonizes anyone who thinks or lives differently than me—combined with the gifts God has given me, I could be making a lot more money.

In one of my books, I express that there's no union for pastors when the system fails us.[9] This isn't everyone's story, but many ministers have as much or more education than their friends who are lawyers, doctors, engineers, and entrepreneurs—and often more student debt. Unless we pursue big church jobs, it's hard to make ends meet sometimes or to get ahead. And many of us move a lot. Renata and I have lived in Canada and seven U.S. states in the last sixteen years. My point is: despite the hardships, and my prayers asking God—at times begging Him—to let me serve Him in some other way, He hasn't changed His call. Therefore, I persist, because He has persisted. I may not be on covert missions driving

---

8. Eleanor Roosevelt, "It Is Not Fair to Ask of Others What You Are Not Willing to Do Yourself," *My Day*, 1946.

9. See James Ellis III, *Tell the Truth, Shame the Devil: Stories about the Challenges of Young Pastors*.

tent pegs through anyone's temple, but I try to devotedly invest in what God has called me to do. Like Deborah, who stepped up when Barak hesitated, I want to honor God with full submission as best I can. Speaking of Barak, in my early twenties, fresh out of undergrad, I regret to say I wasn't very responsible with money. Once I landed my first few full-time jobs, with benefits and all, I nearly lost my mind. I don't know if it qualifies as "passing the buck," but I acted like money grew on trees and time was unlimited. I learned the hard way that neither was true.

At one point, my vehicle was repossessed—the first one I'd ever purchased on my own. It was a used Mitsubishi Montero Sport SUV with a few miles on it, and I loved that car. *Do you hear me?* Slow in the city, fast on the highway, I zipped all over the DC area. With the music cranked up as loud as I could stand it, I had "Ha"[10] by the rapper Juvenile on repeat. You couldn't tell me nothing! *Do you hear me?* But somebody should've told me (and they very well may have; back then I didn't listen well) that the bank was serious about wanting their money. They didn't care that some of my cash flow had abruptly stopped flowing, as I found myself in between jobs. Although I miss that car, I do not miss that attitude, preoccupied as I was with passing the buck and trying to play a part more than responding faithfully to what I'd been given. Humility comes in various forms, but God always sends it for our sanctification. Mark Twain was right that, "Courage is resistance to fear, mastery of fear—not absence of fear."[11] Remember Annie's daring declaration:

> But God hath promised strength for the day,
> Rest for the labor, light for the way,
> Grace for the trials, help from above,
> Unfailing sympathy, undying love.[12]

---

10. Juvenile, "Ha," 1998.
11. Mark Twain, *Pudd'nhead Wilson and Other Tales*, 72.
12. Annie Johnson Flint, *What God Hath Promised*.

Sometimes We Need to Sing
Judges 5, October 29, 2023

EVERYWHERE YOU GO, IT'S easily detected. In elevators or waiting rooms, you hear it. Karaoke is built around it. At high school, college, and professional sporting events, there's no escaping it. Most of us blast it in the car or at the gym. Personally, I often listen to it while ironing clothes at home—it's therapeutic. In the shower, many of us have delivered spirited renditions of our favorite songs, confident that only God knows how offbeat and out of tune we truly were. Back at Lyndon Hill Elementary School, LaVante Johnson and I once performed our best rendition of the 1989 single "Self-Destruction" during a talent show. The song featured a lineup of prominent rappers, with proceeds going to the National Urban League to support the Stop the Violence Movement. Elton John once said, "'Music has healing power. It can take people out of themselves for a few hours.'" This is true. There seems to be a universal resonance within us that affirms the gift that is music. Whether superficial or awe-inspiring, some song, artist, or genre holds meaning for each of us. Like most things, its expression varies across cultures. In Brazil, there's *Carnival* and the legendary samba dancers. In New Orleans, it's bounce music and jazz, shaped by Mardi Gras traditions and the second-line brass band funeral parades. As expressed in the soundtrack of the 1984 breakdancing film *Breakin'*, many of us know from experience that "music makes you lose control."[1]

Many people, especially students I served while at Hope College, have heard the story of how, when Renata and I were just getting to know each other, I finally worked up the nerve, as an introvert at that, to express my sincere romantic interest in her. I even dared to hope that, if the Lord willed it, she might one day become my wife. Her response? "Oh,

---

1. *Breakin'*, 1984.

you're too nice for me. But I should hook you up with my roommate." Understandably, we didn't stay in regular contact for a while after that. Later, though, once the Holy Spirit had softened her heart a bit, we reconnected. One of my favorite memories from that time is slow dancing with her to Shania Twain's songs "From This Moment On" and "Forever and for Always." To this day, almost any Shania Twain song brings that to mind. Over the years, we've probably logged thousands of miles playing her music playing in the car. Music has a way of marking boundaries in time—it can transport us instantly to a memory, a place, a person, or a specific moment. It's been shown to help regulate stress, anxiety, loneliness, relaxation, and sleep. In good times, hard times, and everything in between, music helps us lament, celebrate, and live. As simple as it may sound, for the sake of others, the vital work we are called to, and the health of our own souls—sometimes we just need to sing. That's exactly what we see happening in Judges 5.

Barak, the somewhat reluctant yet ultimately victorious commander of Israel's army, and Deborah—the powerful judge and prophet you'll remember as the real "shot caller"—sing a song in the aftermath of their triumph over Jabin, the king of Canaan. Their song is like a biblical version of an *ESPN* highlight reel or a poetic *CliffsNotes* summary, preserving their victory in the lyrical annals of history. In many Bibles, including the NIV, Judges 5 is titled something like "The Song of Deborah," and for good reason. While Barak did lead the Israelites into battle against the Canaanites, he did so only under the condition that Deborah accompany him. Though God explicitly ordered Deborah to tell Barak to lead the charge, his response was, "If you go with me, I will go; but if you don't go with me, I won't go." Deborah agreed but prophesied that once they won, the honor would not be his: "The Lord will deliver Sisera into the hands of a woman." That woman, of course, was Jael—who drove a tent peg through the skull of Sisera, the opposing general. Barak is mentioned in the song, but only briefly and almost as an afterthought.

Deborah, by contrast, is honored throughout the song. Before her bold and faithful leadership, "the highways were abandoned," as verse 6 tells us. With Halloween around the corner, it's easy to imagine the scene through the lens of a *Scooby-Doo* episode—mystery, fear, and danger lurking around every corner. People were scared. They avoided the main roads for fear of robbery, assault, or worse. Historical context suggests that many fled the open terrain and sought the safety of walled cities.

Deborah, however, helped unify the people, leading them into a 40-year period of divinely ordained peace.

Verse 7 states, "Villagers in Israel would not fight; they held back until I, Deborah, arose, until I arose, a mother in Israel." When Deborah spoke, people listened. She was a forward-facing force of God's will, and Jael, in turn, became the unexpected hero who delivered the final blow. In Judges 5, God's praises are sung not just in temples but in public gathering places—at taverns, watering holes, and community spaces—where people recounted how the Lord brought victory. Sisera, who had long oppressed Israel with his 900 iron chariots, was brought down in part because the rain, sent by God, turned the battleground into a muddy, mushy mess, rendering the chariots useless, metal tombs. Then came Jael, described in verse 24 as the "most blessed of tent-dwelling women": "She struck Sisera, she crushed his head, she shattered and pierced his temple." But not everyone joined the fight. Unlike past battles, when tribes rallied to each other's aid, some held back this time. Verses 16–17 read, "In the districts of Reuben there was much searching of heart. Gilead stayed beyond the Jordan. And Dan, why did he linger by the ships?" Deborah might've said, "There is some fungus among us." The truth is, division among God's people is a recurring theme in Judges, and throughout the Bible. At times, there's beautiful unity, like siblings ready to stand together against a common foe. Other times, it boils down to every tribe for itself. The song concludes with a dramatic and sobering scene beginning in verse 28. Sisera's mother—who hasn't appeared in the story until now—waits anxiously for her son to return from battle. "Why is his chariot so long in coming? Why is the clatter of his chariots delayed?" she wonders. She imagines him and his men reveling in victory, dividing spoils taken from their defeated enemies. But tragically, she doesn't yet know that her son—her flesh and blood—is gone, now only to be spoken of in the past tense.

The power of song is unmistakable in Judges chapter 5. It's one reason why it's not only wise, but some would argue that it is necessary to musically commemorate victories, losses, setbacks, and even the ordinary moments of life. Think about your prom date. The song you played while cruising in your first car. The one that captured exactly how you felt in a moment—expressing something you couldn't quite put into words. I wonder what songs would make it onto the soundtrack of your life? The song played at a loved one's homegoing? The artist you turn to most while sewing, tinkering in the garage, or reminiscing about days gone by? Music is a powerful tool. One of its great benefits is how it can reinforce truths we hold dear—truths we may be prone to forget or deny when we're frustrated. Billy Ocean explained in 1985, "When the Going Gets Out, the Tough Get Going,"[2] but the tough in us sometimes seems slow to activate. Maybe you can identify with that. Given what's happening on the world stage—Russia's invasion of Ukraine and, more recently, Hamas' deadly attack on Israel—the celebratory tone of Judges 5 might strike some as unpleasant or even offensive. In wars like these, there may be a declared winner and loser, but every side loses something. The combatants we read about in the Bible were real people. Savage though he was, Sisera was loved by someone. King Jabin was loved by someone. Jael, Deborah, and Barak had family who cared whether they lived or died. God's people and God's enemies alike had dreams, plans, cakes to bake, and children to tuck into bed at night—children who were afraid of the dark.

War is never pretty, even if, in our broken world, it's sometimes deemed necessary. It always brings damage of some kind—often more collateral than anticipated or admitted. Today, in the long-standing conflict between Israel and Hamas, nearly everyone has an opinion. Amid the chaos, explosions, and stench of damage, even Christians can get swept up in the noise, chasing attention and followers in all the wrong places. But having a platform doesn't make you an expert, and being an expert doesn't make you right. Experts are wrong all the time. Tom Brady was an expert quarterback, but he threw interceptions, lost games, and even lost championships. I've enjoyed films starring Jamie Foxx, Tom Hanks, Jamie Lee Curtis, Samuel L. Jackson, and Eva Mendes—but they've all been in some duds, too. And meteorologists? Well, we all know how that goes. If we are to be spiritually mature, responsible, compassionate, and intellectually honest—and I believe the Holy Spirit enables us to be—we may need to stop exhausting ourselves trying to make sense of senselessness. What happened to God's chosen people then may, in some ways, be linked to what's unfolding today, but how, exactly, is rarely something we know with certainty. And that's okay. It's okay to stay in that uncertain place while yet praying, weeping, and celebrating where, when, and how we can. The book of Judges repeatedly reminds us, "In those days Israel had no king; everyone did as they saw fit." That line diagnoses the

---

2. Billy Oean, "When the Going Gets Tough, the Tough Get Going," 1985.

condition of God's people then, and it resonates still. The difference is that today, we don't just have a king—we have *the* King, the King of Kings and Lord of Lords: Jesus. So, we need to sing more than ever.

In her 2022 Pulitzer Prize–winning novel *Demon Copperhead*, Barbara Kingsolver writes, "I'm hopeful because you have to be. We cannot give up. We must work at it. Hopeful is something you do. It's your job."[3] Renata shared that quote with me last week. Singing, I believe, is one way we practice hope. That's why, as best I can tell, there's always a reason to sing, alone or together, in thanksgiving to God. When someone's birthday comes around, we should sing. The classic recitation comes to mind, of course:

> Happy birthday to you,
> Happy birthday to you,
> Happy birthday dear [Name],
> Happy birthday to you.

But there is also the spirited refrain of Stevie Wonder's 1980 version, created as a tribute to the late Reverend Dr. Martin Luther King, Jr. It is worth checking out if you are unfamiliar. If you think long enough, you'll find a reason to sing. In 1779, deeply convicted by the Holy Spirit of his own wicked and wretched condition, John Newton, at the age of 47 and once a trader of enslaved people along the African coast, penned the hymn "Amazing Grace." In the third stanza, he wrote:

> Through many dangers, toils, and snares,
> I have already come;
> 'Tis grace hath brought me safe thus far,
> And grace will lead me home.[4]

This is a fitting reminder for any Christian—and also appropriate for someone still on the fence—who longs to taste the victory of eternal life offered by Jesus, the only one able to lead us from being lost and blind to being found and finally able to see clearly. One reason, among countless others, not to forsake gathering together as a church body, both locally and in spiritual unity with believers around the world, is the support we give and receive through singing. We sing to encourage one another at times, but most importantly, to give thanks to God.

Sometimes, we simply need to sing.

---

3. Barbara Kingsolver, *Demon Copperhead*, 495.
4. John Newton, "Amazing Grace," 1779.

The Weight of Asking God to Wait

Judges 6:1–18, November 5, 2023

HE DID NOT NOMINATE himself, no votes were cast, and he was not consulted at all—yet Gideon still finds himself handpicked as the next judge, a rescuer of his countrymen, God's covenant people. Inducted into the Rock and Roll Hall of Fame in 1989, The Shirelles—a vocal quartet of African American female classmates from Passaic, New Jersey—back in April of 1961 released a wonderful song: "Mama Said."[1] Parents and others can warn us of impending tribulation, but they can also be the cause. In either case, challenging days are ahead for all of us, in one way or another, whether we have advanced knowledge or not. The Israelites, who endured roughly 2,555 grueling days, or seven years, under an oppressive Midianite regime, all because *they* had done "evil in the eyes of the Lord." As we've seen in previous chapters, their immediate ancestors were no strangers to this nauseating pattern of rebellion. They just wouldn't do right, it seems. By that, I mean they continually violated God's prohibition against worshiping other gods—those lesser, false, and nonexistent deities whose astrological, fertility, or sexual cults were all the rage. Whether they never took this command seriously or on rare occasions when they might have, they still gave in to internal and external pressures. Like foolish radicals following Frank Sinatra's advice to its natural end, they were all about doing it, "My Way,"[2]—even though their way was never the right way.

---

1. The Shirelles, "Mama Said," 1961.
2. See Frank Sinatra, "My Way," 1969.

It all comes down to this: the people of God did not listen to God. This tragic truth, stated plainly in verse 10, echoes throughout the book of Judges. In this instance, having chosen mutiny against the one true and living God, His people were hanging on by a thread. Things were so dire that, as a basic survival tactic, as found in verse 2, "they prepared shelters for themselves in mountain clefts, caves, and strongholds." For the Israelites, anything of value—if found—was taken. Crops? *Taken*. Sheep, cattle, and donkeys? *Taken*. Like swarms of locusts, the Midianites would sweep in and strip the land bare, leaving the people destitute, depressed, and dejected. Without a holy interruption, death would surely be next on the docket. As it has been said, "Courage is not the absence of fear, but rather the assessment that something else is more important than fear."[3] Unfortunately, cowardice—not courage—defined the people of God. They were utterly terrified of the Midianites. If Aleksandr Solzhenitsyn was right in *The Gulag Archipelago* when he wrote, "The simple step of a courageous individual is not to take part in the lie,"[4] then the Israelites failed that test miserably. Their lives were marked by deceit, defiance, and the dishonesty of betrayal. Let's be honest: these weren't Teenage Mutant Ninja Turtles living underground in the sewer system, misunderstood and shunned despite their passion for justice, martial arts, and pizza. No, the Israelites were a people hard-pressed on every side, not because of injustice or misfortune, but purely because they had convinced themselves that God was not enough.

You might remember the 1984 film *Red Dawn*, featuring young up-and-comers Patrick Swayze, Charlie Sheen, and Lea Thompson. It depicted a violent, gruesome World War III scenario, beginning in Colorado with an invasion by Cuban, Soviet, and Nicaraguan forces. With their town and way of life under siege—and many of their parents imprisoned or executed—a group of teenagers fought to survive in the wilderness. Gideon felt just as ill-equipped for his task of liberation as they did for theirs. We don't like to hear this, but not everyone can be the indominable Coach K, Mike Kryzyzewski, of former Duke University basketball fame. Not everyone is a Deion Sanders—who won state honors in football, baseball, and basketball in high school, then excelled in multiple sports at Florida State, and later became both an NFL legend and a Major League Baseball player. God wasn't calling Gideon to be Oprah Winfrey, Colin

---

3. Ambrose Redmoon, "No Peaceful Warriors!", *Gnosis: A Journal of the Western Inner Traditions*, Fall 1991, 11.

4. Aleksandr Solzhenitsyn, *The Gulag Archipelago: 1918–1956*, 1973.

Powell, Elliot Ness, Madam C.J. Walker, Garrett Morgan, or Joan of Arc. Nor is He calling us to be any of those titans of entrepreneurship, battle, and strategy. But God *was* calling Gideon. As verse 12 says, God identified something in Gideon that He had already placed there: "The Lord is with you, mighty warrior." The odds didn't matter. His background as a member of the weakest clan in Manasseh, and as the least significant member of his family, meant little in the face of what God had created him to accomplish. The same goes for anyone who surrenders to God. That's why Christ said, "My grace is sufficient for you, for my power is made perfect in weakness." Whether you're naturally gifted or have to work "like the dickens" at your calling, if it's the task God has placed before you, you'll be fine. Just do your part—and trust Him.

When the angel of the Lord appears to Gideon, verse 11 tells us he's in hiding, just like everyone else, threshing wheat in a winepress, tucked away to avoid detection, "to keep it from the Midianites." What follows is a back-and-forth exchange: the angel speaks, Gideon responds—three times this pattern repeats—until finally, in verse 18, the angel concludes with, "I will wait until you return." Gideon's frustration is evident. His words reveal both confusion and anger. He knows that he and his people have abandoned God, that they've been unfaithful and disrespectful. Yet, instead of owning that truth, he blames God. In verse 13, he rightly points out that the Lord has handed the Israelites over to Midian, but he fails to appreciate the bigger picture: this hardship was meant to be temporary, a season designed to correct and redeem, not to destroy. Though God guarantees victory, Gideon remains skeptical. He requests a sign—confirmation that this encounter is a true *theophany*, a divine appearance where God reveals Himself directly to a human. He then asks the angel to stay while he prepares an offering, as a gesture of honor and consecration. "Please do not go away until I come back and bring my offering and set it before you," he pleads. Some people depict God in the Old Testament as harsh, wrathful, and unloving, in contrast to the supposedly gentle, grace-filled Jesus of the New Testament. Despite Jesus' own words—"Do not think that I have come to abolish the Law or the Prophets; I have not come to abolish them but to fulfill them"[5]—this dichotomy persists.

---

5. Matt 5:17.

Many imagine Jesus as an all-accepting figure whose love erases judgment, while viewing Yahweh, Jehovah, El Shaddai, or Elohim of the Old Testament as insecure, jealous, or even cruel. But this is a false distinction. The New Testament does not replace the Old. It's not like changing your oil or swapping clothes. Rather, the Old and New Testaments exist in partnership, forming a theological and historical continuum. Texts like Judges 6:1–18 make this clear. In this story, we see not only God's power but also His patience, compassion, and mercy—qualities consistent with His character throughout Scripture. Through His angelic messenger, God speaks directly to Gideon. And what does Gideon do? He questions, complains, and hesitates. To give him the benefit of the doubt, maybe he was just overwhelmed. Still, Gideon dares to push back: "Pardon me, my lord," he says in verse 13, "but if the Lord is with us, why has all this happened to us? Where are all His wonders that our ancestors told us about? . . . But now the Lord has abandoned us and given us into the hand of Midian." God could have shut him down. He could have said, "Look, I don't have time for this. You're hiding in a corner, acting like I'm the problem—when it's your disobedience that got you here." To borrow the voice of Martin Lawrence's iconic TV character, God could've said, "I'm out." But He didn't. Instead, He said, "I will wait until you return." If that isn't love expressed through restraint, I don't know what is.

Speaking of restraint—let me just say, I don't know about you, but if I had ever responded to my mom or dad growing up with, "Uhhh, let me get back to you on that," after they gave me an instruction or invitation, all I would've seen, heard, or felt was tough love. And if their message had come through someone they'd entrusted—say, my sister, my cousin, my aunt, my teacher—and I decided not only to respond with some juvenile, discount sarcasm but also to question the whole premise? Trouble would've become my middle name. Because from their perspective, I would've been showing out in front of company or acting like they hadn't raised me right. What Gideon did, and lived to talk about, was similar. But let's be clear: just because God worked with Gideon doesn't mean we should copy him. Gideon's back-and-forth with the angel of the Lord—who is, in effect, God's messenger and voice—is not an endorsement to tell God, "Hold on while I get comfortable with what You've said." Instead, it reveals something powerful about God's character: His sensitivity toward our humanity. God never lowers His standard. There's no "dumbing it down" for us. As the popular saying goes, "Wrong is wrong, and there ain't no right way to do wrong." Insecurity and fear are never valid excuses. If God tells you to jump, the only acceptable answer is, "How high?" And this—this willingness to work with us, to show grace without compromising His holiness—is just one reason why God stands alone. There's no one better. He understands us.

In Christ, through the Holy Spirit, each of us has the capacity to say "yes" to God the first time. But being the Alpha and the Omega, He already knows we will not always get it right. So, in accordance with His will and wisdom, He adjusts—not by lowering the bar, but by offering grace within the limits He's already determined. He knows the end from the beginning.

That's both a mystery and a miracle—one that the wise among us will never take for granted.

An unknown devotional writer once described grace this way: it's as if God "bought the mortgage on your life and paid the bills completely." Grace is "a sovereign gift for every contingency…unmerited, undeserved, and unending." And that's a perfect reason to live in gratitude. Because God, having created us, knows us—and for Him to know us is to love us. He alone embodies perfect truth, and even when He delivers accountability we'd rather avoid, He does so with unshakable kindness.

Nevertheless, there's a weight—w-e-i-g-h-t—to telling God to *wait*—w-a-i-t. A few chapters ago, we read about Barak negotiating with God through the prophetess and judge Deborah. Many of us are also familiar with the moment in the book of John when the resurrected Jesus told Thomas, "Stop doubting and believe."[6] Then He added, "Because you have seen me, you have believed; blessed are those who have not seen and yet have believed." And in Genesis 19, we see the story of Lot's wife, who, in fleeing the judgment of Sodom and Gomorrah, defied God's instruction by looking back, and turned into a pillar of salt. Here's the point: God *will* accomplish what He intends to accomplish. He can use you, but He's not obligated to. So, when He does call you into a task, assignment, or calling, it should be treasured. It should be protected. It's not healthy to walk on pins and needles with God. As we've already discussed, in Christ, He loves us and works all things together for our good.[7] But the last thing you want to do is test divine providence—because how He chooses to

---

6. John 20:27.
7. Rom 8:28.

respond is His alone to know. "In those days Israel had no king; everyone did as they saw fit." Gideon is no different at this point in his journey. Whether it's entitlement, disillusionment, or aloofness, he exhibits attitudes that are not of God. And the same applies to us when we presume that today's opportunities will patiently wait until tomorrow—that the offer, the relationship, the vision, the resource, the gift, our health, or the job on the table will still be there next week or next year, while we sow our wild oats or wait for more confirmation. That's not how life, or faith, works.

Trying to negotiate with God is never the right posture, even if He mercifully accommodates our hesitation. If we're not careful, we'll wake up one day and realize we've let too many moments pass, convincing ourselves we need more time, when in truth we're just afraid to move forward. Asking God to wait isn't an act of reverence—it's a delay that only burdens our relationship with Him. And for what? Over the years, I've spent a lot of time with young men and women navigating personal and professional milestones. Our culture has shifted. Many traditional gender norms have changed before our very eyes. Some of those changes are good, but not all. I can't count the number of young women who've come to me in frustration, wondering why men their age never seem to initiate. A guy likes a girl but never asks her to lunch, dinner, a movie, bowling—anything. He just waits. And because young men have expressed their own frustrations about dating—I've heard their hearts, too. Many say, in all honesty, they've never really had to initiate. In high school, college, or even in their early careers, it was the women who made the first move. "The girls are aggressive," they've said—not as a complaint necessarily, but not with applause either. After processing things, some of these young men will say something like, "James, I really like this one girl on the volleyball team," or "She's in my internship program," or "I always see her at the gym, and I want to ask her out. But I'm afraid."

Part of what I tell them—and here's where I land—is this: "Look, I can't promise that this woman will be your wife. I don't know that. But I *do* know this: the odds of anything meaningful happening with her—or anyone else—are slim to none if you won't respond to the opportunity in front of you. If you sit on your hands long enough or keep meeting with me long enough without ever stepping up, eventually someone else might—and then it's too late." Gideon didn't realize that there's no time like the present. In asking the angel of the Lord—therefore, asking God—to prove Himself, he risked forfeiting the blessing. Tomorrow is not promised. So, if you don't yet know Jesus Christ personally, today, right now, is your opportunity. And if you already belong to the King whose kingdom has no end, let Gideon's story remind you: though God lovingly understands our struggles, *immediate* obedience is never the wrong path to take.

Fear's Familiar Tentacles
Judges 6:19–40, November 12, 2023

BEFORE WE SHIFT OUR focus to Thanksgiving, Christmas, and then New Year's, especially now, with mid-November just around the corner, let's pause to acknowledge a holiday that has only recently faded into the rearview mirror: Halloween. Originally established to mark the end of summer and the beginning of the long, dark, frigid winters that the Celtic people of what is now modern-day France, and the United Kingdom knew all too well, Halloween was also believed to be a time when the spirits of the dead returned to earth to torment farmers' crops. As power in the region changed hands, and Christianity spread through Western Europe, this pagan festival was reshaped by traditions like All Souls' Day, a Roman Catholic observance honoring baptized Christians believed to be in purgatory. This belief stems from Catholic doctrine that unrepented "lesser" sins must be atoned for after death. Most Protestants, however, reject the idea that a Christian who has not confessed every single, specific transgression before dying must then endure a kind of spiritual debtor's prison, or purgatory, to make amends before being allowed into heaven. Instead, we trust in the words of Scripture: "All have sinned and fall short of the glory of God, and all are justified freely by his grace through the redemption that came by Christ Jesus."[1] We believe one's eternal destination is determined by our response to the call of salvation—either we accept God's gift and spend forever in His presence, or we reject it and spend eternity apart from Him. There is no postmortem holding pattern where souls circle while making last-minute adjustments. All Souls' Day, with its parades, bonfires, and costumes of angels, devils, and saints, is observed on November 2. The day before, November 1, is All Saints'

---

1. Rom 3:23.

Day, celebrating the great cloud of believers who have gone before us into glory. Historically called Alholowmesse or All-Hallowmas, this led to the night before, October 31, being known as All Hallows' Eve. Over time, this name evolved into what we now call *Halloween*.

When you think about it, Americans are deeply devoted to fear—we even profit from it. In a land led by supply and demand, it's not surprising: if there's a market for something, we will market it to death and sell it so long as people cough up the dough. In 1993, the Wu-Tang Clan put it bluntly with their song, "C.R.E.A.M.,"[2] which stands for, "Cash Rules Everything Around Me." For how we operate in America, they were only telling the truth. If you guessed that Halloween spending this year would reach $12 billion, you'd be correct.[3] As over-the-top as our spending may be, there's something to be said for being scared by what is purely make-believe for a change—not by a medical bill, a car accident, a job loss, illness, armed conflict, or food insecurity. Whether it's dressing up in a goofy or ghoulish costume, watching a scary movie, or being startled by a friend or grandchild jumping out from the shadows, it's good to laugh—like really laugh. But as we know, real life isn't always so carefree. The great American poet Robert Frost, in his 1936 collection *A Further Range* wrote, "There's nothing I'm afraid of like scared people."[4] When bound by fear, we're capable of anything. Last week, we looked at Judges 6:1–18 and were introduced to Gideon, a man with serious trust issues, who was full of excuses and sass. The angel of the Lord appeared and informed him that, despite his insecurity and doubt, God had chosen him to deliver Israel from Midianite oppression. After going back and forth with the angel—three times, in fact—Gideon finally said, ". . . give me a sign that it is really you talking to me. Please do not go away until I come back and bring my offering and set it before you."

In today's verses, Judges 6:19–40, I count three more instances of Gideon operating out of fear, personifying the attitude behind this notion: "It is no measure of health to be well adjusted to a profoundly sick society." In a way, Gideon is "the rose that grew from concrete"—or at least that's the identity God sought to awaken within him. Otherwise, he was simply a product of his environment. After seven years of state-sponsored

2. Wu-Tang Clan, "C.R.E.A.M.," 1993.

3. National Retail Federation, "Halloween Spending to Reach Record $12.2 Billion as Participation Exceeds Pre-Pandemic Levels," *National Retail Federation*, 2023.

4. Robert Frost, "A Hundred Collars," 1936.

poverty, bondage, and humiliation—living in constant fear of Midianite raiders—Gideon had adapted to a survival mindset: *go along to get along.* We're sensitive, as God was, to the trauma he carried as a casualty of institutional oppression. But just as we must own our baggage, Gideon had to own the fact that he struggled deeply to trust God—God's reasoning, God's choices, God's provision, and God's presence. Gideon was suspicious. He lived with one eye open. He didn't take anyone, or anything, at face value. When God visited him, Gideon stalled; unwilling to get with the program unless it was on his own terms. This fear-fueled control showed up again when he tore down his father Joash's altar to Baal "at night rather than in the daytime," because, as verse 27 informs us, "he was afraid." Later, in verses 36–38, Gideon asks God for a sign. Then, in verses 39–40, he asks for another, saying, "Do not be angry with me. Let me make just one more request. Allow me one more test with the fleece. . ." This is a judgment-free zone—but let's be honest: by this point, it's starting to look a bit pathetic, even insulting. God only wants to rescue him and commission him for holy work, yet Gideon keeps dragging his feet. Say "ouch" if saying "amen" is too hard—because you know you've also thrown a temper tantrum or two with God yourself.

Gideon wasn't just trying to verify that he was dealing with a real messenger of God. He didn't ask the angel for an ID badge or two-step authentication. He just kept pushing, asking question after question—not because he was bold, but because he was afraid. And that fear stirred a kind of self-righteousness in him. Yet God met each of Gideon's many requests—not out of obligation, but out of a desire to communicate love in a way Gideon could receive. This is a picture of grace—not the kind we should antagonize, but the kind that humbles us.

God met Gideon where he was, but that doesn't mean we should use his story as an excuse to stay stuck in our fears. Instead, through grace and by faith, we're called to face our fears with God. Some fears will be overcome. Others will be fought for a lifetime. But all of them can be faced in God's power. As 2 Timothy 1:7 says, "For the Spirit God gave us does not make us timid, but gives us power, love, and self-discipline." Still, don't walk away thinking all fear is bad. That's not true. If you're severely allergic to nuts, pet dander, penicillin, or latex, you *should* have a healthy fear—it keeps you alert and alive. If a fire alarm goes off, you're right to think of evacuation plans, 911, and stop-drop-and-roll. However, there's a difference between preparedness and paranoia.

Fear can sharpen your focus or fog your brain. It simmers within us like soup in a crockpot, always whispering semi-sweet nothings for the sake of control. Its grip is familiar to cowards and kings, champions and cheaters alike. We fear missing out, not belonging, growing old, and growing old alone. Some here this morning have had to face the fear of losing a spouse, child, sibling, or parent—because it became their reality. And many live with the fear of being alone or rejected. Maybe your fear is shingles, taking a bad fall, memory loss, or walking down the aisle again. Maybe, if you're honest, you're terrified of death—because while you know it won't skip you, not knowing *when* or *how* it will find you, keeps you up at night. Or perhaps you're afraid of being hurt, of not loving well, of letting people down—so you invest in avoidance more than intimacy. Love, with all its vulnerable sacrifices, keeps slipping through your nervous, sweaty hands. Fear leaves fingerprints wherever humans live.

I don't want us to justify Gideon's misconduct. There's enough of that happening today, where Christians smother situations with so much grace—like sausage gravy poured over chicken-fried steak or biscuits—that the real substance of the situation, the sanctifying lesson to be learned, is obscured. Such an approach is careless and damaging. Still, I urge you not to look down on Gideon. We have a lot in common. Accountability is always important, but we should also be quick to affirm that:

> It's me, it's me, O Lord,
> Standin' in the need of prayer.
> It's me, it's me, O Lord,
> Standin' in the need of prayer.
>
> Not my brother, not my sister, but it's me, O Lord,
> Not the preacher, not the deacon, but it's me, O Lord,
> Not my father, not my mother, but it's me, O Lord,
> Not the stranger, not my neighbor, but it's me, O Lord,
>
> Standin' in the need of prayer.

Just like Gideon, the fighting hasn't even begun yet, and here he is, organizing 40 verses of delaying, dodging, and doubting. A mentor to me and many others, as James Earl Massey would sometimes say, "Of all our emotions, fear is the one that weakens our judgment the most." Whether the decision you face demands upfront evidence or the "substance of things hoped for, the evidence of things not seen," fear has a way of annihilating both every time. But let's be real—what God summons and invites us to do can be downright petrifying. If I am a Christian, I am not sanctioned to curse people out, hate people, or hoard what I've been delegated to manage. However, God will issue instructions to you that He does not issue to me and vice versa; calling you to a new business or ministry venture, to relocate somewhere you're not excited to go, or to speak when you'd prefer to remain silent, or to remain silent when you think you have a lot worth saying. But remember, we've not been given a spirit of fear.[5] It's vital to understand that when fear is given the microphone in our lives, we are, in some way, inviting the enemy of God to speak to us and for us. Fear, left unbridled, can cause incredible harm.

Affectionately known as "Black Wall Street"[6] because it was built for Black people by Black people, this area had a thriving economy where "a dollar circulated 36 to 100 times" within the community and stayed there for "almost a year before leaving." It boasted numerous Black professionals, including doctors, lawyers, educators, and entrepreneurs. There were five Black hotels, banks, churches, movie theaters, 31 restaurants, two dozen grocery stores, a library, and lavish homes. Even though at the time Oklahoma had only two airports, six Black families from this area owned their own planes. Sadly, what took decades of sacrifice, hard work, discipline, faith, courage, and innovation to build was erased over two days of violence, starting on May 31, 1921. The historic 35-city block stretch of Greenwood, a part of Tulsa, Oklahoma, was burned to the ground in what became known as the 1921 Tulsa Race Riot or Massacre. With the help of deputized city officials and mobs of White citizens, a wave of terrorism, killing, murder, and firebombing was unleashed. What had been a formidable, flourishing, and profitable Black community was soon plundered, and that valuable property ended up in White hands. "What sparked all this?" you might ask. A Black man was accused of attacking a White woman in a downtown elevator, although he was proven innocent, the charges were dropped, and the woman later exonerated him in a letter. But the damage was done. All that came too little, too late. In the aftermath, 10,000 Black people were left homeless, and over 300 were murdered, their bodies dumped into mass graves. Remember Dr. Massey's words: "Of all our emotions, fear is the one that weakens our judgment the most."

5. 2 Tim 1:7.
6. See Tim Madigan, *The Burning: Massacre, Destruction, and the Tulsa Race Riot of 1921.*

"In those days Israel had no king; everyone did as they saw fit." Our days may look different from Gideon's, but fear remains a cancer that can steal, kill, and destroy. Years ago, Renata and I toured New Bethel Baptist Church in Detroit, where Aretha Franklin's father, C. L. Franklin, pastored until his death in 1984. In its heyday, it was a megachurch—seating 3,000 in a former theater, with a massive balcony. One of the employees showed us around, and he had his daughter with him. Julia couldn't have been older than four years old. At her dad's request, she led us down a long, dimly lit hallway. Her little legs moved with crazy quickness. Between trying not to trip over anything in an unfamiliar place, it was hard to keep up. She did this multiple times, taking us to different rooms as her dad stayed behind. My best guess is that she had spent so much time in that building, that navigating it no longer terrified her as it may have in the past. When I grow up, I want to be like my little homegirl Julia. I think we *all* should strive to be like her. She didn't say much, but she was confident and purposeful. Fear is a part of life, but because of Christ, we can respond to it much better than Gideon did. And that always begins with accurate transparency about what we're feeling and what the situation is that we need help with. It is virtually impossible to be healed from what you refuse to reveal, which only advances fear's tentacles. As the English proverb says, you may end up trying to master someone else's life because you despise your own. Face your fears with God now, while you still can.

A Tale of Two Testimonies
Judges 7, November 19, 2023

"It was the best of times, it was the worst of times, it was the age of wisdom, it was the age of foolishness, it was the epoch of belief, it was the epoch of incredulity, it was the season of Light, it was the season of Darkness, it was the spring of hope, it was the winter of despair."[1] Charles Dickens wrote these words in his 1859 novel *A Tale of Two Cities*. Indeed, much of life seems to swing between extremes, at times in clear opposites, and at other times in collaborative pairs. Interestingly, the Bible has already weighed in on this subject. King Solomon, thought to have authored the book of Ecclesiastes, wrote in verse 9 of chapter 4, "Two are better than one, because they have a good return for their labor." This sentiment was echoed in 2009 by Taylor Swift and the band Boys Like Girls, who released their song "Two Are Better Than One." But it doesn't end there. Many others, in their own ways, have affirmed the value of two. "The Boss" Bruce Springsteen has sung about "Two Hearts," and Brad Paisley has his song "Two People Fell in Love." There's *Two of a Kind*, a 1983 romantic crime comedy starring Olivia Newton-John and John Travolta; *Two Weeks Notice* (2002), with Hugh Grant and Sandra Bullock during their prime; and, not to be outdone, we can't forget the 1970 western *Two Mules for Sister Sara*, starring Clint Eastwood and Shirley MacLaine.

Understanding that today's trending battle against ableism is separate from hardwired biological imperatives, not to mention God's idea of standardized human flourishing, we all hope for twos: two hands and two feet, two eyes and two ears, two arms and two legs. And we desire not just for two generic adults to assume responsibility, but the exclusive

---

1. Charles Dickens, *A Tale of Two Cities*, 3.

two biological parents, which of course both the Bible and science say can only be one male parent—we call him father—and one female parent—we call her mother—to produce and rear the child. Two, exemplifying an incontrovertible binary that fits hand in glove. Furthermore, its highest ideal is found in one husband being wedded to one wife until only death separates the two who have become one.

Twos are all the rage. Dr. Seuss proved it with Thing One and Thing Two. In arithmetic, there are even and odd numbers. Two. A fraction consists of two parts: the numerator and the denominator. We need day and night. Two. In 1991, with cool dance moves and parachute-sized pants, MC Hammer declared, "2 Legit 2 Quit." To use chopsticks, you need two. Twix candy bars come in a pack of two. There's 2Pac Shakur, Finesse2Tymes, and 2 Chainz. And in today's text, we come across two testimonies. For a change, the first one isn't about our friend Gideon, but rather about his comrades—his family members, and the nation of Israel. "The Lord said to Gideon, 'You have too many men. I cannot deliver Midian into their hands, or Israel would boast against me.'" God knew that His people would say, "My own strength has saved me." Imagine how you would feel if God called you to a colossal task—one of life and death—and though He assured victory, He suddenly pumped the brakes just as you were coordinating provisions, people, and next steps. God told Gideon, in short, "You're doing too much. You've planned too well. Too many ducks are perfectly lined up in a row." It was too neat, too proper, too crowded. And God knows His creation. He knew that if He allowed things to stay that way, the people of Israel would misappropriate His power, acting as if it was by their own strength—through their will, bravery, sacrifice, skill, and generosity—that they were positioned to defeat their enemies.

That won't work for God. He will not accept anything less than preeminence in our lives, and He does not tolerate others siphoning credit that belongs solely to Him. Sin has fragmented us, leaving us with an ever-throbbing internal compulsion to oversell our piety and intellect. As a result, God creates, or allows, conditions that forcefully demonstrate how reliant we are on Him for our triumphs, both big and small. Yes, we have a role in the play, but we are never the lead.

In verses 1–8, the army Gideon was poised to lead—quicker than you can say "Jehoshaphat Jones"—was reduced from 30,000 to 10,000, and then finally to 300 who made the cut to face the Midianites. Everyone else was sent home. Some of you may remember the scene in the 1979 film *The Warriors*, when David Patrick Kelly's character yells, from one gang to another, "Warriors, come out to play!"[2] Now, Gideon is ready, willing, and able to do the work after all the hesitation. With thousands of warriors ready to fight in God's name, he might have said, "Midianites, come out to play," when God pulls the rug out from under him, shrinking his fighting force first to 33%, then to a mere 3%. In the end, after starting with 30,000, Gideon is left with a pitiful 1%—just 300 men. Those are outrageously ridiculous odds. But remember our theme: "In those days Israel had no king; everyone did as they saw fit." God is laboring to get His people, called by His name, to stop worshipping themselves, stop following the whims of popular or powerful groups, and focus entirely on Him.

The first testimony focused on the collective—the macro, big-picture view of the people of God—and their tendency to quickly claim glory that does not belong to them. Verses 9 through the end of Judges 7 chronicle how God, once again as in chapter 6, gently shepherds Gideon through his fear. Knowing Gideon's particular struggles, God offers him an invitation—not because He must, but because He chooses to: "Get up, go down against the camp, because I am going to give it into your hands." God adds, "If you are afraid to attack, go down to the camp with your servant Purah and listen to what they are saying. Afterward, you will be encouraged to attack the camp." This second testimony arises from God's gracious prompting—a reassurance that He sees Gideon, loves him, and can be trusted. As Scripture reminds us, God "is not a human, that he should lie, not a human being, that he should change his mind."[3] In other words, God thoroughly knew Gideon's DNA: his limitations, his trauma, his fears, and his strengths. And God responded with compassion, engaging him in a way that took all those factors into account. Sometimes, God meets us in uniquely tailored ways to help us stay the course on that "long road of obedience in the same direction."[4]

Through divine diversion—what you might call holy confusion—God caused the Midianite camp to turn on itself. By the end of the chapter, Gideon's 300 men, divided into three companies, strike just as the enemy changes guard. This surprise attack causes panic, and many Midianites fall

---

2. *The Warriors*, 1979.

3. Num 23:19.

4. See Eugene H. Peterson, *A Long Obedience in the Same Direction: Discipleship in an Instant Society*.

to friendly fire, as verse 22 notes: "The Lord caused the men throughout the camp to turn on each other with their swords." Two of the Midianite leaders are killed with their severed heads brought to Gideon as crude proof of victory. But the turning point began the night before, with God's words: "If you are afraid. . ." And by now, we all know—it wasn't a matter of "if." God knew Gideon *was* afraid. Yet in His mercy, God provided secondary and even tertiary layers of support to help Gideon obey. God's call alone should have been enough, and in truth, it should be enough for us too. But He told Gideon to approach the Midianite camp under cover of darkness, where he would overhear a soldier expressing terror—saying in verse 14, "God has given the Midianites and the whole camp into his hands." God knew this would encourage Gideon. And instructing him to take his servant Purah along was yet another layer of comfort—an extra hand to steady him, to help ease the grip of anxiety and attune him to the Spirit's work. Each one of us can land in a place of desperation or depression, that implores us to cry out, saying, as Carrie Underwood did in her 2005 song, "Jesus, Take the Wheel."[5] Gideon was no different. He obviously wasn't petitioning for Jesus to save him, but he was exhausted and terrified.

In her devotional book *A Lamp Unto My Feet: The Bible's Light For Your Daily Walk*, missionary-turned-Bible teacher Elisabeth Elliot wrote, "The Bible is full of examples of people doing what they could do and asking God to do what they couldn't do."[6] She's right—there is a clear point where our capabilities end and where God calls us to trust Him more fully. You see this dynamic throughout Judges 7, and really across the entire book. Yet, what we often prefer to do is avoid what we *can do*, then sulk, criticize, or even discard God when He doesn't tear open the heavens and fix things like a genie. On a broader, communal level, it is essential that we—as people adopted through Jesus' incarnate, redeeming blood—both surrender to and proclaim the truth that God knows exactly what He is doing. He has been doing what He does far longer than we've been doing anything, and He has never lost, nor will He ever. Rocky Marciano retired 49-0, Floyd Mayweather Jr. went 50-0, and Muhammad Ali's daughter, Laila, was 24-0—but they were all beatable. God is not. In fact, humanity's flawed and limited hands are far too short to even think

---

5. Carrie Underwood, "Jesus, Take the Wheel," 2005.
6. Elisabeth Elliot, *A Lamp Unto My Feet: The Bible's Light For Your Daily Walk*.

about boxing with Him. That's why we must continually return to Scriptures like Psalm 37:23-28—passages that not only remind us of what we know to be true, but confront us when we're tempted to abandon that truth during hard times.

> The Lord makes firm the steps
> of the one who delights in him;
> though he may stumble, he will not fall,
> for the Lord upholds him with his hand.
>
> I was young and now I am old,
> Yet I have never seen the righteous forsaken
> or their children begging bread.
> They are always generous and lend freely;
> Their children will be a blessing.
>
> Turn from evil and do good
> then you will dwell in the land forever.
> For the Lord loves the just
> and will not forsake his faithful ones.[7]

The longer we live, the more we'll form our own commentaries and convictions—and that's a good thing. But part of where Israel went wrong was in failing to keep their priorities aligned with God's. They tried to do God's job for Him, which never ends well. Or they spent so much time envying their enemies that they continually sold their souls down the river. As a community, our testimony should reflect a readiness to recognize how God chooses to resolve our situations using resources that, to human eyes, appear insufficient. It may be uncomfortable, but it is sanctifying. On a more personal, private level, we need to cultivate a posture of obedience that responds to God the *first time*. We must hold ourselves accountable to that standard, rather than expecting God to keep repeating Himself—as if we're merely "toddlers with long legs," needing constant love taps on the backside, timeouts, and nap after nap to calm our wayward wiggles. God knows precisely where, when, and how you struggle, just like He did with Gideon. He knows the sickness weighing you down, the relational stress that's causing your heart to skip a beat. He knows your difficulty in attending church, serving, or prioritizing fellowship—especially if you feel unwanted or undervalued. And yes, church can be a messy hospital filled with sinners who don't always want the

---

7. Ps 37:23-28.

Great Physician to heal them. He knows that you can believe He'll do the impossible for others, but struggle to believe it for yourself. He sees your misery and mystery, your cowardice, and every other chaotic character flaw you're wrestling with. And none of it scares Him. Principally, He does not want your performance, your perfectly wrapped holiday gifts, your pretend piety, or your polished appearance. He wants you—*all of you*, so yield to Him today.

Leadership Woes
Judges 8:1–21, January 7, 2024

THIS MORNING, I'M ASKING you to do me a small favor: *just throw your hands in the air and wave 'em like you just don't care* if you've ever rubbed shoulders with a bad leader. I'm talking about someone steeped in incompetence, fluent in manipulation, or who hides a shady, shoddy true self behind a charming public veneer. With his iconic backup ensemble, The Wailers, Bob Marley made what we already knew even clearer, that there is, "So Much Trouble in the World."[1] He declared this in 1979, the year I was born. Who among us can deny that poor leadership is often the source of preventable drama and suffering? Bad leadership can ruin any environment or experience. While some leaders are rightly focused on efficiency, the best among them also serve the people in their care. They ensure their teams have what they need, work to reduce or eliminate unnecessary red tape, and lead with fairness, flexibility, and empathy. They set an example worth following. Others, however, are driven by self-interest. For them, exploitation is the name of the game.

A classic film that portrays toxic leadership is *9 to 5*, starring the legendary Jane Fonda, Lily Tomlin, Dabney Coleman, and the unforgettable Dolly Parton—whose song of the same name became a major hit. The movie follows three female office workers who bond over the systematic harassment, exploitation, and devaluation they endure in a workplace dominated by bigotry, misogyny, and unprofessionalism. Their conniving supervisor, Franklin Hart, embodies the good ol' boy culture they ultimately unite against, giving him a long-overdue taste of his own medicine. The film serves as brilliant cinematic evidence of Anglo-Irish political thinker Edmund Burke's observation: "When bad

---

1. Bob Marley, "So Much Trouble in the World," 1979.

men combine, the good must associate; else they will fall one by one, an unpitied sacrifice in a contemptible struggle."[2] Like Burke's warning, the women of *9 to 5* choose action over silence, resisting unacceptable leadership in all its immoral, illicit, and incompetent forms. If you've paid any attention lately to American industry, government, or—perhaps most disturbingly—American church life, then you know I'm not, as the late comedian Bernie Mac said, "puttin' 20 on 10" when I say we're facing a leadership crisis. But as the story of Gideon reminds us, "there is nothing new under the sun."[3]

At the beginning of chapter 8, Gideon actually starts off pretty well. After being confronted by the Ephraimites—his fellow Hebrews and brothers-in-arms—about feeling excluded from the battle against Midian, Gideon, to his credit, stays remarkably cool. But make no mistake: they were *heated*. As verse 1 puts it, "they challenged him vigorously." Some biblical commentators are critical of the Ephraimites, suggesting they were focused on the wrong things—bitter they missed out on the honor, the spoils, and the pomp of victory. I get that perspective, but we can't say for sure what their motives were. What we *do know* is that, back in chapter 6, Gideon had recruited fighters from Manasseh (his own tribe, including the Abiezrites), as well as from Asher, Zebulun, and Naphtali. Then in chapter 7, God intentionally reduced Gideon's army from tens of thousands to just 300 men—so that no one could boast that their own strength had won the battle. That reduction wasn't Gideon's idea; it was God's. And it frustrated him. So, when the Ephraimites showed up later in the campaign, helping cut off Midianite escape routes and capturing two of their leaders, it's understandable they may have felt like an afterthought. Maybe they thought they were being given scraps, treated like kids with chores rather than trusted warriors.

While that wasn't Gideon's intent, and it certainly didn't reflect his heart according to the text, we can still appreciate their frustration. They weren't privy to Gideon's private orders from God—they could only interpret what they saw. Still, to their credit, the Ephraimites did the right thing. They didn't gossip behind Gideon's back or roast him with memes on social media. They went directly to the source. That's a powerful example—not just for Christians, but for anyone. Nothing grinds my gears more than when someone has an issue with you, but tells everyone except

2. Edmund Burke, *Thoughts on the Cause of the Present Discontents*, 106.
3. Eccl 1:9.

you. Addressing a concern directly doesn't mean you have to agree on every point—but at least the air gets cleared, as both sides speak their mind. Now, whether Gideon was using flattery to smooth things over or genuinely meant what he said, we can't know for sure. Nonetheless, his response calmed the situation and affirmed the Ephraimites' value: "God gave Oreb and Zeeb, the Midianite leaders, into your hands. What was I able to do compared to you?" That response showed tact, humility, and a desire to keep the peace. Problem averted. This was an early win for Gideon—a display of maturity and restraint that suggested wisdom. Unfortunately, as the story continues, his leadership begins to falter. As the book of Judges repeatedly reminds us: "In those days Israel had no king; everyone did as they saw fit."

The next thing you know, Gideon ends up in a heated conflict with the men of Sukkoth (verses 6–7) and then with the men of Peniel (verses 8–9). From where I'm standing, it looks like he was trying to bully his fellow Israelites. Back-to-back, he demands from both groups, "Give my troops some bread; they are worn out." It's important to understand the context: this was a time when pleasantries weren't exactly standard in the vocabulary of military leaders—especially during wartime. Leaders were accustomed to taking what they needed without asking. Some scholars argue that Gideon's words were actually a respectful request, and only sound like a demand to our modern, more delicate ears. That may be partially true. Still, as a follower of Yahweh—the God of Abraham, Isaac, and Jacob—and as a leader representing Him, Gideon should have gone out of his way to show respect to the very people whose help he and his men needed. One mark of good leadership is *not* throwing your weight around to get what you want. Great leaders don't lean on fear or threats, to motivate others. There are moments when a firm word, a reminder of authority, or even a righteous confrontation is necessary, but that's not what Gideon was doing here. He was simply offended that someone dared to say *no* to him. And instead of showing restraint, he escalated things into a pointless, prideful showdown—a "urinating contest," if you will—y'all can talk among yourselves after church about the more colorful version of that phrase.

The people of Sukkoth and Peniel didn't respect Gideon. That's obvious! They seemed to mock him. After he publicly asked for their help, they basically called him a failure. In verse 6, they ask, "Do you already have the hands of Zebah and Zalmunna in your possession? Why should we give bread to your troops?" Petty? *Definitely*. Messy and foolish? No doubt. Poking the bear is never a smart idea. Gideon had just said in verse 5 that he and his troops were exhausted but were still chasing down two Midianite kings. And instead of helping, they hit him with two rhetorical questions, trying to embarrass him. Provoking someone in the middle of a mission—especially your own leader—is reckless and absurd. But if it counts for anything, Gideon followed through on his word. After capturing Zebah and Zalmunna, he disciplined the men of Sukkoth, tore down the tower of Peniel, and "killed the men of the town" (verse 17). What stands out is that the diplomatic tact he used earlier with the Ephraimites is now completely missing. If you're like me, you're probably wondering: what happened to Gideon? In chapter 6, we found him hiding from the Midianites, timid and insecure, convinced his clan was the weakest and he was the least in his family. He was sarcastic, doubtful, and needed repeated signs to believe God was really calling him. Even after multiple encounters with the Divine, he only dared to destroy his father's altar to Baal *at night*, because he was afraid of his family and townspeople.

In chapter 7, God had to guide him every step of the way—through dreams and signs—just to get him to carry out the mission. How is it that, in just a few chapters, Gideon goes from being paralyzed by fear to acting like a man who's *about that life*. He became a thug or mobster overnight. What changed? I think life happened—that fast. It doesn't take much for pride to trick us or for our egos to take over. Just like a quiet, reserved person can flip and turn into a loud, belligerent so-and-so under certain conditions, a hesitant, insecure leader like Gideon, once given power and influence, can just as quickly go off the rails. In the Old Testament, where mercy and grace weren't expressed as explicitly as they are through Jesus in the New Testament, values like self-control still mattered. In that cultural context, however, keeping the covenant through the Law was the highest aim. Therefore, when Gideon learned that Zebah and Zalmunna were responsible for killing his brothers, all bets were off. That's how things worked back then.

Still, what's striking is what happens next. Gideon asks his son Jether to kill the captured kings. But when Jether hesitates—understandably so—the two kings actually rebuke Gideon. They shame him for asking a child to do what was universally understood to be a man's job. Wielding a sword strong enough to end a life requires not only physical strength, but also emotional and spiritual resolve. Gideon's failure here wasn't just tactical, it was personal. In letting his emotions get the better of him, he dishonored his son, his enemies, himself, and ultimately his God.

Despite his issues—and we'll see more of them as chapter 8 concludes—I'd caution you against thinking of Gideon as the worst leader of all time. The truth is, all of us lead at some point and in some capacity. Everyday John and Jane Does lead. We lead as uncles and aunts, as members of the PTA, in neighborhood associations, or simply by how we conduct ourselves in the workplace. Laypeople lead. Clergy lead. Even babysitters lead. With Gideon, it seems he simply got caught up—and that happens. It can happen to any of us. Maybe it already has. Perfection isn't a requirement for leadership because, frankly, it's impossible. There are no perfect leaders. There are leaders who are weak in some areas, strong in others, and exceptional in a few. Leadership comes in all shapes and forms. But there's a key distinction: there's a difference between a leader who struggles because they lack experience or expertise, and a leader whose approach is fundamentally broken—whose unresolved internal issues spill into every part of their leadership responsibilities. Part of why we often end up disappointed in leaders is because we assume leadership can be bought or manufactured. We think that if you go to the right school, earn the right degree, read the right industry journals, land the right jobs, and rub shoulders with the right people, leadership will naturally follow. That might get you a paycheck or a title—but it doesn't make you a leader.

You can listen to every TED Talk, subscribe to all the top podcasts, and still miss the mark. The leaders we admire most lead from the *inside out*—not the outside in. They have conviction and compassion, neither of which can be bought. They hold others accountable because they don't run from accountability themselves. They sacrifice for the greater good when and how they can. They don't run from a fight, and they don't hide the light of their faith under a bowl. Gideon's leadership journey is messy and flawed—but Jesus' leadership is not. His leadership was steady, trustworthy, and without harm. At times, he spoke with directness; other times, he taught through parables. But always, he was honest, welcoming, and fully present. He experienced the worst in people while seeking the best for them. Ultimately, he gave up His life to offer humanity its only path to redemption. Following is the best path to leading—and, in the grand scheme of things, it's the only way to truly live. So today, would you consider being the kind of leader who first chooses to follow? Whether you're coming to Jesus for the first time or returning after a long absence, remember this: only his love can cover a multitude of sins.

Welcome to the Club
Judges 8:22–34, January 21, 2024

THIS MAY FEEL LIKE too invasive a question—impolite, even—but here it goes: When was the last time you were in a club? For our purposes, it doesn't really matter whether the space is defined by booze, music, sports, or dancing. Whether it's a lowbrow dive bar, a high-end hookah lounge, a retro speakeasy, or a venue with fireman's poles despite no fire in sight. Regardless, minimally, people gather in clubs for similar, simple reasons: to relax and unwind. Some go—rightly or wrongly—to let loose, have a few drinks, enjoy a meal, or watch a game. Clubs come in all shapes and sizes. Skiles on 8th Street, I've heard, used to be a little unsavory—not the most family-friendly spot—long before downtown's upscale makeover. When we lived in Holland years earlier, I remember occasionally, or maybe more than occasionally, seeing student-athletes from a nearby Christian college coming and going from Parrots on South River. Three years into our now 17-year marriage, Renata and I lived in an apartment complex on the same street as—you guessed it: a club. Club Luckie, right on Luckie Street in Northwest Atlanta. We were at 451; it was down the block at 375. We never stepped inside, but we knew it was packed. Cars were everywhere. A long line was outside. From Thursday night through Sunday, the soundtrack of our evenings was loud music, fights starting or ending in the parking lot, and, unfortunately, the occasional police siren or even gunshot.

There's another kind of club, though. You might not know it by name, but you probably know it in practice: Club Doing Too Much. At this club, you can do as much of whatever you want—because that's the whole point. It's the place for being bold, reckless, and unapologetically self-governed. No dress code here. Club Doing Too Much prides itself on keeping you *comfortable*. Don't expect bouncers or off-duty cops either. Everyone's too busy navel-gazing—like Narcissus from Greek mythology, mesmerized by their own reflection—to start any trouble. The drinks? Bottomless and free, as long as you keep doing too much. The last thing anyone wants is for some sober killjoy to find religion, gain perspective, or grow up and disrupt the vibe. Doing too much is the *culture* here. It's what gets you in and what keeps you there. Some people show up to prove their worth—to feel relevant, superior, or untouchable. Others go to convince themselves they're fiercely independent. Here, you don't need people—people need *you*. There's no rest, no restraint, not even for God. At Club Doing Too Much, *you do you*, however you want to do it. Part of the appeal? You like marching to the beat of your own drum—or at least, you think it's *yours* alone. But the truth is, Club Doing Too Much has an owner, and he insists there never be a cover charge. Your dysfunction, the wake of destruction it leaves behind, and the delight he takes in watching it unfold are payment enough. They say misery loves company. But misery loves it most when the company doesn't realize it's miserable.

Gideon was a reluctant leader, remember? From the very start of his service in Judges 6, he spends valuable time putting God through the paces, almost like someone test-driving a used car. You kick the tires, press the buttons, and fiddle with the features. You want to give it some gas and see what kind of get-up-and-go it has. "What is it capable of?"—inquiring minds want to know. Is it as advertised? Verse by verse, chapter by chapter, Gideon gradually warms to the mantle of leadership—though even then, he takes the remedial route, needing constant reassurance and handholding from God just to make progress on the basics. But once the light finally clicks on, it doesn't take long before some of his deeper issues—particularly a stubborn streak of individualism—begin to resurface. As it's been said, "Those who do not move, do not notice their chains."[1] In Gideon's case, he chose messy comfort over lasting honor. Still, in Judges 8:23, he has at least one clear and commendable moment. After leading Israel to a stunning victory over the Midianite oppressors, the people ask him to become their king. His response is striking: "I will not rule over you, nor will my son rule over you. The Lord will rule over you." These words are not just symbolic—they're substantial. They serve as a valiant vision statement of humility, submission, servant-leadership,

---

1. Commonly attributed to Rosa Luxemburg; original source unverified.

and alliance with God. As judge, Gideon was determined to keep his eyes fixed on the Lord—to be led by Him, to do His work, and to resist becoming a mere ruler seeking power over people. God was the one true King, and Gideon, in that moment, had not forgotten.

But then—he opened his big mouth. He couldn't leave well enough alone. So quickly after such a noble declaration, he spoiled it by asking the Israelites for gold earrings. And it wasn't a donation to his 401(k) or a reward for his hard work in delivering them. This was about ego—an unchecked pride that had been festering, like black mold, just beneath the surface. In verse 27, we read that he melted the gold down and made an ephod, a ceremonial priestly garment, and placed it in his hometown. This lavish, bedazzled piece was no simple religious relic. "All Israel prostituted themselves by worshiping it there, and it became a snare to Gideon and his family."[2] Industrialist Andrew Carnegie once said, "As I grow older, I pay less attention to what men say. I just watch what they do."[3] The proof is always in the pudding—not in what you say about the pudding. To avoid becoming a regular at *Club Doing Too Much*, we have to root ourselves in Scripture. We need to remember: "Faith without works is dead"[4] *and* "Without faith it is impossible to please God."[5] Hypocrisy isn't just saying one thing and doing another—it's defending that contradiction as though it's okay. We're all flawed. That's life. But the goal is to be honest about our inconsistencies and seek God's help in correcting them. Gideon, like many of us, started seeing himself as above God, and that pride contributed directly to Israel's spiritual downfall. After his death, "the Israelites again prostituted themselves to the Baals."[6] When you're living *la vida loca*, popping bottles at the club, it's easy to forget the Lord your God who rescued you. You start believing you rescued yourself.

I wonder if this refrain is familiar by now: "In those days Israel had no king; everyone did as they saw fit." None of us can afford to live by empty mottos. In pursuing holiness, we should instead be driven to cultivate meaningful, transformed lives that align with the teachings of Scripture. The truth will set us free—but many of us prefer distraction. Like Martha, whom Jesus gently corrected for being "worried and upset

---

2. Judg 8:27.
3. Commonly attributed to Andrew Carnegie; original source unverified.
4. Jas 2:14–26.
5. Heb 11:6.
6. Judg 8:33.

about many things,"[7] we often avoid confronting life. Instead, we try to control it, micromanage it, or escape it altogether. "The land," verse 28 tells us, "had peace forty years," but as soon as the desert hospice chaplain at Gideon's bedside announced his passing, that peace died with him. And while the people were certainly accountable for their descent into idolatry, you can trace much of the blame directly to Gideon's failings. During those four decades following his military triumph, his pride, idolatry, and moral compromise were no secret: the request for gold, the crafting of the ephod, the false worship that followed. He had many wives and children—"70 sons," to be exact. This wasn't incidental; it was a lifestyle he engineered.

As God's appointed leader, instead of acknowledging his errors, seeking forgiveness, and making things right, Gideon let it all ride. He basked in the glow of earthly success that would not survive him. Gideon—how did you get here? Maybe Gideon gave up. Maybe his trauma was too deep, and his life too comfortable. He was fine. The nation was fine. His children were fine. If it wasn't broken—why fix it? Maybe Gideon believed his compromises weren't that serious. After all, he had risked life and limb to save his people—he had put love on the line. But here's the truth: the legacy you leave—whether to your spouse and children, nieces and nephews, your community and church, or the friends and strangers who may one day be influenced by your witness—is only as redemptive and meaningful as your courage to acknowledge where you went wrong, and to make changes while you still have the chance. Gideon didn't do that. Many of us don't either. We're too busy living our so-called best life, dodging honest, hard conversations and the responsibility they require—while no one calls us out, because everyone making it rain at Club Doing Too Much is just as guilty.

Like many African American kids now of a certain age, I grew up loving the 1988 comedy *Coming to America*, starring Eddie Murphy. It became an instant cult classic. The sequel, featuring most of the original cast, even the supporting characters, returned in 2021, with everyone now older. As sequels go, which we all know can be hit or miss, it wasn't my favorite for more reasons than I have time to list. Still, the ending was beautiful. I watched it last week while on the treadmill at the gym. In the sequel, the prince has taken over for his deceased father, who ruled

---

7. Luke 10:41.

the country in the first film. But instead of delivering on his youthful promises of bold change and innovative diplomacy, it becomes painfully clear that he's spent most of his royal tenure full of hot air—sacrificing integrity for comfort, and trading substance for the illusion of prosperity and fragile peace. He has lived a life dominated by fear, simply masking it with a smile. Eventually, however, he comes to recognize the error of his ways. And to his eldest daughter, he says with humility, "Forgive an old fool; an old fool who loves you very much."[8]

Hear me when I say this: leaving behind living trusts, life insurance, land and homes, stocks, cash, and even a long era of peace—that's all good. It has its place. But it all fades and it only takes the right mix of poor choices, addictions, or crises—and in one generation, it can all disappear. So, if that's *all* you leave behind, then your memory—and the memory of the God you served—may fade with it. But God has deposited far more in you to give to the world in His name. That kind of legacy requires honesty about where you've fallen short, and the willingness to make amends wherever possible, in the name of Jesus. But also know this: *Club Doing Too Much* is always calling. Sin doesn't sleep. In the spirit of the U.S. Postal Service motto—"Neither rain, nor snow, nor sleet, nor hail shall keep the postmen from their appointed rounds"—the club is open 24/7/365. All ages are welcome. One way to keep that club at bay is to plant yourself in a healthy church community—to both invest in others and allow them to invest in you—learning from the strengths *and* the failures of those who've walked the road before you.

---

8. *Coming 2 America*, 2021.

The Smokescreen of Sameness
Judges 9:1–29, January 28, 2024

I'M GRATEFUL THAT THE Spirit of God saw fit—and you agreed—for us to serve together, for you to invite me to be your pastor. Maplewood, you've allowed us to laugh together often and have both uneasy and uncommon conversations. And every Sunday, you show up not knowing whether I'll reference Cardi B, John Calvin, or Dolly Parton; the Heidelberg Catechism or James Weldon Johnson's 1900 anthem "Lift Every Voice and Sing"; quote Rabindranath Tagore or Voltaire—or whether you'll see some smooth dance moves as I try to faithfully proclaim biblical texts from this pulpit, that are often thorny and packed with potentially explosive issues. Thank you for not only sticking with me but encouraging me to be myself. Today is no different than most of our Sunday mornings together. Although it is a statement that is difficult to verify, we think that Fred Allen, a popular host during the Golden Age of American radio (from the 1920s through the late 1940s), once quipped, "Most of us spend the first six days of each week sowing wild oats, then we go to church on Sunday and pray for crop failure." While it's tempting to view Sunday as an especially sacred day—set apart from the rest—Scripture reminds us, "Do not be deceived: God cannot be mocked. A man reaps what he sows."[1]

Last week, we looked at Gideon's final moments in Judges 8. As heroic yet deeply flawed as he was, Gideon closed out his judgeship by collecting loot from the people, building a golden idol, and returning to his hometown to settle in—and, quite literally, get busy. He was ahead of his time. During the 40 years of peace that followed his military success, Gideon had 70 wives. Scripture adds: "His concubine, who lived in

---

1. Gal 6:7–8.

Shechem, also bore him a son, whom he named Abimelek."[2] None of this, as you can imagine, was a good look for a man of God. And now, like a Ring Video Doorbell alert, we can see the chickens of Gideon's poor example coming home to roost. "In those days Israel had no king; everyone did as they saw fit." Abimelek—an illegitimate son among many others, all likely struggling with their own tattered identities—wants to keep power in the family; *his* version of family. This is where nepotism enters: showing preferential treatment to family, particularly for power or gain. He appeals to his mother's brothers—his uncles—and her entire clan for their bloody allegiance and financial support in making him his father Gideon's successor. His pitch is that it's better for them to be ruled by "one of their own" than by any of Gideon's half-brothers, with whom they share only a father.

It might sound harsh, but if you've lived long enough or remember how unforgiving kids can be, you can think of the kinds of names Abimelek was called, to his face or behind his back. "Bastard," or some variation, was likely common. And you can be sure his mother, perceived as a floozy, or wanton jump-off—maybe even an ancient equivalent of an OnlyFans star—wasn't spared ridicule either. Whether accurate or not, people had opinions. And while Abimelek's conduct shouldn't be excused, we must admit: he got it from his daddy. Gideon set the stage for his son's dysfunction through his own life—idol worship, polygamy, and reckless behavior. To top it off, he gave the one son born to the woman he *didn't* marry a name that means "my father is king." Abimelek, then, was both a chip off the old block *and* a man with a chip on his shoulder.

The son of a concubine—a sexual slave—has risen to the top. In his father's hometown of Ophrah, he coordinated the massacre of his brothers with the help of "reckless scoundrels" he hired using silver donated by his relatives. Only the youngest brother, Jotham, escaped by hiding as we read in verse 5. In verses 7–20, we hear Jotham's bold speech from atop a mountain, where he calls out Abimelek and the people of Shechem for the wickedness they've committed. Afterward, Jotham flees to a place called Beer, exiling himself to avoid revenge. From there, he watches as God "stirred up animosity between Abimelek and the people."[3] Jotham emphasizes that Abimelek rose to power not because of proven

---

2. Judg 8:31.
3. Judg 9:3.

leadership, military skill, or wisdom—no Ph.D. from Harvard Business School here—but solely because of family loyalty. His argument? "Better me, your kin, than the 70 sons of Jerubbaal." It was a fear-based appeal, not a merit-based one. Abimelek's campaign was not about honor or love. It was a calculated move to eliminate competition—an unprovoked strike to ensure his brothers couldn't do to him what he did to them. Yes, there may have been long-standing tension among the brothers, a natural by-product of their complex family dynamics, but Abimelek took it further. He acted preventatively, irresponsibly, and ruthlessly at that, to keep all power for himself, cloaking ambition in the guise of ancestral allegiance. It wasn't about righteousness—it was about ease, manipulation, and control. Tragically, this isn't just the way of the world—it's often the way of Christians, too. Like Gideon and Abimelek, we plot and scheme, fight and fuss, rob, steal, and worse; sometimes immorally, sometimes even unlawfully—to gain or hoard power. All the while, we convince ourselves and others that our sameness gives us a divine competitive edge.

Jim and Kay Havenga are beloved members of this congregation. You and I know how humble, hilarious, and hospitable they are. One thing you can always count on: if Jim and Kay are around and free, any visitor to Maplewood Reformed is likely to be invited to their home, just a few blocks away, for lunch. They're phenomenal hosts who offer prayers, homemade bread, a brief devotional, meaningful conversation, and—if God really favors you—some of those dehydrated apple slices to take home that Kay makes, not to mention the bread. They love God and love people—*all* people. Their home is a vessel of hospitality used to point others to Christ. It's the opposite of sameness; they welcome everyone because they value everyone. That said, Jim and Kay also share a good deal of sameness, which is perfectly fine. They met in graduate school and are now semi-retired veterinarians—both of them. They're biking enthusiasts—again, both of them. They've biked across states, cities, and towns, logging thousands of miles in all kinds of weather. Recumbent bikes, electric bikes, road bikes, Peloton bikes, tandem bikes, touring bikes—they know bikes. Sameness isn't a problem unless it gets in the way of drawing a wide, invitational, servant-hearted, sanctifying circle for the sake of the Gospel.

Following the breadcrumbs down the yellow brick road of Abimelek's condemnable actions, we see not only familial favoritism but a deeper craving: the desire to use sameness—broadly defined—as a vehicle for securing power. I'm convinced that some of the trouble we face today, especially here in the Western world we know best, stems from too many people having inhaled the fragmented powder of fraudulent faith for so long that sin now masquerades as wisdom. It becomes the standard operating procedure for so-called discernment. Despite Abimelek's argument, a mix of emotion and logic completely devoid of godliness, I don't see him as a wolf in sheep's clothing. He was just *a wolf doing wolf things*. What's even more troubling is that, among Christians, we often refuse to admit our own wolfish tendencies: how we'll manipulate, push people aside, and even wound others if it gets us closer to power, money, prestige, comfort, or control. Some of us know exactly what it's like to chase after the spoils that sameness can provide. And because people are everywhere, this kind of manipulation exists everywhere: in big cities and small towns, in storefront churches and megachurches, in matriarchal and patriarchal families, across all professions and institutions. It's a slice straight out of the 2004 *Stepford Wives* remake—we long for communities of clones, unthreatening cronies who look, speak, and think like us, who share our alma mater, our taste in meatloaf, and our institutional affiliations. We shape our circles not to reflect God's kingdom but to manufacture our own controlled utopias.

Instead of submitting to God's call to be transformed so that we might glorify Him in building something new, we often wrap ourselves in spiritual language while denying others their inalienable rights. We shut doors that should be open, not based on character or calling, but on comfort and control. All for the love of supremacy. Thankfully, God can and does use anyone and anything to accomplish His will. That's something to celebrate. But if we claim Christ, then we are accountable to live by the Word of God, not according to whatever feels good, sounds popular, or benefits us personally. Jeremiah warned, "The heart is deceitful above all things and beyond cure,"[4] and I get genuinely concerned when Christians argue that no structural response is needed to correct historical wrongs—particularly those rooted in privileged sameness. As if it were somehow godly to trust that people will naturally do the right thing in matters of justice, integrity, and leadership. That's wishful thinking, not biblical realism. Whether affirmative action—or any form of equity-building—is always the best tool, I can't say in every case. But I *can* say that telling people to "pull themselves up by their bootstraps"

---

4. Jer 17:9.

while modern-day Abimeleks, sometimes invoking Jesus' name, build empires of sameness on the backs of those they've systematically kept from owning boots, shoelaces, or socks—that is not the way of the cross.

Even so, love cannot be legislated. Systems of accountability matter, and we absolutely need people monitoring those doing the monitoring. But no system will ever manufacture genuine compassion or selfless concern. That kind of care doesn't come naturally to any of us—and that's exactly why we need the transforming grace of God. Released in 1978, I owe my familiarity with the lyrics from Bobby Caldwell's song "What You Won't Do for Love" to my parents.[5] In our home, music played in the background unless it was time for homework. To this and songs from artists like Earth, Wind, and Fire, or Parliament-Funkadelic, or Michael Jackson, or Prince, or The Whispers, Tina Turner, Luther Vandross, the Dazz Band, or The Isley Brothers, my parents would dance. Every so often, they would begin doing "the bump" together and when we children, my sister and I, would protest at the sight of them being in such near proximity to one another, they'd always say something like, "Ummmm, how do you think you two got here?!" That never made us feel better, but as we got a little older, we stopped protesting and learned to just let them be. Maplewood, the Gospel of Jesus Christ, described as the Bible does as ". . .alive and active. Sharper than any double-edged sword,"[6] penetrating even to divide soul and spirit, joints and marrow, judging the thoughts and attitudes of the heart—through the Holy Spirit's work, we can do for God what is at first uncomfortable or outside of our character. Similarity is fine. Sameness has its place. But we must mature to be okay approaching life very differently than we often do, so that we aren't following Abimelek's poisonous notion of how to wield power. If people wonder what is wrong with us because we refuse to let go of God, and therefore His standards, then we are on the right path.

---

5. Bobby Caldwell, "What You Won't Do for Love," 1978.
6. Heb 4:12–13.

The Company You Keep
Judges 9:30–57, February 11, 2024

Maybe you have heard of the saying: "Birds of a feather flock together." It simply means we tend to gravitate toward those with whom we share commonalities. If someone's a jerk, chances are they spend time with other jerk-ish individuals who oddly appreciate and reinforce that behavior. If someone loves ham radio, bowling, or devours books like an anteater devours ants, it's no surprise they might belong to a group or community centered around that interest. Likewise, if someone is a charismatic, verbal-processing extrovert who can fire off more words in 20 minutes than an introvert might manage in two days, they likely have their best conversations with fellow motor-mouths—people who we might say, like the rap trio Whodini said in 1984, have a "Big Mouth."[1] That's just how it goes. If you're the adventure-seeking type—into hang gliding, 200-mile ultramarathons, or skydiving—then it stands to reason your inner circle will be made up of like-minded daredevils. Who we are and who we invite into our inner circle speaks volumes. Leading up to Judges 9, we meet Abimelek, Gideon's illegitimate son—born more out of lust than love. He's the impulsive antagonist we love to hate or hate to love. And Scripture does not spare him from criticism. Early in the chapter, we saw Jotham—the youngest half-brother who escaped Abimelek's massacre of their 70 siblings—climb Mount Gerizim to deliver a searing word of rebuke. Not long after, we read that "God stirred up animosity between Abimelek and the citizens of Shechem" because of his persistent, unrepentant violence. The people of Shechem were wicked and compromised in their own right, so after a brief honeymoon period when their

---

1. Whodini, "Big Mouth," 1984.

alliance seemed divinely aligned, God set them against one another—and Abimelek, ever impulsive and insecure, turned on his own people.

While hanging out "eating and drinking" with his friends, a man from Shechem named Gaal, son of Ebed—probably emboldened by alcohol's liquid courage—starts running his mouth about Abimelek. That's where we left last time in verse 29. Gaal basically says, "Abimelek this, Abimelek that," followed by the classic tough talk: "If only this people were under my command!" Yada yada yada—you know the type. In typical Abimelek fashion—like father, like son—he snaps. He gathers his men, divides them into three companies, and sets an ambush in Shechem. We see this unfold in verse 43. He launches a full-on assault against the very city that once backed him, his home base no less. And he doesn't stop at military targets. This wasn't a clean battle by any stretch. The Geneva Convention hadn't been written yet, but even so, what Abimelek did went far beyond what was common or necessary, arguably. Like a horror movie villain—think Jason or Freddy Krueger—he hunts down the people hiding in the temple and burns them alive, killing around a thousand men and women. Not satisfied, his forces go on to destroy the city, even pouring salt on the fields to prevent future crops from growing—a cruel, strategic move to make rebuilding nearly impossible. Yet, it doesn't end there. Abimelek then heads to the nearby town of Thebez to carry out another atrocity. And just when he's about to unleash more barbarity, a woman drops an upper millstone on his head, cracking his skull. Mortally wounded, he tells his armor-bearer to kill him so no one can say, "A woman killed him." It's a desperate move to protect his ego, but let's be real: everyone knew he was taken down by a woman. The injury was fatal—it was only a matter of time.

Some of us may be quick to rage and fly off the handle like Abimelek—but thankfully, that's probably more the exception than the rule, or I hope so. And even if we do identify with Abimelek, it might not be in the way we think. My sense is that many of us relate to Abimelek as the one being provoked, or to Zebul—the governor of Shechem and one of Abimelek's top officers—as the one doing the provoking. Abimelek is fully accountable for his depraved actions, just as we are when we act foolishly. Even without Zebul stoking the firestorm of preemptive warfare, chances are Abimelek would've still chosen to sin. Still, as 1 Corinthians 15:33 reminds us, "Bad company corrupts good character." And sometimes, we are that bad company. We invite, tolerate, or cling to people whose values and behavior should disqualify them from being close to us—often because of issues within ourselves that we've left unaddressed. When I was a kid trying to make sense of the world at Lyndon Hill Elementary in Capitol Heights, Maryland, I witnessed, and got into, my fair share of schoolyard fights. Two people would square off, chest to chest, walking in circles and muttering things like, "What do you wanna do?" over and over. Then, someone's so-called friend would sneak up and push one into the other—escalating tension into violence. That's Zebul: the worst kind of pretend friend. The kind who enjoys the blood—yours or your enemy's. The kind who thrives on drama, chaos, and suffering. The kind who preaches loyalty, but whose loyalty is only to self, not to your well-being or maturity.

In verse 30, after overhearing Gaal's drunken rant, what does Zebul do? He doesn't try to defuse the situation. Instead, he goes out of his way to get word to Abimelek—and even suggests a plan of attack. Judges 21:25 says, "In those days Israel had no king; everyone did as they saw fit." Once the fight becomes inevitable, Zebul taunts Gaal in verse 38: "Where is your big talk now, you who said, 'Who is Abimelek that we should be subject to him?' Aren't these the men you ridiculed? Go out and fight them!" Who knows how many lives might have been saved if Zebul had been a better friend, or a better official? So, be cautious around people who behave like Woody Woodpecker or Shakespeare's Mercutio in *Romeo and Juliet*—those who poke and prod, scheme and stir trouble just to get a rise out of others. If you didn't know, there's even a children's book about this kind of behavior. *Isaac the InstiGator*, written by Jeff Tucker and illustrated by Brian Martin, tells the story of an alligator who creates conflict wherever he goes—simply because he's lonely, angry, and miserable, and wants everyone else to be the same.

Instigators like Zebul do not have your best interests at heart. They reflect the spirit of the ultimate tempter—the devil—who worked relentlessly in the wilderness to get Jesus to trade God's will for fleshly desires.

Your homework this week is to prayerfully reflect on the people you are closest to—and whether they are inclined to step in to help steer you away from avoidable danger or to fight well alongside you when needed, or if they're the type to sit back and just watch the show. I'm not suggesting you surround yourself with bullies—those who want you to be their clone and who, when you're not that, will fuss, fight, and fret in hopes that you'll conform. Some will even use Scripture manipulatively to pressure you into thinking, speaking, walking, and living the way they believe you should. That is not what healthy friendship or godly support looks like. In Zebul's case, he easily could've told Gaal to slow down, calm himself, and sleep off his drunken rant rather than inciting drama that put countless lives in danger. The phrase "snitches get stitches" is clearly a carnal saying—a threat meant to discourage reporting wrongdoing. But in the Kingdom of God, it's not about "snitches" getting punished; it's about those who stir up trouble just to create chaos and pain being out of step with God's will. Plus, let's be clear: being a Christian does not exempt you from fighting—yes, even physically—unless you are fully committed to pacifism or nonviolence in all circumstances, I guess. If someone jumps on you in a Menards parking lot, slaps your mother, shoves your spouse, or breaks into your home, you are going to defend yourself and your loved ones with whatever level of force you deem necessary, I presume. That's not the same as declaring war on another nation, however, but the point remains: fighting is still fighting, in whatever form it takes.

That said, often, the most important battles aren't physical. And with Zebul in mind, we need people close to us who help us fight well—who don't sit back passively when conflict arrives on our doorstep like an Amazon package. You want people who will encourage and, when possible, equip you to fight for your marriage, your peace, your contentment, your simplicity. People who will help you fight for justice, empathy, humility—to fight to become generous, patient, servant-hearted. And, in contrast to Zebul, you also need people who will urge you to choose restraint when that is the right path. People who, when someone is talking reckless about you, will say, "No, Gayle, turn the other cheek. Don't give them what they want. I know they're asking for it, but that's not the way." Or, "George, I know...I heard what they said. But let's just get in the truck and go bowling like we planned. They're not worth the energy." The kind of people who intercept, inspire, and protect—not provoke or incite. Zebul's role in this story—often overshadowed by Abimelek's ongoing disasters—is a lesson in how vital it is to watch the company you keep, because the company you keep is also the company that shapes and keeps you. Marcus Cicero, considered one of Rome's greatest orators and statesmen, wrote in *Laelius de Amicitia*, his treatise on friendship: "Genuine friendship can't exist where one party is unwilling to hear the truth, and the other is equally unwilling to speak it."[2] The reality is, not everyone is committed to truth—in

---

2. Marcus Tullius Cicero, *De Amicitia* (On Friendship), 24.

their own life or in yours. That's why you must be wise, reciprocal, and serious about cultivating a support system that helps you avoid characters like Zebul, or keeps you from acting like Abimelek. Jesus said, "If you hold to my teaching, you are really my disciples. Then you will know the truth, and the truth will set you free."[3] If today, as you sit under the sound of my voice, you sense—for the first time—the truth of Jesus' life, death, and resurrection, the love He displayed for you, for me, and for the world, and you feel compelled to live a new life in Him, then today is your day. This is the most critical step to take to participate in the unfolding of God's already-but-not-yet kingdom—right here, right now.

---

3. John 8:31–36.

Despicable Me
Judges 10, February 18, 2024

THE DECENT GRADES I earned in math and science were mostly the result of pure, white-knuckled effort, not natural ability, because those subjects were never really my jam. I often think of Mr. Kelsey, my high school physics teacher, whom I've stayed in touch with all these years. Now in his 80s, he and his lovely wife, Mrs. Kelsey, have long lived in an impressive, spacious log cabin that he built himself. Yes, built *himself*. He ordered all the logs and assembled the home piece by piece, like a giant wooden LEGO set. He also has a large woodshop in a separate building next door, which he still uses for his woodworking business. Though he's a genius with angles, machines, calculations, and formulas—one of the smartest people I've ever met—I actually learned the definition of *power* not in his classroom, but several years later when I dabbled in Olympic weightlifting at the University of Maryland. Simply put, no matter how you slice it, strength plus speed equals power. Someone might be as strong as an ox but slow as molasses. Someone else might be faster than Speedy Gonzales—or Tyreek Hill, the Miami Dolphins' lightning-quick wide receiver—but so fragile that a strong breeze could knock them over. True power is the fusion of both. One of the most beautiful insights from Judges 10 is its depiction of God's power. The wind and sea, mountains and molehills, mice and men—even when they're operating at their very best—are no match for Him. As beings made in His image, we are distinctively endowed with agency. He permits us to travel north and south, east and west; to take two steps forward and three back; to fuss and fight or to heal and protect—or some combination of it all. We can put on "a form of godliness but deny its power,"[1] or we can choose to follow Jesus,

---

1. 2 Tim 3:5.

denying ourselves and taking up our cross. But rocks don't choose. Tidal waves don't deliberate. Birds, bees, and sycamore trees lack the incarnational dignity and freedom that God has granted us.

Even so, nothing and no one can thwart God. Once "His hand is stretched out"[2]—whether to change the channel on history's remote control or to inspect the messy, damaged, tangled interior of some poor soul—"who can turn it back?" God will wade with us through any worry we face—big or small. And He will dance with us, too, though always unfazed by the darkness, because "God is light; in Him there is no darkness at all."[3] As limitless in power as He is, God does not lord it over us. He feels our pain, even when that pain is self-inflicted. This is the space—this figurative parking lot—where we find God and His people today: present, patient, and near.

Abimelek is dead. Tola son of Puah, who led Israel for 23 years after him, is gone too. Jair, the leader who followed, yes—he's gone as well. By the time we reach Judges chapter 10, it shouldn't come as a shock to hear that, yet again—for what feels like the umpteenth time—"The Israelites did evil in the eyes of the Lord." Once more, they were off serving anyone and anything but God, which, as expected, angered Him. This is the standard fare by now. Still, I've got to say it: "In those days Israel had no king; everyone did as they saw fit." While they were out living what felt to them like their best lives, God, who disciplines those He loves, removed His protection. The result? They were oppressed by the Philistines and the Ammonites. In their desperate, dark, and disheveled distress, they came crawling back to God and said, in verse 10, "We have sinned against you." Yeah—*ya think*? Based on everything we've seen so far, it's not a stretch to assume they thought that merely stating what they'd done would be enough to earn God's forgiveness. No genuine apology, no real repentance. Just: "We have sinned against you, forsaking our God and serving the Baals." It might *sound* humble, but really, it's just stating the obvious. And God wasn't having it. He was done. "Go and cry out to the gods you have chosen. Let them save you when you are in trouble!," He says in verse 14. That might sound harsh to us, but seriously—when is enough enough?

God doesn't respond this way because He's cold, cruel, or indifferent. He is deeply invested in His people. But He cannot allow willful

---

2. Isa 65:2.
3. 1 John 1:5.

disobedience to go unaddressed. The stench of sin was in the room—everyone knew it, but no one was cleaning it up. What God wanted was elementary: He wanted His people back. He wanted them to actually *learn* from their failures—both the isolated slip-ups and the long, ongoing seasons of rebellion. Juli Slattery, in her book *Rethinking Sexuality: God's Design and Why It Matters*, reminds us:

> Throughout church history, Christians have understood that God's love doesn't mean that He blindly accepts or overlooks our sin. However, the modern church speaks of God's love in a humanistic, self-serving light that gives us liberty to live exactly how we want and still claim a right relationship with a holy God.[4]

This issue of selective amnesia mixed with rebellion is not exclusive to any one century. Every generation of Christians has wrestled, in its own way, with holiness—the biblical conviction that a genuine relationship with God includes the paradoxical call to both lay things down and take things up, to abstain and to obtain.

I find verse 16 fascinating: "Then they got rid of the foreign gods among them and served the Lord. And he could bear Israel's misery no longer." Words matter—we know that. And while they're not always cheap, we've been around long enough to admit that sometimes, perhaps more often than we care to confess, they absolutely can be. What stands out here is that God didn't move—and wasn't moved to act—until they made a sincere, sacrificial decision that went against their flesh. Only when they finally called 1-800-GOT-JUNK and tossed out the energy crystals, potions, astrology charts, and golden fertility trinkets of those false Canaanite-Phoenician deities did God take them seriously. It wasn't their words alone, but their corresponding actions that mattered. That doesn't mean that every time we take similar steps of repentance—genuine changes of heart, mind, and behavior—God will intervene exactly how we want Him to. But it does mean it matters to God. We understand this better than we realize. Until we not only buy the gym membership or Peloton subscription but start eating better and being active, it's fair to say we're not truly committed. There's a real difference between saying the right thing and living it out. If someone's words don't align with their lifestyle, we're rightfully skeptical that true transformation has occurred,

---

4. Juli Slattery, *Rethinking Sexuality: God's Design and Why It Matters*, 43.

no matter how sensitive we are to the difficult process of change. And it seems God was operating with that same logic in this case.

It's also deeply moving that the text says God "could bear Israel's misery no longer." This doesn't mean He's some cruel tyrant playing a divine game of "Gotcha," eager to punish. Far from it. God knows more than we do, including who we are and what we truly need. Yes, He sometimes allows pain to sanctify us, but that doesn't mean He takes pleasure in our suffering, even when it's self-inflicted. I recently began reading *The Top Five Regrets of the Dying* by Australian author Bronnie Ware. The book chronicles her experiences caring for people nearing the end of life. Shortly after ordering it, Amazon's eerily accurate algorithm led to a story appearing on my feed from a comedian who joked that "we all know we're dying, but we live like we're not." He suggested we behave as if death might somehow be optional for us, or that the grim reaper will politely check in to see if now is a good time—or at least send a courtesy text. It struck me as painfully true. When confronted with death, we often recoil in fear or denial. And in our confusion and pain, we sometimes make a mess of our own lives—then have the audacity to blame God for not rescuing us on our terms.

Yet God does not change. Just as He patiently and passionately corrects us when we go astray—and we all do—I wonder when the last time was that you couldn't bear someone's misery any longer and chose to act. Yes, it's true—some people don't ask for help. Or they may not want *your* help. Or they may misinterpret your sacrifice, take advantage of your kindness, or ghost you entirely. That's always a risk, but such risk is part of the territory of being holy because God is holy. If we're honest, Renata and I could take quite some time doing a "Shabooya Roll Call" of all the people we've stood in the gap for—whether they asked us to or not. That impulse stems from gratitude for the small circle of mentors and friends who did the same for us, as well as from seasons in our lives when such support was painfully absent. We remember what that felt like, and even if it means being misread, canceled, or ignored while trying to help others avoid avoidable misery, we press on. There will always be a faithful remnant. But unless Christians get serious about loving one another and the world the way God does, Christianity—not Christ, but the cultural expression of Christianity in the U.S.—will become even more nominal and disfigured than most of us can imagine.

There's a 95-minute animated movie from 2010 that's one of my favorites. I can, and often do, watch it over and over again. It's incredibly family-friendly, lighthearted, and genuine. Though there are now several spin-offs, and a fourth sequel slated for release this year, I still think the original is the best. *Despicable Me* introduces us to Gru, an oddly shaped, hardened veteran supervillain who's obsessed with stealing the moon to get rich by selling it on the black market. As part of his scheme, he adopts three sisters—Margo, Edith, and Agnes—from an orphanage to use them as pawns in his plot. The girls try to love him, hoping he might become the permanent parent they long for. But Gru doesn't return their enthusiasm or innocence—he's not interested in caring for them. His focus is on becoming a legendary criminal. Yet he is, unknowingly, miserable. That is, until he begins to grow a conscience and realize that these little girls—brimming with energy, attitude, intelligence, and joy—have become his life. At one point, he misses their dance recital, insisting, "I am the greatest criminal mind of the century! I don't go to little girls' dance recitals."[5] But by the end of the movie, Gru has a change of heart. He apologizes sincerely and takes drastic action to show the girls he's no longer the same man—he's truly changed.

Here's what I'm getting at: Left to ourselves, we are despicable. Despicable you, despicable me. Despicable Bill, Despicable Diane. Despicable Jan, Despicable Renata. Despicable Dick, Despicable Angie. Despicable Gloria, Despicable David. We are the Church Despicable—"for all have sinned and fall short of the glory of God."[6] Only the Lord redeems. Only the Lord can turn suffering into celebration and tame temptation. Maybe we're not miserable every moment of every day, thank God. But we are, in our own ways, just like Gru—hardheaded, prideful, and double-minded. Hallelujah that we no longer serve the Baals, and that eternal life is available to all who would confess their mess, turn to the one true and living God, and walk away from whatever false security previously held power in their lives. This morning is a perfect time to turn to God.

---

5. *Despicable Me*, 2010.
6. Rom 3:23.

The Consequences of Rejection
Judges 11:1–11, April 7, 2024

"Birds of a feather flock together," as the saying goes, means that among living things there's a basic, insatiable appetite for grouping. For the record, that's not all bad; much of it is an essential part of life. Not everyone makes every team. You don't get every job you apply for or every home you put an offer on. Friendships from second grade rarely survive into or through college. Swiping right or professing love doesn't guarantee those feelings will be returned.

March 15 was Match Day—the moment when students, just months away from graduating from medical school, learn where they'll spend the next 3 to 7 years of residency. Some match into specialties like internal medicine, pediatrics, psychiatry, or dermatology. One student I know matched into neurosurgery. Another, hoping for orthopedics, didn't receive a match and will reapply next year. Sometimes, what you hope won't happen is exactly what does. Other times, what you pray for comes true. The ability to process life when it doesn't go your way—skillfully, wisely, and with resilience—is being undervalued and is rapidly disappearing nowadays. Beyond the typical wins and losses, the Christian worldview also describes sin—through us—as giving voice to a spirit whose divisiveness is catastrophic. Without much effort, we default to defining people by race, background, clothing, education level, or physical appearance. Then we categorize them, separate ourselves, or assign them a place in an invisible pecking order—placing a figurative sticker on their back, marking whether they're in or out of the "cool club" we think we're gatekeeping.

Lysa TerKeurst addresses this in her book *Uninvited: Living Loved When You Feel Less Than, Left Out, and Lonely*. Renata often uses this resource to help women confront the distorted thinking they carry into young adulthood—especially around the basic human desire to belong. It's normal to want community, but it's dangerous to be willing to lose your soul, sanity, or self-respect to gain it. Rejection can push people to do harm while believing they're doing no wrong at all. In the *Peanuts* comic strip, Lucy has rejected lovable Charlie Brown for years—inviting him to kick the football, only to pull it away at the last second, sending him flying and yelling, "Ahhhhhh!" The misfit teens in *The Breakfast Club* knew the sting of rejection. So did Cinderella, Shrek, and The Ugly Duckling. Then there's the 2004 film *The Incredibles*, now a cult classic. Early in Mr. Incredible's superhero career, he has a run-in with a kid named Buddy. Insecure but brilliant, Buddy invents rocket boots, hoping to impress his hero and join him as a sidekick—Incrediboy. But one night, Buddy interferes with Mr. Incredible's mission to stop a thief named Bomb Voyage, endangering the whole city. Though Mr. Incredible saves the day at the last second, Bomb Voyage escapes. Mr. Incredible tells him, "Fly home, Buddy. I work alone."[1] Rejection is hard and left unaddressed, it can send any of us into a tailspin of despair and destruction.

Jephthah had grown into a "mighty warrior" by the time his native tribesmen came asking him to return and lead them into battle. The thing is, unlike them, he hadn't forgotten what went down back in the day—how his half-brothers had thrown him out of the house, saying in verse 2, "You are not going to get any inheritance in our family because you are the son of another woman." The memory is likely etched in HD for him—what he was wearing, how his heart ached, the tears he shed during or after being so harshly and publicly rejected. This wasn't a polite eviction. We don't know whether it came to blows or if Jephthah refused to go quietly. What we do know is that his own blood—his brothers—forced him out, changed the locks, and emphatically kicked him to the curb. It seems he was in his teenage years, a time when a boy begins transforming into a man, and the thirst for inheritance, power, and recognition grows stronger. Whether from fear or pride, the brothers cast him out like a threat. Perceived as an illegitimate outsider, Jephthah was left to survive on his own.

He likely did some things he wasn't proud of in the land of Tob—what we now call the West Bank—where he found himself in exile. That's

---

1. *The Incredibles*, 2005.

often the story when someone is ripped away from all they know and forced to do life with a "gang of scoundrels." Scripture tells us these men "gathered around him and followed him." He found community in chaos. We're not given a resume of what Jephthah accomplished during his exile, but the text points to a man who had become respected, scrappy, and resourceful, a kind of rogue leader unafraid to do what needed to be done. A survivor. A tactician. A fighter. The irony, of course, is thick: the very elders of Gilead who once rejected him now return, desperate. "Come be our commander, so we can fight the Ammonites," they say. Desperation is a great equalizer. Because of his mother's reputation, Jephthah had been disgraced and sent away. His countrymen didn't care what would become of him—what he'd eat, where he'd sleep, or whether he lived or died. That rejection forced him into a life of hustling for survival, hungry for protection, living on the margins. But now the tables have turned. He's running his own operation with a loyal crew, living comfortably in Tob. Then suddenly, here come the hypocrites—those who had caused his deepest wounds—asking him not only to forgive and forget but to risk everything he's built to fight their battle, one that technically isn't his anymore. If you've been following this series through Judges, then these words should sound familiar: "In those days Israel had no king; everyone did as they saw fit." Repeatedly, God's people did their best to not act like God's people. And yet, even as they rejected Him, God continued extending His hand, His incarnational olive branch, inviting them back.

Rejection is especially difficult when it stems from factors we can't control. Some of us know what it's like to be singled out because, as the saying goes, "If you ain't Dutch, you ain't much." Or maybe because you came from a Reformed household and married someone Christian Reformed, or vice versa. Maybe rejection came because of your skin color, your accent, your language, or even where you sat in the cafeteria. Perhaps in your family, your parents were divorced, or they were never a couple at all. Maybe you're single, and every so often someone feels the need to comment on it. The divisions are endless. But let's be honest: we've also done the same thing, passing improper judgment on others. Jephthah's father, Gilead, was something of a "rolling stone"—wherever he laid his hat was his home. He had 70 sons. So, when the convoy of elders approached Jephthah, who had been cast aside as his father's illegitimate firstborn, it would make sense for his hand to be close to his sword. After all, these were the very people who had rejected him, now standing on *his* turf. Jephthah brings this up in verse 7. The elders want him to sign on the dotted line, but he refuses to be rushed. He counters their initial offer, and by the end of verse 11, he raises the stakes: if things go according to plan, he will become their recognized commander-in-chief. That's significant, because the elders had tried to lowball him.

Jephthah was chosen, it seems, more by men than by God, which is not a positive development. Another odd detail in this story: neither party consults God. They are too proud. It's only when Jephthah makes vows at Mizpah in verse 11 that God is even mentioned—treated not as the One to seek for guidance, but merely as a witness to the deal they've already made. There's no record of even one prayer or petition for God's direction from the elders or from Jephthah. Desperate people in desperate times tend to behave desperately, but they don't have to. We don't have to. Proverbs 16 offers this reminder:

> Pride goes before destruction,
> a haughty spirit before a fall.
>
> Better to be lowly in spirit along with the oppressed
> than to share plunder with the proud.
>
> Whoever gives heed to instruction prospers,
> and blessed is the one who trusts in the Lord.
>
> The wise in heart are called discerning,
> and gracious words promote instruction.

To keep rejection from running roughshod over us, we must be willing to be vulnerable and respond to it honestly, admitting that a connection we were hoping for or depending on didn't work out. For God's healing to reset our spiritual system and remind us of our unshakable identity in Him, we can't let pride and stubbornness take control. When they do, we start leading ourselves, chasing our own agendas, and striving to elevate our position. Before long, it becomes all about "my kingdom come, my will be done"[2]—just like Jephthah and the elders: selfish and shortsighted. And that's never a good place to be.

Depending on your background or the questions weighing on your heart, it may not always be obvious—but Christianity is not like Tic-Tac-Toe, chess, construction, or assembly-line manufacturing. Yes, much of it

---

2. Matt 6:10.

is clearly laid out for us, but still, we won't always be able to pinpoint what went wrong, who's responsible, or why one thing happened and another didn't. The sooner you choose to trust God with all of that, the better off you'll be, believe me—regardless of your specific situation. Unlike the characters in this story, we must pray—talking to God and listening to what He has already said and is still saying. Prayer isn't about handing Him a glittered list of wants, as if He were Santa Claus. It's about rooting yourself in humility, service, and devotion to the unmistakable power of His Word—because that's the means by which we conquer our own demons, so they don't turn us into what we hate. As Friedrich Nietzsche wrote in his 1886 work *Beyond Good and Evil: Prelude to a Philosophy of the Future*, "Whoever fights monsters should see to it that in the process he does not become a monster. And when you look into an abyss, the abyss also looks into you."[3]

God wants to speak through you. He wants you to dream dreams and see visions. He wants to pour out His Spirit on you and your circumstances to accomplish His will. Your job—and mine—is to give Him the rightful position of authority in our lives. Jephthah and the elders of Gilead got it wrong. The Lord God Almighty is the true "head and commander" over our lives, and we must seek Him—not only to avoid rejection, but especially in the very midst of it.

Rejection is a funny thing. Sometimes, the chickens come home to roost with fiery intentions to avenge wounds from long ago—because the body keeps score, and the mind remembers the names and faces of those who hurt us. Buddy, the once-annoying little kid desperate for Mr. Incredible's approval, eventually became his greatest nemesis. He became an evil genius.

Under the covering of grace and by the Spirit's power, let's be incredible in a different way. Let's invest in the lives of others for the sake of the Gospel—careful never to "call evil good and good evil."[4]

---

3. Friedrich Nietzsche, *Beyond Good and Evil: Prelude to a Philosophy of the Future*, 146.

4. Isa 5:20.

A Desperate Pledge
Judges 11:12–33, April 14, 2024

Let's take a stroll down memory lane. Think back to childhood. Have you ever been dragged into a dispute, a soap opera-level drama, or some chaotic conflict of epic proportions that, when you really looked at it, had little or nothing to do with you? Maybe your younger sibling, staring down someone who'd upset them, said something like, "Okay, that's fine. I'm gonna go get my brother!" Whatever was said or done before that moment—you didn't start it, you didn't see it happen, you were just minding your business. Then suddenly, you found yourself pulled into the middle of someone else's mess. That's a lot like how we were introduced last week to Jephthah, in Judges 11:1–11. Scripture doesn't give us much about his personality or motivations, but we do know his father: Gideon. Gideon first appears in Judges 6, handpicked by God to lead Israel. Remember, it was an angel who appeared to him with the message. At the time, Gideon was hiding, tucked away in the agrarian underground, separating edible wheat from inedible straw. Eventually, though, he rose up to lead the people to victory, until his downfall came through ruthlessness and idolatry. Judges 8 tells us he had 70 sons, with Jephthah being his eldest, born to a woman the Bible refers to as a prostitute.

Jephthah's start in life was rough. His brothers rejected him, declared him unfit, and cut him out of the family inheritance after their father died. So, understandably, he fled to a land far away—the land of Tob—a kind of rugged, untamed wilderness. Against all odds, Jephthah carved out a life for himself there. Then, wouldn't you know it: the same people who disowned him came crawling back when they needed help. The enemy was knocking, and suddenly Jephthah, the outcast, started to look like their best hope. He agrees to help them fight the Ammonites, but nothing in life is free. His terms? If they win, he becomes their ruler.

Now, it would be presumptuous to call Jephthah a "chip off the old block," as if his father's flaws automatically transferred to him. Just because Gideon fell into some dark places doesn't mean Jephthah did. The truth is, we don't really know—and it's perfectly okay to admit that.

You might say Jephthah, like many of the judges in the Book of Judges, fits the profile that Taylor Swift sings about of an "Anti-Hero."[1] Characters played by John Wayne in various Westerns, or James Gandolfini's Tony Soprano from HBO's *The Sopranos*, are great examples of the anti-hero. Enigmatic and intricate, they operate with an irregular moral code. You're cheering them on one minute and shaking your head the next. They're hard to pin down.

Jephthah, in a similar way, is not easy to categorize. On one hand, if he believed that blood is thicker than water, perhaps he stepped in to save his people from a deep sense of loyalty. He certainly doesn't waste any time confronting the Ammonites. In Judges 11:12, he asks directly, "What do you have against me that you have attacked my country?" But on the other hand, maybe he accepted the role purely for the irony of it. It was the perfect opportunity for revenge, with him now holding power over the very people who once so recklessly discarded him. So, what would *you* do? If you haven't seen it, *What Would You Do?* is a long-running hidden camera show hosted by John Quiñones on *ABC*. Unlike prank shows that aim for laughs by scaring or tricking people, this one takes a deeper approach. With actors, it stages real-life moral impasses and watches how unsuspecting bystanders respond. After the big reveal, participants reflect on their actions, and the audience is left to consider what they might have done in that same situation. It's compelling TV. Imagine this: while shopping, you overhear a mother berating her 11-year-old daughter for not being "skinny enough." The girl retreats into a dressing room, eyes filled with tears, and then timidly asks for your opinion. In another scenario, you're at a restaurant when a manager threatens to call immigration authorities on an employee who refuses to work a double shift. Or maybe you're in a doctor's waiting room, and a man loudly tells his mistress he's beginning to regret their affair. Trying to cover his tracks, he looks at you, throws his hands up, and jokes, "Marriage. Hey, what're you gonna do?" When reading about Jephthah—and other biblical figures

---

1. Taylor Swift, "Anti-Hero", 2022.

placed in morally gray, emotionally charged situations—it helps to step outside ourselves for a moment. These aren't just ancient stories. They're human ones. And just like *What Would You Do?*, Scripture invites us to wrestle with the same question: *What would you do?*

As we read earlier, Jephthah finds himself in the middle of a land dispute with the Ammonites, a type of conflict that has long been a flashpoint between nations and still is today. The situation stems from a chain of defeats: the Ammonites originally lost the land to the Amorites, who were later defeated by the Israelites. As a result, the land naturally passed to Israel as a spoil of war. Now, the Ammonite king is saying, in so many words, "Give it back peacefully." But let's be clear—that was a thinly veiled threat. What he's really denoting is that Israel has two choices: surrender willingly or prepare for battle. Either submit or be defeated and shamed. Jephthah responds diplomatically, yet firmly. He basically says, "Look, we don't have a problem with you. But what the God of Israel gave us is ours. And what your god Chemosh gives you is yours. You're the one making this into something bigger than it needs to be." Then, starting in verse 26, Jephthah presents a compelling historical argument: "For three hundred years Israel occupied Heshbon, Aroer, the surrounding settlements, and all the towns along the Arnon. Why didn't you try to take them back during all that time? I haven't wronged you, but you are wronging me by waging war against us. Let the Lord, the Judge, decide the dispute this day between the Israelites and the Ammonites." The Ammonite king responds by cutting off negotiations—an immature and rude signal that war is now fated. And remember, "In those days Israel had no king; everyone did as they saw fit."

Then, in verse 30, Jephthah makes a vow that exposes what seems to be desperation. He says: "If you give the Ammonites into my hands, whatever comes out of the door of my house to meet me when I return in triumph...I will sacrifice it as a burnt offering." Israel does end up victorious, but what's especially interesting is that the Spirit of the Lord comes upon Jephthah before he makes this vow, which makes the promise feel even more needless, and perhaps foolish. For reasons the text doesn't explain, Jephthah chooses to make this open-ended, solemn promise to God. What's telling is that this is only the second time in the entire story, which begins at the start of Judges 11, that Jephthah even mentions God. In both cases, he reaches out to God only when he needs something: help, validation, or divine backing for decisions he's already made. Without overreaching or psychoanalyzing him too much, it's clear Jephthah carries formative trauma. He was his father's firstborn—Gideon was a prominent figure—but his mother was a prostitute, and that damaged his social standing. So, here he is, doing his best to lead, to fulfill his role as a judge. But his approach is dangerously utilitarian. He treats God like a tool—someone to call on for help when needed—rather than a sovereign to constantly be sought for guidance, wisdom, and relationship.

With its infamous, plutonium-powered flux capacitor, the DeLorean manned by Marty McFly and the ever-eccentric Doc Brown in *Back to the Future* reminds us that sometimes we need to go "back to the future"—to return to a moment when we thought or acted like Jephthah, letting worry or misguided logic cloud our judgment. It's easy to say what you *won't* do, but that conviction remains an untested theory until you're face-to-face with temptation: that job, that relationship, that trip, that bottle, that needle, that indiscretion. Suddenly, your desires begin bartering with your values, convincing you it's not *that* bad—and anyway, no one has to know. Remember, though: there is no testimony without a test. When we're exhausted—spiritually or otherwise—distracted, isolated, stuck in a funk, or clinging to poor theology, desperation becomes especially dangerous. Jephthah's vow was like telling God, "Send me a spouse, and whoever comes along, I'll marry them without hesitation—and as a token of my thanks, I'll cut off all contact with the first person who congratulates me." It was wild and irrational. Honestly, it was worse than the infamous fleece Gideon laid out back in Judges 6. Gideon, scared and insecure, demanded God prove Himself with a series of miraculous signs just to confirm his calling—only to later unravel in foolishness himself. God is perfectly reliable; we are not. There's nothing wrong with asking for God's help or favor, but it's something else entirely to make our obedience conditional—to say, "If You do this for me, then I'll do that for You." That's *quid pro quo*—a transactional mindset that's out of place in a relationship with the Divine. The truth is, we have nothing God *needs*. Yes, He desires our obedience and holiness, but He deserves those regardless of whether He grants our requests or not. When we bargain with God like Jephthah did, we're saying, "I've decided this plan is so brilliant, so worthy, that if—and only if—You approve it, I'll offer You something in return." That kind of pride never flies.

We are not God's equals. I don't care how blood-bought, blood-washed, Holy Ghost-filled, fire-baptized, or sanctified you believe yourself to be, you better know that you need God. God does not need you. You cannot manipulate the Creator of the universe, who is at once intimately near and utterly beyond reach. Can I tell you what I wish? I wish God's people, those who've genuinely subscribed to the Good News paid in full by Jesus, would be honest. Because if we're honest, we've all had moments—whether two or three, 75, or too many to count—where we were ready to make a decision we shouldn't, under the illusion that doing so might compel God to give us what we want. In that way, we are no different from Jephthah. We're just as likely to place anything on the altar if we think it will guarantee a win, however we define it. But I'm here to tell you—it's not worth it. As Thomas Fuller said, "They that worship God merely from fear would worship the devil too, if he appears."[2] The same goes for those who worship God only as a bargaining chip. There's a hymn, based on Psalm 86, that offers guidance both universal and essential—guidance we would all do well to remember.

> I need thee, O
> I need thee
> Every hour I need thee!
> O, bless me now, my Savior
> I come to Thee

It may feel simple, but it's sacred:

> I need thee, O
> I need thee
> Every hour I need thee!
> O, bless me now, my Savior
> I come to Thee

It is true, and good, and profitable for us to honor God always and often, by saying in desperation:

> I need thee, O
> I need thee
> Every hour I need thee!
> O, bless me now, my Savior
> I come to Thee[3]

---

2. Thomas Fuller, *Good Thoughts in Bad Times and Other Papers*.

3. Annie S. Hewitt, "I Need Thee Every Hour," in *The Hymnal of the Methodist Episcopal Church*, 273.

No More Passing the Buck

Judges 11:34–40, April 21, 2024

It's fair to say that Jephthah shared some of his dearly departed father's calamitous traits, but he managed to avoid one of them. Unlike Gideon, who had 70 sons and numerous wives, concubines, and prostitutes—making his life and legacy unnecessarily complicated and sullied—Jephthah did not follow that path. St. Augustine, in his classic text Confessions, wrote, "What I live by, I impart."[1] Augustine, who had indulged in scandalous, carnal activities during his earlier years, recognized the truth of this statement. It's clear in Judges that each of us contributes to a legacy shaped by who we've lived for and how we've lived. While we should not idolize the legacy we leave behind, the quality of what remains when we depart is ultimately up to us. Thankfully, Jephthah made different lifestyle choices, possibly to avoid the messy relational fallout he experienced with his father. Scripture does not give us many details about Jephthah's child's mother—whether they were married, cohabiting, or in any other relationship. What we do know is that his daughter, who is unnamed in the text, is his only child. Last week, we read about the desperate vow Jephthah made, hoping to be victorious over the Ammonites. This came after he was made leader of the same people who, years earlier, had banished him from his home, citing his illegitimate status because his mother was never married to Gideon. Despite being the firstborn son, Jephthah was denied any inheritance. It was a cold, ruthless act. Like some of us at various points in life, Jephthah seemed willing to do anything to secure his future.

As we begin, let's acknowledge that this can be a difficult text. Studying the Bible is not a spiritual test like the ACT, SAT, or state assessments. These 66 books are not meant to be a quick fix or a simple resource like

---

1. Augustine, *Confessions*, Book 10, Chapter 6.

Google. Instead, they are God's Word to guide, instruct, challenge, comfort, and care for us as we fulfill God's calling in the world. Just because I don't grasp every nuance of every verse doesn't mean I should create an alternative gospel. There are two major interpretations of this text. The first interpretation is that Jephthah literally sacrificed his daughter—blood for blood—honoring his vow to God by killing her. It sounds outrageous, especially from a modern perspective, but it's still a possibility. When we look at Judges 4:17–21, we see how Jael, a woman, drove a tent peg through the temple of an enemy general, Sisera, after briefly harboring him. The point is that strange and horrifying things happen when sinful, depraved people act on their desires in every generation, every nation, and every family. However, it's important to note that God did not command Jephthah to make this vow. The vow was his own idea, stemming from his desperation for success. Whether it's winning a battle, getting a promotion, or earning approval, people sometimes make absurdly harmful decisions to achieve their goals. This is how many have traditionally understood the story: Jephthah made a literal sacrifice. The second interpretation is that Jephthah's vow did not involve killing his daughter but dedicating her to lifelong service in the tabernacle or church, living as a celibate and unmarried woman. Scholars who support this view suggest that the two months of weeping with her friends, mentioned in verse 37, were not due to her impending death but because she would never marry or have children.

During that time, marriage and motherhood were key aspects of a woman's social significance and survival. For her, this would have been a heartbreaking loss, as she could never experience the joys of marriage or motherhood. Furthermore, women in her time were often denied the opportunity to undo Jephthah's decision. They could advocate for themselves in their own way, but their hands were largely tied. One point of irony is that Jephthah, who was unjustly expelled from his rightful home and future, is now doing the same thing to his only child. This battle against the Ammonites, a fight that wasn't his daughter's and wasn't her fault, is the one for which she is supposed to pay the price. Someone might say, "That's not right!" To God's credit, the text portrays her as a heroine, showing unyielding strength, dignity, and character in the face of injustice. Throughout Scripture, women like Abigail in 1 Samuel 25 or Queen Esther in the book of Esther rise above their male counterparts, demonstrating grace, hope, resolve, courage, and obedience.

There will always be aspects of the Bible that we don't fully understand, but one thing we do know from Judges is this: "In those days Israel had no king; everyone did as they saw fit." This is a good anchor to prevent us from getting lost in the weeds of every interpretive detail. I can't confidently say which of the two interpretations of Jephthah's vow is correct, but I can tell you that, just like his brothers and the elders of Gilead, who refused to own up to their mistreatment of him, Jephthah attempts to pass the buck and avoid responsibility for his actions with his beloved daughter. Returning home from victory, Jephthah's daughter rushes out of the house to celebrate with him, which was customary. When Jephthah sees her, he tears his clothes and cries, "Oh no, my daughter! You have brought me down and I am devastated. I have made a vow to the Lord that I cannot break."[2] This scene reminds me of Hulk Hogan back in the day. When facing opponents like Sergeant Slaughter or Randy Savage, the wrestling star—dressed in his signature yellow and red attire with a blond mustache—would rip his shirt off and ask, "Whatcha gonna do when Hulkamania runs wild on you?" Instead of protecting his daughter, Jephthah has dragged her into a foolish situation that has nothing to do with her. And I'd argue that he has the nerve to then be rather flippant, dramatic, and surprisingly self-righteous about it.

He goes full Hulk Hogan by tearing his clothes, but not to say, "Lord, forgive me. What have I done?" No, instead, his response is all about *him*. It's only "I, I, I. Me, me, me." His posture is, "You brought this on yourself"—which is not the right response when your poor choices lead to agony, disruption, or other burdens in someone else's life. Beware: this is not how a repentant heart behaves. It has been said, "People do profoundly stupid things. When they have to pay the price, and there's always a price, they blame God, their parents, the universe, and everything under the sun except themselves."[3] From 1993 to 2001, William Jefferson Clinton served as the 42nd U.S. president. Many of us remember when allegations of an affair or extramarital conduct surfaced. Clinton initially denied everything, a tactic that often works—wearing people down until they feel like they're going crazy and move on to something else. But on December 19, 1998, Clinton was impeached for high crimes and misdemeanors, though he was eventually acquitted. A four-part *Hulu* documentary[4] about the scandal was released a few years ago, with

---

2. Judg 11:25.
3. Anonymous.
4. *The Clinton Affair*, 2018.

both new and old footage. In it, Clinton admits to the affair with Monica Lewinsky, but stops short of taking *full* responsibility. He comments that it all happened because he was trying to manage his anxieties. None of us get it right all the time, but when we mess up, especially as Christians, we must be quick to come clean and accept the consequences. This is even more important for those in leadership.

One possible translation of verse 35 is, "I have made a solemn and unusual vow to Yahweh, and I cannot take it back." But my question is, why not? For us today, as we are bound by the Law but reconciled through the grace of sacrificial love, why shouldn't we stop in our tracks when we realize we've done wrong—even if that wrong is an immature, misguided, deadly promise—and ask God for help? Shouldn't that be the song our hearts sing? We'll never know how the story might have unfolded had Jephthah been more concerned about his daughter's well-being after making such a colossal mistake, rather than saving face. Now is always a good time to face the music of our errors, and then repent, repair, resign, repay, or redo whatever we can, however we can, to whomever we can. I'm not suggesting that you take the blame for actions or misdeeds that aren't yours. You should only own what you've caused, but trust me, that's enough. I also know that, as you may, that some people today subscribe to the "snitches get stitches" mindset—that you should turn a blind eye to wrongdoing, whether it's criminal or moral. I don't want to be called a "snitch" any more than you do, and I try to stay away from situations where I might end up needing stitches. But I'm not going to risk my peace of mind, integrity, job, marriage, or life to cover for someone else. Just because God is gracious enough to meet us where we are, in the messes we create, doesn't mean He celebrates every decision we make. That's true both in Scripture and in our everyday lives.

Obituaries, Hypomnesia, and Eternity

Judges 12, April 28, 2024

In recent years, anyone I've had more than a brief conversation with has likely heard me, at some point, remark that life is short. This is hardly a groundbreaking discovery—life has always been short—but with each birthday, every step forward and backward, and the constant chaos surrounding us, it feels more pressing. And the mirror doesn't lie: aging and all its companions are not abstract fantasies. They are real, persistent, and they'll win on a fleshly level. *Hands down.* We are here today, gone tomorrow. Our skin is temperamental at best, stretching in ways we never asked it to. From how your hair no longer cooperates as it once did, to your eyesight fading, to flipping through an old family photo album and reflecting on the vigor, curiosity, and patience you once had, only to realize it's long gone. Our once-reliable memory starts slipping away. And friends, loved ones, and even strangers—at some point, it seems—begin to drop like flies. Life is short. Whether you live a godly life or a carnal one, the time you have, or that has you, is borrowed. It allows you to write many parts of your story, but rest assured, it has never asked for your input on how it ends and it never will. In the end, it will be what it will be. If you've ever been under anesthesia, you know how it drives home the fact that no event, no milestones, no experience, is guaranteed on the way to the inevitable. This is a difficult topic to consider, let alone discuss, but it's as real as it gets—and it won't go away. I think this is why the Lord has us addressing it today. Just because something is hard doesn't mean avoiding it is beneficial. When we avoid the hard topics, we do so to our detriment. A society that insists on "soft landings" is partly to blame for why so many people, of all ages, are convinced that whatever they want or don't want to do must be the best choice. You even have Christians convinced that staying stuck in that state of escapism is perfectly fine with God.

Speaking of death, Judges 12 begins with Jephthah's last chapter. He gets into a confrontation with the infamous Ephraimites, who essentially call him a fool and threaten him with violence, even death. When someone belittles you and your people, lies about you, and says, "We're going to burn down your house over your head," let's just say a response is needed. So, Jephthah, perhaps being accommodating in this instance, gives them what they want. They wanted a fight, so, as they say, "When in Rome..." It's interesting that when these Israelites needed victory once again, this time from within their own ranks, one method they used to distinguish friend from foe was to have them pronounce the word "Shibboleth," which means "flood" or "ear of corn." If they mispronounced it as "Sibboleth," leaving out the "h," they knew the person was an enemy. I understand they were doing the best they could, but goodness, isn't that the least scientific and trustworthy method for determining life or death? What if you had a cold, pneumonia, or simply spoke with an accent from the east side of Gilead that made it hard to pronounce? What if you had a lisp? But who am I to talk? It worked.

Scattered throughout the Book of Judges, beginning in chapter 3, continuing through our text, and beyond, there's a consistent pattern: as each judge's tenure concludes, a brief note typically appears summarizing their accomplishments, their death, and the effects of their absence. Some of these summaries are more detailed than others; they vary. In verse 7, for example, we read, "Jephthah led Israel six years. Then Jephthah the Gileadite died and was buried in a town in Gilead." The same formula is used for Ibzan, Elon, and Abdon, the judges who followed him. One of them had 60 children—30 sons and 30 daughters. One led Israel for 10 years, another for eight. But regardless of those personal details, the same truth applies to all: they died, and they were buried. I don't mean to be a party pooper, but that will be our fate too.

On a biological level, it doesn't matter how you lived—only that you lived. And like all living things, there is a beginning and an end: birth and death. It's not personal; it's simply how life works. These brief summaries—like the ones closing many judges' reigns—are essentially ancient obituaries, succinctly marking what someone did, and the legacy they left behind.

Obituaries, as we know them today, often take a different shape. Some are highly technical or formal. They function as both a death notice and a brief biography, alerting the public that someone has passed. Maybe you've done this, or maybe your parents did, but oftentimes people of a certain age are known to flip through the newspaper to see who's died and when. Most of the time, the names and faces belong to strangers. But every now and then, it hits closer to home: "Oh Lord, you remember Mr. Johnson's wife, Judith? She passed. It says her ovarian cancer came back." *Something like that*. As it goes in our country, the rich and famous get more space and attention for their final farewells. But once the fanfare fades—no pun intended—the core facts are the same as for everyone else. *Veni, vidi, vici*—"I came, I saw, I conquered," as the Latin phrase says. Each life boils down to this: they were here, they did some things—good or bad—and now they're gone. No one escapes death, no matter the time or circumstances God ordains.

If the term *hypomnesia* is unfamiliar to you, that lyric captures its essence in a nutshell; it refers to a poor, or abnormally poor, memory. I think it's only natural to want to be remembered, to remain like shrapnel embedded deeply in the hearts and minds of our loved ones, friends, and broader community. We hope to be remembered by the people we invested in at work, those we served through our professions, and the individuals at the shelter whose faces and stories became familiar through our care and prayers. We hope our church family will remember us, too—the ones we've served alongside on too many committees to count. The people we raked leaves with, baked for, tithed with, encouraged, cleaned nursery toys with, prayed with, and played pickleball, volleyball, or Bible trivia games with. Together, we've fought the good fight of faith, each of us a little crazy in our own way, but doing our best. Average Joes and Janes like us know our names probably won't go up in lights. *The New York Times* isn't likely to publish an obituary detailing our contributions to society. Still, we hope someone, somewhere, remembers our example or body of work with fondness.

That friend, mentor, or favorite aunt or uncle who's always looked out for us is often the one we visit the least. The spouse whose steadfast support kept us afloat—whose love, rooted in God's grace, covered a multitude of our sins—we take for granted. We leave too much unsaid and too much undone until it's too late. And if we *are* the spouse, the mentor, the aunt, uncle, or friend, chances are we won't be fully appreciated in the moment either. That's just how people are. Even after we're gone, we'll be spoken of less and less as time goes on. That's the way the human cookie crumbles. We are forgetful. Your job, believe me, will have a search team interviewing for your replacement quicker than you think. Back in 1964, the incomparable Nina Simone recorded the classic song "Don't Let Me Be Misunderstood,"[1] a tune that's since been covered by countless artists. It speaks to a deep human longing—to be seen, to be appreciated, to be chosen, and to be remembered when memories are all that remain.

What I'm getting at is this: it's unwise to live for applause or reciprocal acknowledgment. The brief obituaries we see in Judges 12 remind us how limited such remembrances are, no matter how long or detailed. People's memories, ours or others', fade. Verse 7 reads, "Jephthah led Israel six years. Then Jephthah the Gileadite died and was buried in a town in Gilead." But was he a coffee lover? Did he volunteer at the local Boys & Girls Club? Was he a Kids Hope mentor? Did he grill for his neighbors on summer weekends? Nobody knows! The same goes for Ibzan, Elon, and Abdon, who followed Jephthah. One had 60 children—30 sons and 30 daughters. One led Israel for 10 years, another for eight. Yet the text only tells us: they died and were buried. No mention is made of how one of them may have spent 30 years as a recovering alcoholic, reconciled with a son, or struggled to reconnect with a daughter who wanted nothing to do with his amends. We don't hear how war trauma from Iraq, or time spent as a detective in Gary, Indiana, haunted him silently, nor how surrendering his life to God, though not solving every problem, changed everything. Obituaries, like *church online*, can only offer so much. They don't capture hugs or high-fives given at the right moment, prayers whispered in hushed tones, meals delivered in times of crisis, tuition or rent quietly paid, the Bible studies led, or the countless unseen sacrifices made in love. Even our own memories are too shallow and inconsistent to fully remember (or know) all that. That's why it's essential to live with eternity in mind.

As Judges repeats, "In those days Israel had no king; everyone did as they saw fit." But if today you trust the King of Kings—if you belong, body and soul, in life and in death, to your faithful Savior—then don't waste time trying to make your mark just to be remembered. We all fade from memory in time. What matters most is that which is done for

---

1. Nina Simone, "Don't Let Me Be Misunderstood," 1964.

Christ, because it alone outlasts human remembrance. So, devote your time, gifts, and heart to God. Let the Spirit lead you. Apologize when needed. Take good care of yourself because your life is a gift from a good, good Father. Dance, laugh, sing, cry, confess. Go bowling. Go on walks. Travel up north or down south—wherever you must to invest your days in carrying your cross for Christ. The eternal dividends from that investment are the only legacy that truly endures.

The Calm Before the Storm
Judges 13, May 5, 2024

WHAT FIRST AND FOREMOST connects us to Samson isn't just his behavior—though that certainly matters and we'll get to it later. What draws us in is the incredible transparency of his story. We're given a rare, behind-the-scenes look at his life, from the dramatic circumstances of his birth to his rise as a judge, his peak as a hero (even a kind of superhero), and then his terrible downfall and death. In many ways, he died as he lived—occasionally faithful as a Nazirite follower of Yahweh, but often emotionally reckless, violent, and, by today's standards, toxic.

Scripture lets us be a fly on the wall in Samson's life in ways it doesn't always allow with every biblical character. Take, for instance, the Samaritan woman at the well in John 4. Jesus, without invitation, uncovers her deeply personal history in a single statement: "The fact is, you have had five husbands, and the man you now have is not your husband."[1] It's a fascinating and powerful moment—but the entire encounter unfolds in just 26 verses. Samson's story, by contrast, spans four chapters—96 verses in total—giving us not just snapshots, but a sweeping narrative. We get to see him in the weeds of everyday life, and that detail gives us a more extensive, nuanced picture of who he was. As for his behavior—which I said I'd circle back to—Samson is not usually counted among the Bible's most likable or admirable figures. We need to be honest about that, although there's still plenty to learn from him. The depth and specificity of the biblical account lend him raw humanity that's relatable. Not because we all make the same choices, but because his mindset, habits, and heart posture reflect the same tension we all carry: made "a little lower than the

---

1. John 4:18.

angels,"[2] yet given dominion over creation. Samson's life, like ours, is a mixture of divine purpose and very human failure.

Much like Abram's one-night stand with Hagar in Genesis 16, at the encouragement of Sarai, there's no attempt in Samson's story to sanitize the details. No trigger warnings. No PG-13 rating. The text is unfiltered and messy. And that's the point: we can see ourselves in these flawed figures. Their strengths, yes—as well as their pain, dysfunction, and destructive patterns. If you ever need an unflinching, no-nonsense case study of what to avoid in your own development or in evaluating someone else's growth, Samson won't let you down. His sojourn reminds us that ignoring wisdom—like the old saying, "If you don't want the fruits of sin, stay out of the devil's orchard"—always comes at a cost. For Samson, as you'll see if you've read ahead, trouble is lurking. But before the unraveling begins, his arrival marks the fulfillment of a long-deferred hope. Israel has been under Philistine oppression for 40 years because of their repeated betrayal of God.[3] Meanwhile, Samson's parents are childless, a condition that—in a society where children represented social, spiritual, and economic vitality—was deeply painful. The more children you had, the more favor you were thought to possess: more to trade with, more to fight with, more to continue the family name, and more to care for you in old age. But then comes divine intervention: an angel tells them they will have a son, and, in verse 5, declares, "His head is never to be touched by a razor because the boy is to be a Nazirite, dedicated to God from the womb." You can imagine someone in that moment saying, "Finally, our miracle is here." A storm is around the corner, one they'd have no way of knowing was there, but for right now, they are in a season of calm.

Manoah, Samson's father, has a name that interestingly means "place of rest" or simply "rest"—something that, ironically, would largely escape his son. Just because rest or calm is promised for one season or another doesn't mean—and I believe the text supports this—that it will come without discomfort or taxing work. Rest doesn't automatically equate to "having it made in the shade, sippin' a glass of lemonade." Sometimes it may feel that way, but it's unwise to expect or demand it. Assumptions of that kind, as many of us have learned the hard way, tend to make a mess of things. Though relatively calm compared to what was to come

---

2. Heb 2:7–9.
3. Judg 13:1.

for Samson later in life, his parents were not coasting. They were deeply engaged in the work—the ministry, really—of raising a son whom God had suddenly and sovereignly assigned to a future of leadership, without asking for their input or consent. It's safe to say that being "barren and childless" was not their preference. And even if they had hoped God would bless them with a child, they probably never imagined it would happen in this way—one that would drastically impact their lifestyle and parenting approach. Because their son was to be a Nazirite, at least during his formative years and ideally for life, his parents also had to adapt their lives to fit that sacred calling. This took maturity and discipline. There would be no first haircut to record and post on social media—because, of course, today everyone is expected to care about your child's every milestone and moment.

And unlike Mary, the mother of Jesus, who conceived without ever having been with a man, Samson's birth was not immaculate. Manoah and his wife conceived in the usual way, only it had never resulted in pregnancy until now, when the Spirit intervened. Still, she had to carry the child, nurture him, and risk her life in childbirth. During her pregnancy, she had to abstain from wine, vinegar, grape juice, grapes, raisins, and probably jelly donuts. More importantly, Samson's consecration as a Nazirite was lifelong, as stated clearly in verse 7. This was not like the temporary Nazirite vows taken voluntarily by others. Samson didn't volunteer; he *was* volunteered—by God. That reality meant his parents had to help him uphold restrictions that weren't negotiable or elective. He couldn't eat unclean food, go near a corpse or carcass, and his hair had to remain uncut—giving him a kind of John the Baptist, hippy-dippy, long-haired appearance. All of this formed the foundation of a calling that demanded their ongoing obedience and sacrifice as much as his.

I wonder if this phrase sounds familiar yet: "In those days Israel had no king; everyone did as they saw fit." It's fair to say that the Nazirite prohibitions weren't the harshest ever known to humanity, but we shouldn't overlook the fact that they still required effort and discipline. Anytime your child can't fully participate in the cultural norms of their generation, it's hard. Raising a Nazirite was no walk in the park. Our text doesn't state that Samson's divine calling was a secret, but you can easily imagine the constant comments and questions from others—some well-intentioned, others just nosy. "You really need to get control of your son," one mother might say. "My kid offered Samson some trail mix—raisins, cranberries, nuts, chocolate chips—and Samson knocked the bag right out of his hand! What's his deal?" Everything suggests that parenting Samson may have been an isolating, lonely experience. It's not exactly something you'd want to go around advertising—that your child has been marked from before birth to be the one who "will take the lead in delivering Israel from the hands of the Philistines." And yet, to their credit, his parents seemed to take it all in stride.

As the text continues: "The woman gave birth to a boy and named him Samson. He grew, and the Lord blessed him, and the Spirit of the Lord began to stir him while he was in Mahaneh Dan, between Zorah and Eshtaol." Setting aside catastrophizers and doomsday fatalists for the moment, most of us don't walk around consciously calculating that today will be *the* day—the day that calm ends and chaos, pain, or tragedy storms in to kick down the door and take names. On April 29, 2024, in Charlotte, North Carolina, at 1:30 p.m., the Fugitive Task Force of the U.S. Marshals went to serve active felony warrants on a man located on the 5000 block of Galway Drive. This, supported by local officers and other agencies, is something they do literally every day, multiple times every day. But that day was different. Walking into an ambush, eight officers were struck by gunfire, and four were killed.[4] Miguel Raul Zamudio's loved ones didn't know that here in Holland, Michigan, on April 13, 2024, he would die after being shot in the back of the head by a stranger with a shotgun.[5] Earlier that day, on the 300 block of West 19th Street—before what turned out to be a false bomb threat made by the suspect during his arrest—Miguel had been with his family, listening to music, laughing, and enjoying the weather. There was calm before the storm. In general, and often enough, there is a quiet before the diagnosis, before the life-altering car accident, before the fire, before the orders to a far-off land, before HR calls you in just to let you go, before your identity is stolen, before your loved one is robbed, before a pandemic shuts the world down overnight, before the road rage erupts, before your parent starts slurring their words and forgetting your name, before the first bomb drops, the first punch is thrown, or the first slur is barked out—in the moments before all of it, life is . . . alright.

---

4. Devon M. Sayers, "4 Law Enforcement Officers Were Killed in Shooting at a Home in Charlotte, North Carolina," *CNN*, 2024.

5. John Agar, "Family Devastated by Apparent Random Killing by Neighbor," *MLive*, 2024.

Samson's parents did their part. They didn't try to bargain their way out of God's mission for them. They asked the angel for clarification where needed, offered their sacrifice in obedience, and got on with their Father's business—an instructive example for us all. Storms may visit your life or mine more often than someone else's, whether that's real or just how it feels. *Fair enough.* But still, storms are more irregular than regular, even though they are promised. Jesus said, "In this world you will have trouble."[6] Both the human experience and our eternal adoption into God's family, as cross-bearing Christians, mean that storms will come. Some are unavoidable. Yet, in His perfect will, mercy, and grace, God will often reroute some storms. He will sometimes block the enemy's plans to stir up trouble—but not always. In the end, while storms are inevitable, they don't last forever, and they're not present 99% of each day. That's why Manoah and his unnamed wife serve as a strong example: they show us how important it is to steward the calm before the storm. The calm, whatever it looks like for you, is the norm far more often than the exception. Yet too often, we do the opposite. We hyperfocus on the "what ifs," the "whens," the "hows," and the "whys" of a possible or approaching storm and neglect the persistent present—the right now.

At 8 minutes and 33 seconds long, "American Pie"[7] by Don McLean was released in October of 1971. McLean has said the song was largely inspired by what he calls "the day the music died," referring to the 1959 plane crash in Clear Lake, Iowa, that killed Buddy Holly, Ritchie Valens, and J.P. Richardson. McLean, then a teenage newspaper delivery boy, was devastated—especially by the loss of his idol, Buddy Holly. But perhaps even more powerfully, when he was 15, McLean had an eerie feeling that his father was going to die. Within days, that feeling became reality when his father suddenly dropped dead right in front of him.[8] Between those tragic days and dark seasons, however, are the ordinary ones. And it's those ordinary days, often overlooked, that we are wise to savor and steward well. Doing so helps fill our emotional and spiritual tanks so that, when the world inevitably sours and sends its wind, rain, and sorrow our way, we are not entirely undone.

---

6. John 16:33.

7. Don McLean, "American Pie."

8. Rob Walker, "Don McLean on the Tragedy Behind 'American Pie': 'I Cried for Two Years,'" *The Guardian*, 2020.

It Is Too Late to Say "Sorry" Now?
Judges 14:1–9, Mother's Day, May 12, 2024

WHILE SOME OF US apologize more often than others, we all know what it's like to say we're sorry—and to be on the receiving end of an apology. Maybe you lied, got caught up in gossip, or lashed out in unwarranted anger. Maybe you accidentally cut someone off in traffic. Perhaps your neighbor knows their party got too loud and lasted entirely too long. Or someone stepped on your brand-new, fresh out of the box shoes. These situations vary in severity, but it's not a competition. By "apology," I mean acknowledging wrongdoing with genuine regret—a recognition that, given the chance, you'd choose to act differently. This doesn't mean groveling or begging for forgiveness (though depending on the offense, that might be warranted), but it does mean your conscience is stirred enough to feel remorse. Still, finding yourself in a bind because of the consequences of your actions doesn't automatically mean you feel remorse for the actions themselves. Those with emotional maturity often point out the nuanced difference between offering an apology and asking for forgiveness. This is the territory explored by researchers, therapists, and even armchair philosophers. Books like *Mea Culpa: A Sociology of Apology and Reconciliation* by Nicholas Tavuchis, *Sorry, Sorry, Sorry: The Case for Good Apologies* by Marjorie Ingall and Susan McCarthy, and *Art of the Apology: How, When, and Why to Give and Accept Apologies* by Lauren Bloom all delve into this subject. Professional organizations such as the American Psychological Association, the Association for Psychological Science, and the National Institutes of Health have also contributed valuable insights.

If you remember when pop star Cyndi Lauper declared in 1983 that "Girls Just Want to Have Fun," Samson might be seen as her Old Testament male counterpart from the days of old. As a kind of Prodigal

Son living impulsively, "sorry" never seemed to be part of his vocabulary. Yet from his first mention in today's passage through Judges 16, sorrow, apology, and changed behavior *should* have been central themes of his life. Samson's love for God is questionable at nearly every turn; his love for himself is not. He consistently excels at avoiding responsibility. As we'll see in the coming weeks, Samson was quick to hold others accountable for their wrongs—but never himself and that's a disastrous trait for any leader. In our society, we often avoid apologies while simultaneously romanticizing them—especially in music and pop culture. Anita Baker's 1994 hit "I Apologize" is an R&B classic. Then there's "Apologize" by OneRepublic featuring Timbaland (2007), Prince's "Purple Rain", and Cher's "If I Could Turn Back Time." Go further back and you'll find Connie Francis's "Who's Sorry Now?" (1958) and Brenda Lee's "I'm Sorry." The list goes on. Respectfully, from the time that Samson appears in Judges, basically, until the end, he lives as someone who is a sad sack of potatoes, who lacks any interest in apologizing. He does not value admitting when he is wrong, *no matter the godliness of his parents.* In that maladaptive mind of his, full of cowardice and cockiness, he hardly, if ever, considers that he is wrong about anything in any situation. *Ever.*

Now all grown up, Samson returns from a trip to Timnah and spots what Michael Jackson might have called a "P.Y.T (Pretty Young Thing)"[1] from among the Philistines, Israel's sworn enemies. That doesn't necessarily mean she, individually, is a horrible person—not at all. But God repeatedly told His people, the Israelites, to remain faithful to Him. That included not intermarrying with spiritual enemies—those who opposed Yahweh, the One True, Living God, their salvation and protector. The people understood what God was saying, but they weren't moved enough to obey, and that's always a serious problem. To the mother and father who, in faithful submission to the Lord, took on the responsibility of raising a Nazirite son, predestined to be used to deliver Israel, Samson said in verse 2, "Now get her for me as my wife." I don't know about you, but where I'm from, we'd say, *"Oh, Samson's on that stuff."* Because whether it's cannabis, crack, alcohol, PCP, LSD, heroin, fentanyl, or prescription opioids, only someone deep in an addict's manic psychosis would speak to their parents like that, much less still live to tell the story after being helped back to their feet. And since raw rebellion sounds almost too

---

1. Michael Jackson, "P.Y.T. (Pretty Young Thing)," 1982.

outrageous to accept, we might prefer to give him the benefit of the doubt and assume it was the drugs talking—for his sake. But no, that's what he said. And I think you'd agree—that demands an apology. But even after his parents tried to lovingly redirect him in verse 3, he doubled down and repeated himself: "Get her for me." Yet another missed apology.

Verse 4 offers some privileged, insider information from heaven: God was allowing Samson's disobedience to fester, knowing it would eventually serve His greater, perfect purpose—a divine setup to confront the Philistines. As in so many biblical accounts, this isn't God endorsing bad behavior. He's not saying, "Hey, follow Samson's lead." Instead, God shows that He can work through anything—whether it's rocks, tulips, a donkey, a flicker of faith, or even someone's reckless choices. He doesn't take days off from shaping history, seen and unseen, according to His will, even when it doesn't make sense to us. More often than not, He simply uses what we give Him. And what we give Him, post-Fall, is flaky, flawed, and filthy—like rags stained with sin. We've been chosen—"predestined according to the plan of Him who works out everything in conformity with the purpose of His will."[2] So, as Samson travels with his parents to Timnah, past vineyards he shouldn't even be near because of his Nazirite vow, what happens? "A young lion came roaring toward him," ready to make a meal out of him. If you've ever seen *When Animals Attack*, you know a wild animal—especially one that must hunt to eat—can rip anything to pieces in an instant. Lions can grow up to 11 feet long and weigh over 800 pounds. Yet, in verse 6, with the Spirit empowering him, Samson easily kills the lion and continues searching for his bride-to-be. But he tells no one—not his father or his mother—what he's done. That silence? Another missed opportunity for honesty. Another missed apology.

Later, passing by the lion's carcass, he notices that, somehow, bees have made a hive inside it. In verse 9, we're told, "He scooped out the honey with his hands and ate as he went along. When he rejoined his parents, he gave them some, and they too ate it." In doing so, Samson not only violated his Nazirite consecration, but he also caused his parents to unknowingly do the same. And nothing in the text suggests that he felt even a twinge of guilt. That's two more apologies owed—one to God, the other to his parents—but neither one was offered by Samson.

---

2. Eph 1:11–12.

Taken from a line in Erich Segal's novel *Love Story*—and its 1970 film adaptation—countless people have come to earnestly believe the saying, "Love means never having to say you're sorry."[3] I wonder if that belief played a role in Samson's emotional immaturity. I can't say for sure, but I can confidently echo Scripture: "Pride goes before destruction, a haughty spirit before a fall."[4] In other words, Samson lived as though he were untouchable. And as the Spirit of the Lord came upon him time and time again, he grew increasingly brazen, idolatrous, and wild—much like us, when we veer off course, traveling "a way that appears to be right, but in the end, it leads to death."[5] The Israelites are not us, and we are not them, but we share a spiritual lineage of stubborn revolt. So, when we read, "In those days Israel had no king; everyone did as they saw fit," we should hear echoes of our own restless desires—in our time, our context, and our lives—where we, too, are tempted to treat God as an afterthought and feel no shame about it. I don't say that with judgment. We're all in the same boat. None of us can claim to be free from that depraved, wretched condition on this side of heaven. Until Jesus returns, we need the Holy Spirit and the beautiful brokenness of one another in Christ to help us wrestle our way toward holiness—to be *different*, not *better*.

With "Sorry," Justin Bieber offers invites us to consider if the time to apologize has reached its expiration date. The answer, when it comes to people in real life, is: *Maybe*. You never know until you try. So, when you mess things up with others, you have to be willing to try, and keep trying, to make it right. You can say the words "I'm sorry," but if your heart, actions, delivery, instincts, and desires do not change to support those words, you'll keep running into the same self-inflicted issues. And the truth is, not everyone can survive the fallout of being close to someone who refuses to take responsibility for the damage they cause—whether in a friendship, a workplace, a family, or any other kind of relationship. Sometimes, loving people like Samson—hardheaded, rageful, and willfully unaware—means loving them from a distance, so you don't end up in spiritual ruin yourself. With people, sometimes your "Sorry" is a day late and a dollar short. It depends. But with God? There's no expiration date. There's no "too late" with Him. There's no healing or freedom without surrendering your will to Him "so that you may be reasonably happy

---

3. Erich Segal, *Love Story*, 121.
4. Prov 16:18.
5. Prov 14:12.

in this life and supremely happy with Him forever in the next."[6] And one of the most beautiful truths about God is this: In the economy of a divine kingdom, there is always time to come clean. You can be 8, 18, or 88 and still say, "Sorry" to God. You can be a felon, a fraud, a hypocrite, a Pharisee, or even a Philistine—and if your apology is genuine, God will accept it. Saying "I'm sorry" to the Maker of heaven and earth, who knows the number of hairs on your head and who knew you before you were formed in your mother's womb[7]—that is a powerful place to begin. Whether you're starting a relationship with Him today or returning to one you walked away from years ago, it all begins with, "I'm sorry."

---

6. Reinhold Niebuhr, "The Serenity Prayer, 1943," in *The Essential Reinhold Niebuhr: Selected Essays and Addresses*, 251.

7. Jer 1:5.

Dumb, Dumb, and Dumber
Judges 14:10–20, May 19, 2024

HAVE YOU EVER KNOWN someone who's a glutton for punishment, who seems to crave self-inflicted friction, turmoil, and pain, and maybe even, in some strange way, enjoys it? No matter the consequences, they keep coming back for more. To be clear, we're not talking about those who've suffered physical or emotional abuse or individuals engaged in sexual masochism, as these represent highly specific, clinical contexts. Instead, our focus is on those who, without any formal diagnosis, seem to translate pain and suffering as pleasurable. On a basic level, this is more common than you may think. Consider runners. Most of us know that a marathon covers 26.2 miles. God bless those who take that on, because I have no desire to run that far for anything *ever*. But ultramarathons, have you heard of these? These crazy races stretch to 100 miles, and the longest one—at 3,100 miles—is run over 52 days or less. It's been held annually in Queens, New York since 1985, and in its current format since 1997. Sure, we understand why Navy SEALs, law enforcement officers, and firefighters undergo intense physical training. Their lives, and the lives of others, depend on their readiness. But ultramarathoners? Well, they do it purely for the challenge. For the thrill. Just for fun.

We've all seen those classic action-movie scenes where, in a testosterone-fueled standoff, someone snarls, "Go ahead, hit me." And then after that first smack, they say something like, "Oh, yeah—do it again." Sometimes they even slap or punch themselves, trying to awaken some inner strength or fury to win the fight. Instead of dodging, countering, or de-escalating the situation, oddly they *need* the sting of the blow or blows to get them going. Then there's the sitcom version—think Steve

Urkel from *Family Matters*,¹ with his famous, annoying question, "Did I do that?" The nerdy character who, despite being rejected 10,845 times, used for his homework skills or taken advantage of at work, still clings to the hope that *this* time his crush Laura will snap-to one day and appreciate him, or, most of all, return his affection. Who comes to mind when you think of a glutton for punishment? Better yet, I wonder if their name rhymes with yours? "Mirror, mirror on the wall, who is the dumbest of them all?" That's the question that came to mind as I read this passage. We meet three main characters here, and honestly, not one of them seems particularly sharp. It's not just a lack of wisdom, it's the absence of basic common sense, manners, and maturity.

These characters aren't being asked to assemble a complicated IKEA bookshelf or quilt hundreds of fabric scraps into something beautiful like the Maplewood quilters do so brilliantly. This wasn't hard work. It should've been very low-hanging fruit. For context, consider Calcea Johnson and Ne'Kiya Jackson—two high school seniors from New Orleans who, in their final year, created an original trigonometric proof of the 2,000-year-old Pythagorean Theorem.² This is an enormous achievement that required serious effort and intellect. By contrast, Samson and the other undisclosed individuals in this part of the story were just trying to host a wedding celebration—and they couldn't even manage that. Why? Because they fed the worst parts of themselves. And when any of us do that, it dulls whatever intelligence, common sense, or self-awareness we might otherwise have. So, decide for yourself: Who's the biggest fool in this chapter? There's no single right answer. It's easy to paint Samson as a violent, rash, sometimes-part-time religious warrior-judge with unbridled lust—and that's all true. But some of his worst decisions wouldn't have spiraled so far if the people around him had refused to participate in the drama. He still could've caused damage, no doubt, but things might've gone differently if someone had had the courage to say, "I'm not joining you in this foolishness."

From the outset, one might think that Samson didn't have many friends or was socially awkward, at least, because he arrived at the party—most closely resembling a modern bachelor's party—without a group of

1. *Family Matters*, 1989–98.
2. Xavier University of Louisiana, "Making the Impossible, Possible: Ne'Kiya Jackson, Who Submitted Proof of 'Impossible' Mathematical Equation, Will Be Attending Xavier University of Louisiana," *Xavier University of Louisiana*, 2023.

friends to celebrate with. The text doesn't mention any family or friends accompanying him. Upon arriving at the customary feast, the people "chose thirty men to be his companions." In other words, strangers he didn't know were arbitrarily assigned to be his friends for the seven-day feast. Is it just me, or does that seem odd? Then, out of nowhere, perhaps trying to make friends—though this isn't the way to do it—or to establish his dominance, Samson introduces himself with a goofy riddle and a wager: "thirty linen garments and thirty sets of clothes."[3] Are you serious? Who does that? At a time when people are supposed to be dancing, eating, drinking, and celebrating newfound love and God's provision, he, the husband, ruins it. What, I wonder, is he trying to prove? Regardless, it seems pretty foolish, and not only Samson's part. Why did none of these thirty men, these microwaved Philistine acquaintances, refuse to participate in the bet? One of them could've said, "No, thanks, Samson. We'll pass on the riddle. Let's just enjoy some good food, dance the wobble and electric slide, and have fun." Only their own pride, recklessness, or cowardice explain how readily they agreed to the terms. As dumb and exceedingly avoidable as this all was, while we read it unfolding in slow motion, times when we started something that didn't need to be started or participated in something we had no business participating in should come to mind.

On the fourth day, these men are still stumped. They are clueless about how to solve the riddle. They don't want to lose face to this cocky Israelite who has intermarried within their people group, being forced in defeat to cough up a bunch of fabric and clothing, although right now that's the most sensible response. "It doesn't need to be the end of the world," I would've told them. "Take the loss," I would've said. "You made the stupid bet and lost, so just pay the man and live to make a better decision next time." Maybe someone did tell them that. But they couldn't leave well enough alone and instead accused Samson's wife of setting them up. They promised to kill her entire family, meaning her home with Samson and her parents' home where presumably siblings and other relatives resided, if she didn't do whatever she needed to do to get the riddle's answer from her beloved Samson. Seven being the biblical number of completion, after a traditional Jewish wedding ceremony begins a seven-day period of celebration and feasting. The couple is husband and wife by this time, which is why this text refers to Samson's wife as "Samson's

---

3. Judg 14:12–13.

wife." By tradition, they ought to be conducting intimate business behind closed doors with one another, interspersed with emerging every so often to party with the guests, who are literally down the hallway or in an adjoining building. There are supposed to be seven full days of this righteous revelry—not schemes and egos running rampant.

Samson's superhuman strength hadn't gone public yet, although it would be viral soon enough. Like how The Hulk underwent his transformation, whenever the Spirit of the Lord comes upon him, Samson could effortlessly toss chariots left and right and kill hundreds, if not thousands, of animals or people as needed. Samson was a natural instigator, it appears, and mouthier than the mild-mannered Bruce Banner—but you get the picture. At the forefront of our biblical thinking should be the conviction that this was not about Samson. It never was. It was about God—Him expertly using the selfishness and rebellion that Samson chose of his own volition to advance the divine agenda to overwhelm the Philistines, thus freeing God's people from oppression. The 66 books we uphold as God's Word are all about God. From Genesis to Revelation, we are central, yes, yet supporting cast members. God creates us. God is patient with us. God is disrespected by us and yet opts not to discard us. God protects us. God provides for us. God saves us by sacrificing His only Son. God forgives us. God empowers us. God disciplines us. God is with us. God loves us. And this is all within the context of what we provide to God being a lackluster afterthought and as incomplete as it is highly circumstantial.

Remember the thematic chorus from the book of Judges: "In those days Israel had no king; everyone did as they saw fit." Fearful as she was, though this doesn't excuse her decision, Samson's wife coaxes the riddle's answer from him as the deadline for the wager approaches. She delivers an Oscar-worthy performance: sobbing, crying a tubful of tears, throwing herself on him, and berating him for daring to keep her in the dark. To Samson, it didn't seem like a big deal. He wasn't moved to share the secret with her; after all, not even his father and mother knew it, he said. Still, verse 17 says, "she continued to press him." Translation: she nagged him to no end. Like Roberto Durán famously, and controversially, said in his 1980 bout against Sugar Ray Leonard, *"No más"*—Samson folded. Between her manipulation and his careless, childish immaturity, we're reminded of Proverbs 25:24, written in bold, graffiti-style letters: "Better to live on a corner of the roof than share a house with a quarrelsome wife." And I'll admit that at least for me, it's hard to imagine that during this standoff, Samson's wife is enthusiastically engaging in the intimate side of their young marriage. If you're married, then you might know what I mean, so that, too—just a hunch—might have influenced him. I wouldn't go so far as to call the wife "dumb," given the vulnerable and complicated mess she's in., but Samson? Oh, that's another story. He doesn't come across as very *into* his wife. Back in verse 7, he said he liked her, but the only other thing he actually says *about* her is that he wanted her. There's no mention that she was beautiful, or witty and wise, a great cook, an industrious entrepreneur, good with children, or someone who inspired him to be a better man. Even though he caused a lot of problems to marry her, it seems marriage, to Samson, was more of a fantasy than a covenant—something he was not prepared to approach as a servant. He wanted what he wanted, and that's about it.

Verse 19 says Samson was "burning with anger" to the point that he abandoned his bride and moved back home, but if he's mad at anyone other than himself, which he clearly is, it reflects a poisoned mindset. He could've accepted the fact that he "got got" when the townsmen solved his riddle—which he had to know came from his new bride—and just moved on. He might have laughed about it someday; how he tried too hard to fit in or let his insecurities drive his behavior. But that wasn't his way. Instead, he traveled to another town, slaughtered 30 men, stripped the clothes off their dead or dying bodies, and brought the bloody garments back as payment to his wife's people, before storming off to Mahaneh Dan. At seminary at Baylor University, one of my early influences was Dr. Levi Price. A pastor's kid who served Baptist churches across Texas for decades before retiring to teach graduate courses, he was also a Vietnam War combat engineer and decorated captain. Down-to-earth and direct, he had seen everything: church fights, splits, staff meltdowns, arrests, megachurch blessings and burdens, and small church grit. A quintessential Texan, Baptist, and Marine, he never minced words. It became a running bond among his former students that he would emphatically and repeatedly say, "Don't be dumb." Still today, I consider that an always-timely word of holy encouragement.

We should see glimpses of ourselves in this passage, because none of us is above the manipulation, pride, and greed on display here. Samson lit the match with his pointless riddle. His shallow companions fanned the flames. His wife poured lighter fluid on it. And Samson refused to put out a fire he had every opportunity to extinguish. He must win—or, if not, he must hurt someone. Imagine playing Monopoly with him! What we often do to others, we, the people of God, also do to God. We sulk. We withhold. We throw adult-sized temper tantrums. In our own ways, we put God on trial, declaring He must not love us because a particular desire remains unmet for a season or a lifetime. And that. . . is d-u-m-b. I realize this isn't polite conversation, this business of being "dumb," so forgive me. But if we're serious about blessing God and being a blessing to others, we must be honest about what we see. As I said, decide for yourself who you think deserves the Dunce Award. But before we go, take note: nowhere in this passage, or in the entirety of Samson's story, do we see him associating with anyone he perceives as spiritually or morally more developed than himself. There's no one he looks up to. No mentor. No one whose counsel he respects. No one unafraid to speak truth to him, who isn't dazzled or intimidated by him, and to whom he actually listens. That glaring absence makes him tragically vulnerable—to living and leading in ways that don't uplift, but that instead degrade, discourage, and ultimately destroy. At the very least, if we want to avoid or mitigate Samson's blundering path—if we want not to be dumb—we have to approach our lives differently.

A Popular Fool's Game
Judges 15, May 26, 2024

SAMSON IS LIKE A heat-seeking missile, hot with rage and locked onto revenge. As far as he's concerned, he's been wronged and that's the end of the story. Someone will pay, and, as is consistently the case with him, his target is the Philistines. He's out for some good old "get back," despite God's emphatic command in Deuteronomy, and repeatedly throughout Scripture, that, "Vengeance is Mine."[1] Once again, Samson shows a disregard for precedent and direct instruction. Inflicting pain or distress on someone simply because they caused you pain or distress runs contrary to biblical belief and practice. That's not how we're called to live. The New Testament ethic, in particular, urges us to love our enemies and pray for those who persecute us. That said, retribution, or getting even, is not the same as reparation, restitution, or restoration. The latter seeks to make things whole again, within reason, for us or for others, in response to a wrong. Whether this looks like turning the other cheek in one case or standing up for justice in another, Scripture is clear: as followers of Jesus, we are called to uphold justice, especially for the vulnerable, no matter what.

And yet, the feeling of being wronged and wanting the source of that pain to suffer in kind is universal. It's the elbow to the gut or the shove in the back during a basketball game, a soccer match, or even in the choir stand at the winter recital—the kind of spark that ignites a fight in front of an auditorium full of drowsy parents. It might be the shady, attention-hungry coworkers who threw you under the bus to get the promotion. Or the next-door neighbor who, after a tense exchange across the fence, uninvited you from their daughter's wedding—prompting you to cancel their confirmed RSVP to your annual backyard BBQ. Revenge

---

1. Deut 32:35, Rom 12:19.

is instinctive. You steal my doll, I steal your crayons. You pull my hair, I spill your juice. You delete my NBA playoff game from the DVR, I delete your saved episodes of *Call the Midwife*, *The Great British Bake Off*, or *Columbo*. This is the way of the world.

Samson is convinced that the world has wronged him and now must pay the price, when it's clear that *he* is the true culprit—the one with blood on his hands. This is not a case of re-victimizing a victim. Samson *is* the problem. After his nonsensical riddle flopped and he went on a brief murder spree, stealing the clothes off the backs of the men he killed, he abandoned his wife and returned to his parents' home. One can easily imagine him there, holed up in the basement, scrolling endlessly through social media, ordering DoorDash, sleeping the days away, feverishly brewing concoctions of homemade beer, maybe playing video games. Later, when he felt like it, he returned with what he saw as a reconciliatory gesture, a young goat, fully expecting to pick things up with his one-time bride right where he left off. He planned to go "to her room," presumably to sleep with her, as though nothing had happened. But by then, everyone would likely have known, or at least strongly suspected, that she had remarried. At the end of chapter 14, we're told she was given to another man, one of the companions assigned to Samson during the wedding festivities. And when a freshly wed husband behaves as Samson did, disappearing without explanation, the customary response would've been exactly what happened: she was free to marry again or considered single and available.

So, Samson's destruction of the Philistines' grain, vineyards, and olive groves was not only petty and juvenile, but it was also completely unjustified. He wanted revenge, when *he* was the catalyst for everything that angered him. This illustrates how, the farther we drift from surrendering to God, though God may still use us for His purposes, we become hollowed-out versions of who we could be. We're so broken, we can't even see it. Unsurprisingly, the Philistines weren't pushovers. They wanted *all the smoke*. They were ready for conflict. In retaliation, they burned his ex-wife and her father to death, just as they'd threatened to do back in verse 15 of chapter 14. Samson responded, in verses 7–8, by vowing revenge and slaughtering many of them. And then, true to form, he ran off and hid, this time "in a cave in the rock of Etam." I can relate to Samson's denial and deflection. I've been in situations where, like him, I blamed others when the fault was actually mine. This past Friday, I spoke to AP

English students at Holland Christian High School about my background as a competitive spoken word poet. During the talk, I shared, which I've told many of you before that halfway through my sophomore year of college, I was academically dismissed.

In high school, I had been a solid B+ to A– student-athlete. But in college, my GPA dropped to around 1.7. I kept changing my major, dropping classes after the drop/add deadline, and getting poor grades because I skipped classes. My sister, two years older than me, had attended community college before transferring to the University of Maryland. By the time I graduated high school, we both entered the university together—she as a junior, me as a freshman. She had once been placed on academic probation before and wrote a letter to the review board that led to her swift reinstatement. So, when I got my dismissal notice, I thought I could do the same. But my appeal was denied—and I was *livid*. Eventually, though, I came to realize that no one was to blame but me. *I* was the one who chose to go to parties instead of studying, to hang out in D.C. clubs instead of going to class. Essentially, I made a bad gamble and lost. Samson lost, too—but he would never admit it. He reminds me of Julian, the kid from the 1999 film *Big Daddy* starring Adam Sandler. In one scene, while playing a made-up card game with Sonny's friends, Julian announces, "I win." When asked why, he says, "Because I win." And when someone asks, "What's the name of that game, anyway?" he replies, "I win."[2] Samson is stuck in that same cycle.

Starting at verse 9, we read how the Philistines came to capture Samson, essentially prepared to go to war and slaughter everyone if necessary. In response, the people of Judah, Samson's own people, send "three thousand men from Judah" to confront him at the cave he's been living in. They try to impress upon him the gravity of the situation he's created. The Philistines, they explain, are their resident oppressors. They can only live, move, or eat with the Philistines' permission. Though viewed by God's people as foreign heathens from the southern coast of Palestine, Judges 13 explains clearly: "Again, the Israelites did evil in the eyes of the Lord, so the Lord delivered them into the hands of the Philistines for forty years." In many ways, Samson's troubles reflect the ongoing punishment and spiritual failure of his people, as detailed throughout the Book of Judges. Both are stubborn, prideful, and idolatrous. When Samson tells

---

2. *Big Daddy*, 1999.

his brethren, "I merely did to them what they did to me,"[3] it's a bold-faced lie. Samson is a bully, and like many bullies, he doesn't expect those he's harassing to fight back. He assumes they'll either submit in fear or let it go. But the Philistines aren't wired that way. They are willing to die for their convictions, their people, their power, and their honor.

Samson, by contrast, seems only committed to whatever feels right in the moment. Honor is a concept he has yet to grasp. He insists that his fellow Israelites not kill him themselves, only hand him over to the Philistines—which they agree to do. But suddenly, "the Spirit of the Lord came powerfully upon him," his bindings disintegrate, and with a fresh donkey's jawbone, he slaughters 1,000 Philistines, avoiding capture. Then Samson has the audacity to say to God in verse 18, "You have given your servant this great victory. Must I now die of thirst and fall into the hands of the uncircumcised?" The entitlement is thicker than the thickest oatmeal. Still, as we've seen throughout Samson's story, God is using him for a greater, perfect purpose—even when Samson's behavior directly contradicts God's character. I don't know if you agree, but our current culture seems to echo Samson's crisis of character. Like him, people today are deeply committed to doing what they want, when they want, especially if it feels good or comes easily. Yet society struggles to uphold, and often avoids, doing what is hard but right. People will spend thousands on fertility treatments, extravagant baby reveals, *push presents*, or supersized playrooms, but then blatantly neglect to parent their child, which is, inarguably, central to parenthood. Others "quietly quit," doing the bare minimum at jobs they hate, enjoying the benefits and pay, but then criticize the economy when things fall apart. Work isn't always fun. Family isn't always a blast. But many of us, especially those of a certain age, have learned—by God's grace—to go to work even when we don't want to, to discipline our kids even when it's hard, cut our grass, consistently serve in church, and say "I'm sorry" even when we'd rather not.

Without promoting legalism, we must acknowledge that Jesus' teaching about letting our "yes" be yes and our "no" no has become increasingly rare, even among His followers.[4] We've become just like the world—and just like Samson: opportunistic, cowardly, two-faced, reckless, unprincipled, and without honor. We treat life like a game, producing generations and a society of fools. Yes, life is complicated; that's not

---

3. Judg 15:11.
4. Matt 5:37.

new. But we must stop over-spiritualizing or avoiding the things God has placed, or allowed to be placed, in our path simply because we don't want to confront or be confronted in love. Take Samson again. Let's just tell it like it is—he's a jerk and a bully. But if he were a member of a church today, would anyone call him out on it? I wonder. And I don't mean a half-hearted, beating-around-the-bush conversation. I mean someone saying, "You've got one more time to act like that around here, Samson, and it's going to be a big problem. It's not of God, and we're not doing that here."

If Samson were a church leader—rageful, manipulative, untrustworthy, vengeful, irresponsible—would we promote the Holy Spirit's work by letting him face the natural consequences of his behavior? Or would we hem and haw, argue about grace, or hide behind prayer? I wonder. Here at Maplewood, I know we're serious about generosity and helping others, but that doesn't change the reality that if you don't study, you're likely to flunk out. If you steal, you may go to jail. If you drive too fast, you could injure yourself or someone else. If you're overly friendly or unfriendly, it will catch up to you. If you argue over everything, joy will be hard to find. If you never stand up for yourself—not in anger, but in maturity—you may find respect constantly eludes you. If God's people run from accountability and the daily rhythm of holiness, we will never develop the strength or dangerous faithfulness required to speak with power about the disruptive Good News of Jesus Christ.

But You Know Better
Judges 16:1–14, June 2, 2024

AFTER ABANDONING HIS WIFE—AND in the backdrop of her remarriage to another man—Samson made choices that ultimately led to her death and the death of her father. To be specific: they were murdered. Even more tragically, they were murdered by their fellow Philistines—burned to death. This wasn't a chaotic, unfiltered reaction to the heartbreak and confusion Samson caused, though he was clearly the root. Rather, it was the consequence of Samson's own deviousness, pride, and lust. Now, seemingly sowing his wild oats, Samson visits a prostitute—her name not given in the text—to do what both sex workers and their clientele do, nothing of which is secret. The town is buzzing with information. People know he's in town, and they know why. As they always do, the streets are talking. "Some time later," we read, he becomes involved with Delilah, a woman he claims to love, though his past behavior shows no evidence of true commitment. This happens "in the Valley of Sorek."[1] So, the same man who once got married and minutes later began demonstrating only self-obsession now contends to have been struck by Cupid's arrow? Samson is present, but not really *present*—would you agree? With the clarity that hindsight often provides, and the benefit of Scripture's detailed retelling, the reasonable conclusion is that Samson isn't thinking straight, if he's thinking at all. And the culprit is the most powerful, destructive force known to mankind, one that no one can outrun: sin.

Samson is stuck in a destructive cycle of defiance that he is completely blind to, harming himself and everyone he encounters. And it's not passive; it's willful. Samson isn't reacting to the death of a loved one, to chronic pain, or to some hidden mental torment. No, he is a walking

---

1. Judg 16:4.

time bomb of poor impulse control and unchecked rage. A "baby boy" who refuses to grow up.

At every turn, there are open doors—ways of escape from temptation, opportunities to resist reactive violence, and chances to return to God. But Samson forever chooses his own path. Of his own free will, he makes his decisions—and he stands by them, regardless of the cost. Yet, God uses his rebellion, just as He uses the rebellion of the Israelites, the rebellion of the Philistines, and the rebellion of humanity as a whole—for His perfect and sovereign purposes. God corrects, interrupts, allows, diverts, protects, comforts, instructs, and redirects—but always according to His perfect timing, method, and measure. As Scripture reminds us: "For my thoughts are not your thoughts, neither are your ways my ways," declares the Lord. "As the heavens are higher than the earth, so are my ways higher than your ways and my thoughts than your thoughts."[2]

Samson's affection for Delilah is significant, especially given his prior treatment of women. He clearly enjoys her company, so much so that the text mentions him falling asleep in her presence multiple times. They share a room, likely a bed, while she repeatedly tries—and fails—to uncover the secret of his great strength. Interestingly, we're never told how they met. And anyone who has ever been in love—or even just a fan of romance, commitment, or *Hallmark* movies—knows that the origin story really matters. Whether a relationship flourishes or flops, it starts somewhere. That "how we met" moment is part of the emotional foundation. It's like that for Renata and me. Renata, an extrovert the likes of which I've rarely seen rivaled, is known in multiple states and counties for her superpower: effortlessly using hundreds, sometimes thousands, of words in rapid succession to tell what could easily be a very, very short story. Back then, she was also the *bossiest*—or, if you prefer, most independent—person I'd ever met. Oil and water, water and oil—that's been us in some ways from the beginning: opposites that somehow defied the odds and ended up holding hands. I was voted "Most Shy" in my senior year of high school. I've never been especially talkative or outgoing. But here's the thing: though I'm quiet, I'm no pushover. As I grew from childhood into young adulthood, the chubby cheeks and deferential demeanor could fool you—but if you didn't like me, I honestly couldn't have cared two tiddlywinks.

---

2. Isa 55:8–9.

So, when I met Renata, by *chance* at a staff meeting, I mustered the courage to talk to her afterward. I took the risk of rejection, eventually asking her out. And later, in no uncertain terms (or in today's verbiage, I "shot my shot"), I made it clear that I wanted to court her—intentionally, publicly, and specifically—with marriage in mind. Her response? "Ummmm, well, thanks, but no thanks," she said. I was, as she put it, *too nice*. In that moment, I wanted to say, "Well, God bless your heart and all your parts, young lady. May He watch over you and bless you real good in your comings and goings, but as for right now, girly, you can forget my number!" Of course, I didn't say that. But I did draw some firm boundaries that led to us being out of touch for several months. God didn't erase our differing values or personalities, nor did He override our free will. However, as He so often does behind the scenes, He prompted us, separately, to keep thinking about each other. And in due time—*His* time—we "fell in love," just as the text says Samson did with Delilah. But what drew Samson to Delilah like a moth to a flame? Was it her beauty? Her charm? Were the measurements 36–24–36 too appealing to resist? Was he humming along to The Commodores' 1987 hit "Brickhouse,"[3] completely entranced?

Did a perfectly timed pickup line seal the deal? Something like, "Are you from Tennessee? Because you're the only 10 I see." Or maybe, "Are you tired? Because you've been running through my mind all day." Or, "If you were a burger at McDonald's, you'd be the *McGorgeous*." Did Samson slide into Delilah's DM? Did she initially ignore him because he was too short, too bald, or didn't have a six-figure income? Was their connection more of a *Lady and the Tramp* moment circa 1955, complete with shared spaghetti and soft glances? With the text's omission of these details, we will never know the exact answers, which is okay., but I find it helpful in situations like this to at least explore the question because it helps us identify with what transpired in the Bible back then, linking it to the relevancy of the humanity we experience today.

What's easy to miss about Samson is that he's a judge—a leader of leaders—*while all of this is happening*. For 20 years he led Israel, remember? That's from Judges 15:20.[4] So, while he's out here slipping and dipping, sneaking around alleys and backdoors, totally out of control—a

---

3. The Commodores, "Brickhouse."
4. Judg 15:20.

poor example of a Nazarite to his people and a poor witness to his enemies—he's both a sexual philanderer and a violent one-man wrecking crew. And yet, at the very same time, he holds the highest position of authority among the Israelites, who are still under Philistine occupation. The truth is—he just doesn't care. Whatever the context or variables, has there ever been a time in your life when, like Samson, you were lost in the sauce of idolatry?

Samson is not a six-year-old at the dentist's office with his mom, pulling the fire alarm while she's out of the room just to see if it works—like I did. Samson is not a teenager testing the limits of curfew, like maybe you and I did, knowing full well there would be consequences if we didn't make it back inside before the streetlights came on (not *at* the same time, not *after* but before). Samson isn't even a young adult making poor decisions while sincerely, though chaotically, trying to heal from pain, stumbling his way through unfortunate hurts, habits, and hangups. That kind of person may be misguided but may also remain *teachable* and *remorseful* as consequences catch up with them. That's not Samson.

Samson lives by the seat of his pants, doing whatever he feels like in the moment, counting on the Spirit of the Lord to show up and empower him to lay the smackdown on whoever gets in his way. As we've discussed, God is using Samson's foolishness to advance a divine agenda that includes Israel's eventual triumph over the Philistines, which connects directly to the lineage of Jesus—His birth, ministry, and atoning sacrifice. But we cannot sanitize Samson's story: There is no sign of a moral compass or authority in his life outside of himself. He willfully and maliciously disregards the ways of God without any sense of conviction or concern. Have you ever been *that* far gone? If so, who have you told the God's honest truth to about it, as a way of giving glory to God and helping someone else avoid your same mistakes? That's part of what testimony is: not just celebrating deliverance, but soberly sharing the path that led you to your need for it.

Samson might have despised the Philistines—*kind of*—but especially when they crossed or irritated him, except he *loved their women*. His loyalties were reactive and shallow. Growing up, the good guys on one of my favorite cartoons *G.I. Joe*, told us, "Knowing is half the battle." And it is. But *knowing* alone guarantees nothing. You can know the plan of salvation—the Scriptures, the mechanics, the theology. You can know who does the saving and what response is required, but if you never act on that knowledge, it will not be yours. Your parent's faith, your friend's testimony, or your Bible teacher's example cannot be credited to you. Only you can do your business with God. Only you can repent. Only you can choose to believe in Jesus, reject the devil, confess Christ, and settle in your heart the conviction to follow God's plan for your life now and in eternity. As Smokey Bear famously said, "Only you can prevent forest fires." In the same spirit: Only you, by grace through faith in Jesus, can receive salvation for you.

"In those days there was no king in Israel. Everyone did what was right in his own eyes" Even as a judge, Samson was no different. He knew better, as did the Israelites, which makes his story a tough but profoundly relevant example of God's patience, providence, and persistence with His people. Information, by itself, gets you nowhere. It must be accurate and then put into practice. Whether we're talking about dollars and cents, zeros and ones, or biblical data, knowledge alone doesn't cut it. Information without transformation is dead, just like faith without works or orthodoxy without orthopraxy. Samson knew better. He knew the stories of the judges before him, and where they failed. He would have known about Barak's cowardice in Judges 4–5, when Deborah—pious, bold, and brave—stepped in to lead with courage. He would've been familiar with Gideon, from the "weakest clan in Manasseh," who struggled with trust in God and eventually fell into pride and idolatry; Abimelek's evil and the bloodshed he caused; Jephthah the Gileadite, who carried unresolved trauma tied to his father's rejection, leading to tragic vows and decisions. Moreover, beyond the judges, themselves, Samson would have been familiar with Adam, who blamed Eve instead of owning his sin; Abraham, who failed to stand up to his wife when she suggested he sleep with Hagar. Not to mention, he wouldn't have been a stranger to the legacies, good and bad, of folks like Joshua, Aaron, and Moses. So, when we read Judges 16:1–14, and really all of Samson's story, if you're like me, it feels like you're watching a slow-motion train wreck. You want to yell, "But you know better!"

By this point, you'd think he'd have learned to stop with the needless riddles. You'd think he'd stop toying with women, especially when they start probing for secrets. A warning sign, brighter than any digital message board, should've been flashing in his mind: "STOP." His past experiences alone should have told him, "If a woman is urgently asking about a secret you haven't shared with her, something shady might be happening." But Samson doesn't stop. He ignores every signal. The spirit may be willing, but "the flesh is weak."[5] And while your supernatural strength from the Spirit of the Lord may have carried you this far, there's a limit. God is not going to let your defiance go unchecked forever and when He addresses it, it won't be pretty. *"But you know better."* Yet knowing better doesn't automatically lead to doing better. Samson's story, the rest of Scripture, and our own lives make that painfully clear. One takeaway from this text is the need to foster rhythms of gratitude and real community in our lives. That way, we're less likely to tolerate long stretches of spiritual carelessness, in ourselves or in our brothers and sisters in Christ. It's a two-way street. If I am truly my brother's and sister's keeper, though they are ultimately accountable to God for their choices, I want to speak words of encouragement and biblical correction when needed. Why? Because I love them. Even when it inconveniences me. And that also means being willing to receive that same correction in return—because they love me, and together, we love God. Samson didn't do that. You and I absolutely should.

---

5. Matt 26:41.

The Tulip That Grew from Concrete

Judges 16:15–22, June 9, 2024

THOUGH ITS ORIGIN REMAINS uncertain, many are familiar with the old military sentiment: "There are no atheists in foxholes." Some atheists, pluralists, and others argue that this phrase misrepresents them, casting their worldview in a negative light and dishonoring the sacrifices of those who have served in combat without subscribing to any religion or belief in a deity. To be clear, it's entirely possible to be just as resolute in unbelief as one is in faith. People can and do commit themselves to Taoism, Hinduism, Christianity, Islam, Buddhism, Satanism, Scientology—or no belief system at all. Each person ultimately chooses the wagon to which they hitch their life. That said, and with full respect to opposing perspectives, as a Christian, I personally find great strength in the synergy of like-minded loyalty, especially when life becomes difficult or the odds seem overwhelming. Despondency is a serious liability. It saps momentum, weakens resolve, and discourages unity, but that doesn't mean we should cling to some delusional optimism either. What we need, and what I hope for, is a deep reservoir of trust, of confidence in the possibility that things can improve; a faith that *remains* intact, regardless of the outcome. I'm not talking about blind denial, as if money grows on trees or hardship never comes. I mean the kind of hope that shows up when life goes sideways, as it so often does. And when it does, don't come to my hospital room if you bring no hope with you—for this life or the next.

I'd rather be in a foxhole with people who are fighting for something. Fighting to live. Fighting for truth. Fighting because they believe there's something worth dying for—and because they're convinced that when the time comes to leave this life, there's a beautiful place of rest prepared for those who are in Christ. *To be absent from the body is to be present with the Lord.*[1] I'd rather be surrounded by those who are governed by a covenant. Samson, as we find him in this part of the text, has no such covenant mindset. He's living for himself. Shacked up with his new *snuggle-boo*, Delilah, Samson is a Philistine-killing machine with no problem attracting women. He's a player. The biblical account of his life reflects the age-old story of women—some, maybe many—being drawn to bad boys, and of men—both sincere and naive—being manipulated by women with hidden, harmful motives, often because of their own brokenness. On paper, Samson's predicament looks grim—hopeless, even. He was undone by his ego with his wife a few chapters earlier, and now with Delilah he's headed down the same self-destructive road. Her nagging, the emotional manipulation, the accusations of lovelessness, the tears she cried on cue—all of it worked. Whether she *withheld* or gave him what he wanted for the sake of control, her tactics were successful. Unbeknownst to Samson, but fully known to God, the player was being played. And for the second time, he folds like a lawn chair. Not once, not twice, but four times, Delilah tries to get the secret out of him. And in verse 17, he finally confesses, revealing the source of his strength: "No razor has ever been used on my head," he told her, "because I have been a Nazirite dedicated to God from my mother's womb. If my head were shaved, my strength would leave me, and I would become as weak as any other man."

"Honesty is," as the saying goes, "the first chapter in the book of wisdom."[2] But for Samson, this kind of transparency is both rare and, in this moment, tragically misplaced. It is improper, even. Despite countless opportunities to learn the value of truthfulness, he hasn't. Being honest, especially with a foreign enemy to whom he's tied by lust, not loyalty, about such a deeply personal and significant truth is not an act of maturity. It's foolish. Just like his riddles, which he believed showcased his cleverness, this confession is another display of ego-driven carelessness. The entire situation lacks the moral grounding and spiritual depth one might expect from a judge or leader of God's people. Only God knows what Samson was thinking. So far, he has been deaf to wise counsel, numb to conviction, unmoved by holiness, and full of himself.

1. 2 Cor 5:8.
2. Thomas Jefferson, *The Papers of Thomas Jefferson*, 51.

Now captured, with his divine strength cut off and his eyes gouged out, Samson is, in biblical terms, reaping what he has sown. What once fed his beasts of lust and pride has been stripped from him like a tree stump ripped from the ground. There's no coming back from gouged-out eyes. This isn't glaucoma or cataracts. It's not diabetic retinopathy either. This isn't an animated cartoon fight, or a dramatic injury in *Die Hard* or *The Hunger Games*. This is permanent, devastating, and real.

His spiritual blindness has now manifested as physical blindness. He can no longer gaze upon the female forms that once so easily enchanted him. He cannot see the faces of his beloved parents, or of the Philistine captors whose friends, family, and neighbors he likely slaughtered. Yes, he has been betrayed, but only because he betrayed first. Samson abandoned the virtues that mark true leadership: Servant-leadership. Love. Maturity. Decorum. Faith. He discarded them all. Worst of all, he departed from God, treating the Spirit of the Lord like a magic trick to be pulled out when convenient. In verse 20, he says to himself, "I'll go out as before and shake myself free," not realizing the chilling reality that "the Lord had left him." He is now a shadow of his former self, lost in memories of what used to be. He's not just in a dark place emotionally or spiritually—he's literally in darkness. And sadly, his story echoes the greater tragedy of his time: "In those days there was no king in Israel. Everyone did what was right in his own eyes."

Starring Jake Gyllenhaal, *Guy Ritchie's The Covenant*[3] is a two-hour action-drama released in 2023 and set in Afghanistan. It follows a U.S. Army Special Forces unit battling to outlast the Taliban—sniffing out bomb-making operations, weapons caches, and tracking down credible tips on attacks in the making. I won't say it's from the devil, but some of you know how much I dislike running. Still, I don't mind doing it on the treadmill—as long as I can watch a movie on my tablet. That's what I was doing the other day when I ended up watching a pivotal scene from *The Covenant*. There are many gripping moments in the film, and I highly recommend it, but in this particular one, the tension was high—you're not quite sure if the troops will make it out. Then, just in the nick of time, help arrives. The tears that welled up in my eyes caught me completely off guard. Crying at the gym was definitely not on my to-do list, but there I was. Admittedly, I carry the weight of childhood memories

---

3. *Guy Ritchie's The Covenant*, 2023.

and personal connections to military service, and the sheer impact of the sacrifices made by those who serve, and by their families, always hits hard. Whether it's in a firefight, responding to an ambush, or racing to help fellow soldiers—where time, grit, and strategy matter most—you want hope. Hope can look like a rose, sunflower, orchid, peony, or tulip growing from concrete. In other words, given the conditions and odds, hope often seems impossible. And yet, it breaks through. Sometimes it emerges even when we've done nothing to deserve it, or even when we ourselves helped create the poor soil it must push through. Samson has made the bed of nails he now has to lie in.

Nevertheless, Judges 16:22 tells us, "But the hair on his head began to grow again after it had been shaved."

Samson's downfall came when he told Delilah that shaving off his "seven braids of hair," which had never been cut since birth, would strip him of his strength. Delilah relayed that information to the Philistine rulers, who paid her in silver and subdued him. They took him to Gaza and sentenced him to grinding grain in prison. Notably, there's no mention in the text, at least not yet, of regret or repentance. *Interesting*. And still: "the hair on his head began to grow again." It's a small detail, but it offers a powerful lens to view life through. Samson's hair begins to grow not because he earned it, not as a reward, but because God was still at work. This doesn't mean Samson's actions didn't matter; they absolutely did. But it reminds us that God "will neither slumber nor sleep."[4] He is always moving forward with His will—offering signs, breadcrumbs, and most of all, His presence—as a nightlight for His people. Samson was given hope when he didn't deserve it. And you and I? We're given hope when we don't deserve it either.

Will we have eyes to see and ears to hear hope? Will we believe that even in concrete-like, challenging situations, tulips can still bloom? Maybe they'll be a different color than what we planted. Maybe whatever vexes us will return, or ultimately become our end, but none of that has to stop us from choosing hope. Hope is not something I have to earn. When I water the flowers I've planted, I can see signs of hope. In my children, or my nieces, nephews, or grandchildren, I look for hope in who they might become and what they might do with their lives. In job loss or job gain, in diagnoses I celebrate or mourn, I am presented with a sacred

---

4. Ps 121:4.

opportunity: *to choose hope*. Hope reflects a sober assessment of reality, yes, and it includes prayers shaped by that reality, yes—but ultimately, it leans on the new covenant in Jesus' blood. So, whether or not the cavalry comes riding in, guns blazing, to rescue me from my material or physical predicament, I can rest in the truth that Jesus' victory on Calvary matters most. He is coming again, and when He does, I'll have a front-row seat to perfection.

God, simply because He is God, provides hope. He loves me, and so I look to the hills for my help, confident that God can, and often does, change my circumstances or my perspective and values, or all of the above. But even if He doesn't, if I have Him and *He has me*, I have more than enough to endure. If we serve the Lily of the Valley, the Bright and Morning Star—if our God still makes a way out of no way when He doesn't have to—if God being for me outweighs the attacks of my enemies or even my own self-sabotage, then Samson's broken story gives us just a glimpse of how God empowers us to choose. And even when we make detestable choices like Samson did, God's providential mercy, grace, and love still shine through. They become the hope He offers during the turbulence—if only we'd pay attention to the details.

Appreciating the Sequel
Judges 16:23–31, Father's Day, June 16, 2024

Life is full of erratic, winding events that somehow stay connected—a continuation of what came before, carried forward by what comes next. The fact that U.S. Presidents 45 and 46 are currently seeking re-election, hoping to join the exclusive group of just 21 out of 46 presidents who have served a second term, reflects our deep-rooted desire for permanence or continuity—for recurrence. It's the same sentiment echoed in the old children's rhyme about Michael Finnegan:

> There was an old man named Michael Finnegan
> He had whiskers on his chinnegan
> Along came the wind and blew them in again
> Poor old Michael Finnegan
> *Begin again*
>
> There was an old man named Michael Finnegan
> He went fishing with a pin again
> Caught a fish but it flopped back in again
> Poor old Michael Finnegan
> *Begin again*
>
> There was an old man named Michael Finnegan
> He ran a race and tried to win again
> Then he fell down and bumped his shin again
> Poor old Michael Finnegan

Think with me about film franchises like *Jurassic Park*, *Star Wars*, *Finding Nemo*, *Rocky*, *A Nightmare on Elm Street*, *The Godfather*, or *The Lion King*. There's *Black Panther* and then *Black Panther: Wakanda Forever*. Or consider Led Zeppelin's sequence of albums: *Led Zeppelin* and *Led*

Zeppelin II, both released in 1969, followed by *Led Zeppelin III* in 1970 and *Led Zeppelin IV* in 1971. Or *The African Trilogy* by Nigerian author Chinua Achebe, beginning with his landmark 1958 novel *Things Fall Apart*. Or *The Life and Strange, Surprising Adventures of Robinson Crusoe* in 1719 and its many adaptations, editions, and spin-offs.

We must realize, however, that a sequel is not a do-over. Certainly, as stories unfold, opportunities for redemption often emerge—for a collapsed bridge to be rebuilt, for fears to be faced with better outcomes, for a second chance at what once failed. But not always. Sequels are not guaranteed.

Let me try to make it plain. Suppose someone has a concealed carry permit. While navigating the summer highway construction common to Michiganders, they're involved in a fender bender on an exit toward downtown Grand Rapids. Words are exchanged. Tempers flare. And not because there's an imminent physical threat that cannot be avoided before police arrive, but because pride, ego, and anger take control, in a fit of rage, they pull the trigger. Seven pounds of pressure are utilized, and a life is lost. For those involved, and their families, in different but shared ways, there will be no sequel. No redo. No reset. Beyond apologies, lawsuits, or imprisonment, what's done is done. Bullets tend to carry a high rate of finality.

Not everyone gets a chance to "control-alt-delete" and try again with their greed, alcoholism, sexual misconduct, or bigotry. Not everyone returns from war zones scattered with IEDs to a quiet job at Home Depot. Not everyone who longs for children can have them, despite the booming fertility industry. Not everyone wins the scholarship, makes the team, or lands the dream job. Not everyone finds healing from their trauma. Not everyone finds a partner. Not everyone goes into remission.

Eunah Kim lost her 16-month battle with pancreatic cancer on my birthday, June 14, in 2015. She didn't live to see her two sons grow up—the youngest a sophomore, the oldest a Ph.D. student both at the University of Maryland, my alma mater. She had 10 years, not 26, or 39, or 50, with her husband Derrick, my friend. There was no sequel for her. However, Adam and Eve did receive a sequel. Lot's wife did not. One act of defiance turned her into a pillar of salt. The Samaritan woman, after her encounter with Jesus, ran into town testifying: "Come, see a man who told me everything I ever did."[1] But Nabal's stubbornness in 1 Samuel 15 led to a stroke and his death. Barak in Judges 4 never quite recovered

---

1. John 4:29.

from the hit to his reputation after saying to Deborah, "If you go with me, I will go; but if you don't go with me, I won't go." And then there's Judas. His guilt drove him to the grave. Through the full counsel of God, across the Old and New Testaments, only Christ's return, reign, and promises are eternal. The unpredictable nature of how and when sequels happen just is what it is. That inconsistency, and the perception of its unfairness, has driven many people into despondency. We mourn the early deaths of the righteous, while injustice, hate, sexual deviance, and misogyny seem to thrive and dominate our feeds. As the psalmist laments, compromise and the prosperity of the wicked often feel like today's love language. We cannot strong-arm God into extending our time or reshaping our circumstances. Yet by contrast, there is much to glean from Samson's experience of receiving what could be considered a sequel.

He was the most feared terror to the Philistines, the great Herculean Samson—son of Manoah and his once-barren, unnamed mother—dedicated as a Nazirite from birth. And now, publicly humiliated and imprisoned in Gaza, verse 15 tells us, he prays. For the first and only time across four explosive chapters and nearly 100 verses, this judge—this spiritual leader—finally acknowledges God. Until now, his greatest contribution has been body-slamming Philistines. And while Samson thought he was using God's Spirit to get what he wanted, God was actually using Samson's reckless brokenness to advance His own redemptive plan, to begin delivering Israel from Philistine oppression. Samson thought he was getting over. But the Spirit of the Lord was doing what the Spirit always does: working everything together for God's glory and our good. "In those days there was no king in Israel. Everyone did what was right in his own eyes." And yet, even then God was at work, as God is at work right now.

Samson's plea in verse 28 is: "Sovereign Lord, remember me. Please, God, strengthen me just once more, and let me with one blow get revenge on the Philistines for my two eyes." We know how the story ends. He positions himself between "the two central pillars on which the temple stood," and cries out, "Let me die with the Philistines!" With his extraordinary strength restored, he pushes, and the entire structure collapses—killing more Philistines in that one act than he had throughout his life. Some estimates suggest that up to 50,000 people may have died in that moment. In his final words, whether sincere or performative, Samson addresses God with language that translates to "Divine Master." He is formal. He is reverent. He is missional, finally embracing the posture he should have all along. Samson recognizes that God's honor is on the line, as Israel's pagan enemies are mocking one of God's own, thereby mocking God's people and ultimately God Himself, while celebrating their false god, Dagon. And so, God shows up through Samson one last time. But make no mistake—it's not *because* of Samson. It's *in spite of* him.

Now, I don't want to be too hard on Samson, or anyone else in Scripture, for that matter. I want to let the text speak for itself. And when the text is silent, I want to leave room for mystery and for the Spirit to work as the Spirit wills. With respect to differing interpretations, and with full awareness of my own limitations as a finite, Western reader, I find it telling what Samson does *not* say. He does not admit wrongdoing. He does not express regret. At the very least, we should be able to agree that this is one of the key lessons God offers us through Samson. When you do wrong, even if you've already yielded to God for salvation's sake, the dried dirt of stubborn living remains your covering until you come clean. Samson didn't deserve a sequel, and neither do we, but repentance should always mark a Christian's response to sin. And repentance demands confession. "God, I didn't control my anger." "God, I took You for granted." "God, I fornicated. I acted entitled. I neglected my responsibilities and calling." Samson *could have* said these things. He should have said these things, but he didn't. Regardless, in our lives, this must be our posture. It is godly conduct to come clean, especially before God. You don't need to carry what isn't yours to bear, but you do need to be honest about what is. God already knows. Confession isn't for His sake—it's for ours. The second thing to note: whether here in Judges 16 or in earlier episodes of Samson's life, we see no evidence of regret, sorrow, or remorse. No contrition over the riddles, the prostitution, the desertion of his first wife, the ego trips, the mistreatment of his parents. He never says, "I'm sorry"—not to God, not to anyone. And we're not talking about regret because you were caught. That's not repentance. That's damage control.

True repentance means acknowledging the violation and its consequences, regardless of what you stand to lose. Consider a nurse or shift worker who lies about being sick to attend a Taylor Swift concert. Their absence forces their coworkers to shoulder a heavier load, and someone ends up injured amid the chaos. When HR investigates and the person admits the lie but can't understand why it's "such a big deal," they still don't grasp the weight of their actions. That's not repentance. That's immaturity. And that's Samson. That's us, at times. To his credit, perhaps Samson did want to strike a righteous blow for God, even if it cost him his life. But let's be honest—he'd already lived his best life. He'd been in the streets. He'd had women in different area codes. He'd manipulated, murdered, and moved on without a hint of remorse. And even here, in verse 28, Samson remains concerned about Samson. His stated motive is *revenge* for the loss of his eyes, even though he brought it on himself. Nothing is ever his fault, which is a lie from the enemy. If you behave like Samson—in thought or in practice—trust me, you *are* at fault. I'm not saying Samson is the worst person in the Bible. But he clearly struggles with acknowledging guilt, sorrow, or responsibility. Without drowning ourselves in shame, it is both appropriate and necessary to feel conviction over how our decisions impact God, ourselves, and others. Real repentance requires more than lip service. It demands contrite, corrective action. Yes, it won't always be neat or linear—we are complicated, messy, fallen people. Fair enough. But "faith without works is dead."[2] Something is off when Christians say they're sorry with their mouths while refusing to do the work of dying to the flesh—daily, repeatedly—so that their lives align with God's will. Clearly, Samson's approach is not the blueprint. God used him, just as God said He would, but it's foolish to tempt divine providence by ignoring God's call to repentance. As John the Baptist said in Matthew 3:8: "Produce fruit in keeping with repentance." Even when it's inconvenient. Even when it's unpopular. Even when it costs you.

It may make you cringe to see Samson listed in the Hebrews 11 "roll call" of faith—the lineup that traces the ancestral lineage of those God used (some more willingly than others) to pave the way for Jesus and the sacrificial salvation He offered. But if that perceived impropriety, or what seems like a mismatch to us, leads you to deny, devalue, or disobey God, you'll end up creating a world of unnecessary trouble for yourself. I say *perceived* because, really, who are we to tell God how to be God? He accomplishes His will when, how, and through whomever He chooses. God is the Judge. He owes no one an explanation, though in His kindness, He often gives us insight in Scripture. We see clearly that He uses all kinds of nouns—*people, places, and things*—to advance His kingdom. Just because we find much of Samson's conduct unworthy of replication doesn't mean we can dismiss him as a useless scoundrel with a heart of stone. We are

---

2. Jas 2:14–26.

meant to learn from his failures, strive to be our best before the Lord, and trust God's purpose in using even flawed individuals.

Author Frederica Mathewes-Green, for example, once considered herself a Hindu. But after honeymooning with her husband Gary in 1974, she encountered Christ. That experience led both to enter seminary, with Gary becoming an Episcopal priest, and eventually converting to Eastern Orthodoxy. He went on to found Holy Cross Orthodox Church in Baltimore, Maryland. Frederica has since authored ten books and written over 800 essays. In a 2002 *Christianity Today* article, she asked a piercing question: "Whatever happened to repentance?"[3] She continued: "We live in a time when it's hard to talk about Christian faith at all, much less about awkward topics like repentance...Try telling a person who's been discipled by modern advertising that he's a sinner." Samson did nothing to earn or deserve a second chance—a sequel, an opportunity for his story to continue. It was an act of pure favor, granted by God simply because He chose to grant it. And when God extends that same mercy to us, Samson's story serves as a case study of what a repentant response should *not* look like.

---

3. Frederica Mathewes-Green, "Whatever Happened to Repentance?," *Christianity Today*, 2002.

The Midnight Train to Georgia
Judges 17, June 23, 2024

THE BIBLE STANDS ALONE—a riveting piece of literature abounding with paradox, courage, precision, and complex compassion. It "is alive and active. Sharper than any double-edged sword, it penetrates even to dividing soul and spirit, joints and marrow; it judges the thoughts and attitudes of the heart."[1] When we examine the 13 verses of Judges 17, a lot unfolds that, like much of the Book as a whole, is not intended for imitation. Rather, it exposes humanity's limitations, lies, and liabilities—demonstrating why Jesus, the Christ, came to rescue souls from the depravity common to man. In our passage, we encounter a virtual cornucopia of broken hearts and bad behavior. From the rural backwoods of Ephraim, we meet Micah, a confessed thief. Perhaps you've heard the saying, "If you lie, you will cheat. And if you cheat, you will steal. And if you steal, you will kill." Even among criminals, stealing from your own—especially your own mother—is frowned upon. Yet, for unknown reasons, Micah's mother takes his betrayal in stride. She chooses to use 200 of the 1,100 shekels he stole, just 18%, to commission a silversmith to craft an idol for worship, despite God's command forbidding such idolatry. Micah then goes on, in verse 5, to appoint one of his own sons as a priest to serve this delusion. Soon after, a man from the tribe of Levi—the tribe responsible for cultivating worship leaders—comes along, searching for a place to stay. Micah, doubling down on his sin, offers the Levite a salary of ten shekels a year, along with food and clothing, in exchange for becoming the *concierge* priest of his homemade religion. In Micah's mind, having a Levite on the payroll gives his operation legitimacy. "Now I know that the Lord will be good to me," he says in verse 13, "since this Levite has

---

1. Heb 4:12.

become my priest." The diagnosis comes midway through the chapter, in verse 6, and it's echoed throughout the book of Judges: "In those days Israel had no king; everyone did what was right in their own eyes." I hope the Spirit compels you to recognize just how effortlessly connected we are to these biblical forebears, and that no one in this narrative chose wisely. This isn't about vilifying the Israelites; rather, it's about recognizing that the nature and tone of their transgressions before a holy God are strikingly similar to our own in 2024. In that way, "there is nothing new under the sun."[2]

Inasmuch as it represents a microcosm, a ⅛ scale model of the broader human condition, Judges 17 offers an unsettling impression of a family, a church, and a society on the brink of implosion. It portrays a world where disorder is celebrated, where messy individualism festers like a cancer no one is trying to cure, and where even grace and mercy, though divinely good, are misunderstood as substitutes for consequence—a word that now feels profane in many circles. It's frightening, isn't it? Much like our present moment, what was once called right is now deemed offensive or dangerous. We live in a culture where foundational truths are under siege. It's now considered wrong to support young children with structure, instruction, guided creativity, and high expectations. It's seen as harmful to affirm the biological reality that men are not women, and women are not men—no matter what one's mind or emotions may claim. We are told humans can identify as wolves, raccoons, bears, chairs, sidewalks, or entirely without gender at all—even as plural persons—simply because they feel that way. But feelings, though real, are not infallible. Logic, science, language, and what used to be known as common sense are being deconstructed by ideologies whose circular reasoning eventually collapses under its own weight—contradicting, betraying, and exhausting those who promote it. Respectfully.

With OnlyFans normalizing hypersexuality on one end and inexcusable incivility being promoted on the other, hedonism and hostility have become our mother tongues. Public education is in question, not just from curriculum standards but also from systemic inequities. Many who can afford it simply opt for privatization, creating wider gaps. Generations are either neglected or overindulged. "Body positivity" is now an all-encompassing term that denies the need for discernment

2. Eccl 1:9.

or accountability. Meanwhile, people of all ages suffer from the curated dopamine hits of social media addiction. The psychological toll is undeniable, with even the U.S. Surgeon General recently issuing warnings about its long-term effects. In cities from Portland to Pittsburgh, Houston to Holland, Boston to Benton Harbor, and beyond, the walking dead—strung out and hopeless—are in plain sight. If none of this keeps you up at night, I wonder what does. We've started living as if freedom costs nothing, and as if hate, so long as it targets those we dislike, might be justifiable. And blaming all this solely on secularism is an inexpensive cop-out. Within the church itself, compromise is rampant. In Heidelberg, Germany, since 2015, a pastor has held worship services featuring the music of Madonna, the Beatles, Michael Jackson, Bob Dylan, and more recently Taylor Swift—all under the banner of attracting young people.[3] But what are we attracting them *to*?

Even among those who once said "I do" to Christ's call, who vowed to believe in Him and follow Him, we are witnessing itching ears and false teachers, violent nationalism, self-absorption, non-disclosure agreements, moral indifference, and chaos masquerading as creativity. We shrug at mediocrity as if it's quirky instead of deadly. Peer accountability has all but disappeared. We're afraid to say anything that could be labeled "judgmental," for fear of being canceled.

Sometimes we grow weary of the present and long to revisit the past, the familiar smells, the values we understood, the unity and excitement we felt even in hard times. As natural as those instincts are, though, we must be cautious. We have work to do here and now. Micah's story, for instance, is a cautionary tale. We don't know where his father was—perhaps he was deceased, unknown, absent, or never married to the mother. But when Micah stole a massive amount of silver from his mother, she didn't discipline him. Instead, she only admitted the theft had affected her after he heard her cursing over the loss, seemingly on the brink of heart failure. That failure to correct him hurt everyone. It gave Micah reason to believe that stealing wasn't a big deal—just a minor bump in the road. And we see how that lack of correction influenced his later decisions. His mother would've been well within her rights to lay down the law, like Cliff Huxtable famously told Theo in an episode of *The Cosby Show*—words many of us heard growing up: "I brought you into this

---

3. Kristen Thomason, "In Post-Christian Germany, Taylor Swift Music Brings People to Church," *Baptist News Global*, 2024.

world, and I can take you out."[4] Beyond words, though, Micah needed to experience the real-life consequences that come from violating a major moral commandment: "Thou shalt not steal."[5] What he took from his mother would have been considered grand larceny. If a decent annual salary was, say, 10 shekels—what Micah eventually paid his priest—then 1,100 pieces of silver suggests his mother was wealthy, perhaps from years, even a lifetime, of careful saving. This could have been her only nest egg, and he ran off with all of it. Can somebody shout, "*Handcuffs*"? Yet instead of confronting his wrongdoing, she rewarded him. She financed his spiritual delusions—his desire for status and legitimacy—by funding the creation of a shrine, an ephod (a ceremonial religious garment), and all kinds of idolatrous figures and paraphernalia. It was irresponsible and counterproductive.

Micah then recruited his own son into the mess—and later, a young Levite from Bethlehem. This Levite, having left the sacred place God had appointed for his ministry, was likely struggling with his own issues. Priesthood came with structure, hierarchy, and accountability. In those days, you didn't just walk away from your post in Bethlehem to wander around seeking your next religious gig. But this Levite had a price, like many of us do, and Micah was able to meet it. The Levite felt renewed; Micah felt powerful and justified, even if it was all a lie. Micah represents what it looks like to be deeply convinced of something, even when we have every reason to know it's wrong. He tries to bribe God into blessing him, thinking that hiring a Levite priest will secure divine favor. As if that mattered to God. As if God would bless what is clearly illegitimate. That's absurd. But it's also a mirror. We, too, can fall into that trap, trying to manipulate God, justifying our own compromises, and convincing ourselves it's all good.

Looking down on others is never a Christ-like posture. *Ever*. You've heard me say before that, as disciples, we don't see ourselves as better than anyone else. In fact, we are the chief among sinners, as the apostle Paul described himself[6]—an awareness that keeps us grounded in gratitude for Jesus' sacrificial love. We're not better than others; we're simply striving to be biblically centered—holy because God is holy, set apart to point

---

4. *The Cosby Show*, 1984.
5. Exod 20:15, Deut 5:19.
6. 1 Tim 1:15.

this world to Jesus. Christians are not the galaxy's police force, nor are we the fulcrum upon which society rises or falls. It's not as if, if we could just get ourselves together, the world would suddenly become a better place for everyone. No—the world is fallen. Our systems are fallen. Our bodies are fallen. There are visible and invisible battles that will only be resolved when Christ returns. Until then, humanity's muddled shenanigans will dominate the headlines. And that can feel overwhelming—like being a hamster running endlessly on a wheel, going nowhere. As one writer put it, in times of stress, our bodies instinctively react with fight, flight, freeze, or fawn (the impulse to comply just to survive another day).[7] In that state, we may find ourselves retreating inward, existing on autopilot, seeking substitute versions of engagement that feel safer but leave us disconnected. You can end up isolated—hoarding your gifts, storing up for yourself "treasures on earth, where moths and vermin destroy, and where thieves," like Micah, "break in and steal."[8] You can become fearful or indifferent toward the very people God has called you to inspire, mentor, care for, and correct—in other words, to *disciple*. In Psalm 139:7–12, a fellow sojourner asks:

> Where can I go from your Spirit?
> Where can I flee from your presence?
> If I go up to the heavens, you are there;
> if I make my bed in the depths, you are there.
> If I rise on the wings of the dawn,
> if I settle on the far side of the sea,
> even there your hand will guide me,
> your right hand will hold me fast.
> If I say, "Surely the darkness will hide me
> and the light become night around me,"
> even the darkness will not be dark to you;
> the night will shine like the day,
> for darkness is as light to you.

I realize you may not see your desire to escape—like Micah's mother, Micah himself, his son, or the traveling Levite—as a desire to escape God, but that's exactly what it is. There are limits to what it means to "mind your own business." Eventually, in one situation or another, choosing not to get involved becomes a communal liability, one that can negatively

---

7. Olivia Guy-Evans, "Fight, Flight, Freeze, or Fawn: How We Respond to Threats," *Simply Psychology*, 2003.

8. Matt 6:19.

impact everyone you know and love, even generations not yet born. That midnight train to Georgia is not the answer—because Micah's mother, Micah, his son, the Levite, and their kind? *They're in Georgia, too.* They're off the grid, too. They live in retirement communities, abroad, and in every place you might imagine escaping to, too. There's no running from brokenness—it's everywhere.

God has placed you here and kept you here *"for such a time as this,"* so you can do your part—impacting your family, your street, your city, your church, your workplace, your nation, and every sphere of society you find yourself in—all for the love of God.

When the Clergy Become Compromised

Judges 18, June 30, 2024

The work of a doctor, lawyer, building contractor, mechanic, or salesperson can be taxing in general—and brutally isolating due to the stigma that many in these professions are seen as shysters. The assumption is that they can't be trusted because what they know best is how to manipulate consumers for greater profit. According to this line of thinking, they underperform, rely on fast-talking, flattery, and misinformation, and get you to sign paperwork in triplicate—all while padding their own pockets by unethically, even illegally, draining yours. And yet, while these roles aren't exactly viewed in the same light as humankind's oldest profession—we all know what that is—pastors, ministers, priests, prophets, or preachers (in other words, any form of clergy), however, might receive just as much, if not more, scorn and skepticism. Speaking as an ordained clergyman myself, I don't want people to make wild generalizations, but I understand why they do at times. Many have had negative, disappointing, or even traumatic experiences with someone in my field. Others may not have had direct encounters but have heard the stories, read the headlines, or followed the court transcripts. As a result, clergy today are often presumed guilty by association—seen as selfish, ignorant, dishonorable, uncredentialed, ungoverned, or rogue. We are often dismissed as spiritual quacks. For those looking to understand the inner life and responsibility of pastoral ministry, there are powerful resources worth exploring: *The Diary of a Country Priest* by Georges Bernanos, *Pastoral Theology: Essentials of Ministry* by Thomas Oden, *The Care of Souls: Cultivating a Pastor's Heart* by Harold Senkbeil, and *The Book of Pastoral Rule* by St. Gregory the Great.

The 1992 film *Leap of Faith*, starring Steve Martin, vividly illustrates how art imitates life in depicting the moral corruption or impersonation of ministry. Martin's character, Jonas Nightingale, is a conman—a wandering evangelist chasing power, money, and fleeting value. At one point, he asserts, "Look, I run a show here. It's a lot of smoke and noise, and it's strictly for the suckers."[1] Tragically, that line reflects what many have come to expect from people who claim—some sincerely, others fraudulently—to be called by God to care for souls. Family therapist and rabbi Edwin H. Friedman wrote in his landmark 1999 book *A Failure of Nerve: Leadership in the Age of the Quick Fix*:

> I believe there exists throughout America today a rampant sabotaging of leaders who try to stand tall amid the raging anxiety-storms of our time...It is my perception that this leadership-toxic climate runs the danger of squandering a natural resource far more vital to the continued evolution of our civilization than any part of the environment. We are polluting our own species.[2]

I think you'd agree that we're in a dangerous place when the people of God not only tolerate but begin to *praise* and *protect* subpar servant-leaders—leaders whose focus is often marked by small-minded exploitation, an unwillingness to *follow* anyone, and a pattern of compromise. Having been led to the slaughter themselves, they now lead others astray. I'm not suggesting that clergy are the linchpin of everything. Far from it. Life does not fall apart if a pastor isn't available to bless a meal, teach Sunday school, or lead a building campaign. But the apostle Paul makes clear in Romans that vocational gospel messengers and shepherds matter a whole lot. He writes:

> "Everyone who calls on the name of the Lord will be saved.'"
> How, then, can they call on the One they have not believed in?
> And how can they believe in the One of whom they have not heard?
> And how can they hear without someone preaching to them?
> And how can anyone preach unless they are sent?[3]

So, while clergy are not saviors, they do hold a unique and necessary role in the Church and in society. And when that role is abdicated or corrupted harm inevitably follows. Judges 18 stands as a witness to that reality.

1. *Leap of Faith*, 1992.
2. Edwin H. Friedman, *A Failure of Nerve: Leadership in the Age of the Quick Fix*, 2.
3. Rom 10:13–15.

In Judges 17, we meet the early antagonists: first Micah's mother, then Micah himself, and finally the "young Levite"—as Scripture describes him—whom Micah hires to serve as a personal priest to bless his mess. As is often the case in Judges, the chapter is filled with egocentric, poor decision-making. Chapter 18 opens with a thematic refrain that should, by now in this series, strike either deep conviction—or become frustratingly familiar: "In those days Israel had no king." You have Micah attempting to launch his own religious venture, a kind of personal kingdom or spiritual startup. While staying in Ephraim (think of it like an Airbnb stopover), the Danite tribesmen recognize a familiar voice—the young Levite priest. Through the course of their conversation, the people of Laish are unfairly marked for conquest. It was an unprovoked and unnecessary assault. These were "an unsuspecting people," as verse 10 tells us, quietly dwelling in "a spacious land . . . that lacks nothing whatever." This is how the five-man reconnaissance team described Laish when they returned to their people in Zorah and Eshtaol.

Laish was situated in the far north of Palestine, a remote, self-sufficient, and peaceful place. You might compare it to Michigan's Upper Peninsula. The people of Laish excelled at staying off of everyone's radar. But after returning to Ephraim, the Danites—now armed with 600 troops—raid Micah's home and steal the idolatrous artifacts that had been financed by his mother (with the 1,100 shekels Micah had originally stolen from her in chapter 17). Apparently, there's no honor among fools or thieves. When the Levite priest sees the theft unfolding and asks what's going on, he's swiftly rebuked. They tell him, in verse 19, "Be quiet! Don't say a word. Come with us and be our father and priest."

This offer echoes the one that Micah made earlier in Judges 17:10–12—"Live with me and be my father and priest"—which came with the promise of "ten shekels of silver a year," clothing, and food. Now the Danites up the stakes: "Isn't it better that you serve a tribe and clan in Israel as priest rather than just one man's household?" The Levite agrees and goes with them. Even without phone lines, express mail, or the Internet, news still traveled fast. Realizing something is wrong, Micah sets out to confront the Danites—a scene reminiscent of John Singleton's 1991 film *Boyz n the Hood*. Doughboy, played by Ice Cube, approaches some guys harassing his brother and calmly asks, "We got a problem here?"[4] Micah attempts something similar—but it doesn't work. The Danites,

---

4. *Boyz n the Hood*, 1991.

hard-eyed and resolute, shut him down. In verse 25, they warn, "Don't argue with us, or some of the men may get angry and attack you, and you and your family will lose your lives." In today's vernacular, it's as if they said, "Micah, don't let your pride get your whole family killed. You don't want *this smoke*."

Verse 27 tells us they left with both the young priest and Micah's stolen religious artifacts, items Micah believed would guarantee him divine favor, even as he opposed God. But his plans crumbled before his eyes. Judges 18 ends in tragedy. The Danites destroy "a people at peace and secure." The city of Laish, faultless and unthreatening, is attacked "with the sword," and its buildings are burned to the ground. Right there, in the ashes and ruins of its rightful inhabitants, a conniving, violent people put their name on the land and took possession. They set up their stolen idols and appointed their own priests, just like Micah had. This moment marks the bitter legacy of Micah's mother, Micah himself, and possibly even his father, if he was absent by choice or influence. Regardless of the details, the point is clear: how we use, or misuse, what we are given in life *always* matters. Yes, everything unfolds under the sovereign, holy, omnipotent, omnipresent eye of God. Nothing escapes His providential control. But that doesn't mean our choices are meaningless. A healthy, godly example can inspire people toward righteousness. An unhealthy, ungodly example can lead people to repeat the same failures—or choose a better way because they've seen firsthand the devastation caused by excused wrongdoing.

This morning, I'm saying that in this land—overflowing with the milk and honey of opportunity, enterprise, and religious liberty, a combination that is arguably a global rarity—part of the reason so many churches are unstable, so easily tossed about in the cultural storms of our day; part of the reason so many so-called Christians have convinced themselves that Jesus died so they could live in catered comfort and convenience—a life that, like a vampire, avoids the light of the cross, much less carrying their own—is because of the rise of clergy who operate like the young Levite priest in this passage. Does Micah bear responsibility? Of course. His mother? Yes, ma'am. His son? Certainly. The savage Danites? Absolutely. But the priest? He was expected to know better. The last thing he should have done was sign on the dotted line to become the supposed spiritual hinge of Micah's desperate, and idolatrous, enterprise. But he was just as thirsty for prominence. He wanted the lights, the camera, and the action of a ministry that *looked* mega—gargantuan and important, that was the talk of the town.

In verses 2–6, we're not told he prayed at all when the nomadic Danites asked, "Please inquire of God to learn whether our journey will be successful." Then, when he saw them robbing the man who had fed, clothed, housed, and employed him, he didn't even blink. He switched sides instantly. Verse 20 says, "The priest was very pleased." Why? Because now he had a shot at serving not just one man, but an entire tribe and clan in Israel. And though the text doesn't explicitly say it, it's evident that in his new role, he would be blessing the same idolatrous behavior—just on a larger scale. His compromise didn't correct the situation; it expanded it. The question I find myself asking from time to time—not first of the masses, but of clergy like me—is this: "What in tarnation are we doing?" Today, anyone can download an ordination certificate online, for free or a small fee—mainly so friends and relatives can officiate weddings without involving a church or, dare I say it, a *real pastor*. Add to that the steady stream of pastoral scandals, and the fact that seminary education is either unaffordable or, in some circles, considered unnecessary or elitist—and it's no wonder the Church in America sometimes resembles an insecure middle schooler, desperate not only for acceptance but popularity. We want the world—and each one another—to think we're cool. And much of that stems from the fact that many clergy, the chief custodians of our communal life of faith, are spiritually lukewarm. Some aren't just lukewarm—they're imitating what they *think* ministry looks like. They never truly believed in the beginning, or they stopped believing years ago but refuse to admit it.

Like the compromised Levite, many endorse their own forms of idolatry. We convince ourselves that if the ministry God gave us doesn't resemble the platforms of T.D. Jakes, Joyce Meyer, Joel Osteen, Michael Todd, or Steven Furtick, complete with tailored wardrobes and assistants to manage assistants, then God must be disappointed with us. We believe lies. That endowments will save us. That steering clear of politics is safer. That firing clergy for destructive behavior is "too risky." But none of that is biblical. Now, while we acknowledge that "all have sinned and fall short of the glory of God,"[5] let me say this: Just because people follow you doesn't mean you're called. Or that you're a pastoral servant-leader.

---

5. Rom 8:23.

Hitler had followers. Putin has followers. People have followed cult leaders into mass suicides. They've stormed the U.S. Capitol. They've turned a blind eye to long lists of offenses—some criminal—all in the name of what some counterfeit preacher said. Too many clergy are playing church, just like the young Levite did, thinking that idolatrous worship, fellowship, and behavior (including a violent kind of landgrab takeover of Laish) can somehow twist God into granting them favor. As if God could be bribed with religious performance. And if today's priests, pastors, and ministers don't grasp the utterly profane nature of this mindset, then those who *do* have eyes to see and ears to hear must have the courage to act on God's behalf. As Scripture says, we must "test the spirits to see whether they are from God."[6] That's why it's critical that we become disciplined students of the Word of God. It is alive—and in it, we find life. Again, as I mentioned already, in the film *Leap of Faith*, Steve Martin's character—playing a con-artist preacher—says, "Look, I run a show here. It's a lot of smoke and noise, and it's strictly for the suckers." It's not everyone. But given the rise in biblical illiteracy, the spread of unchurched and dechurched mindsets, and the declining commitment to the Christ of Christianity, some clergy are indeed having a heyday—abusing the rebellion of those they vowed to love, lead, and grow.

---

6. 1 John 4:1–6.

There's a Flag on the Play
Judges 19:1–15, July 7, 2024

ALTHOUGH THE SPECIFICS VARY from one society to another, one thing is clear: in the midst of life's messy, uncomfortable, catastrophic, and downright crazy moments, human beings still know how to celebrate. From quinceañeras to birthdays, engagements to promotions, Olympic victories to favorable haircuts, family reunions to potty training, Comic-Con to new homes, retirements to anniversaries, and holidays like the Fourth of July—we're quick to fire up the grill or make a reservation to *eat, drink, and be merry*. And if you ever need an excuse to shake your groove thang—with positive, kid-friendly lyrics—look no further than Kool & The Gang's "Celebration," which hit number one on the Billboard Hot 100 on February 7, 1981. Music is almost always central to our celebrations, and the same can be said of gifts. According to *USA Today*, Americans were expected to spend roughly $22 billion last month on Father's Day—about $13 billion less than what was spent on Mother's Day.[1] Sorry, dads, but that's just how the cookie crumbles. And of course, we can't forget food. As a chunky kid, I'd celebrate almost anything—so long as there was food. Give me some Twinkies, fried pork chops, macaroni and cheese, and a half-dozen HUGs (those colorful little barrel-shaped drinks for kids), and we could party forever.

But these days, I'm sad to say, we've gotten good at celebrating the lowest common denominator—what might generously be called *mediocrity*. We hand out participation trophies and offer applause for completing the most basic tasks. Because a child "graduates" from preschool—if we can even call it that with a straight face. Because someone took what they

---

1. Betty Lin-Fisher, "Mother's Day Gift Budget: How to Celebrate Without Going Into Debt," *USA Today*, 2024.

proudly call an "everything shower" before a date (a head-to-toe cleanse instead of a quick rinse). Because a co-worker shows up on time, or you and a friend complete a 48-hour social media fast—and then immediately post about it. Because someone tried halibut or brussels sprouts for the first time—suddenly the earth must stop turning, the red carpet must be rolled out, and paparazzi armed with confetti and finger food must descend in a congratulatory swarm. This is our reality. Now, don't get me wrong. I'm poking fun, but I'm also the first to admit—life is hard. And within reason, it's a beautiful thing to find ways to celebrate big and small wins, in big and small ways. There is value in appreciating life's mundane sequences. Gratuitous lightheartedness can tattoo joy onto your soul, giving you strength for the taxing—and at times terrifyingly cruciform—moments that lie ahead. Still, an excessive preoccupation with celebration, even when well-intentioned, can lead us into dangerous territory—distractions or detours that might have otherwise been avoided.

Take Judges 19, for example. The chapter opens by introducing us—so it seems—to a new Levite, different from the one we encountered in chapters 17 and 18, who, you'll remember, signed on as a priest-for-hire in Micah's spiritual Ponzi scheme. This is not that man. There's no backstory here—no explanation for how, why, or when he took a concubine. We're simply told that he had one, and that she was from Bethlehem. As a follower of the one true and living God—and even more so as a Levite, a man set apart to lead worship and guard the tabernacle—this arrangement was disgraceful. He had entered a cohabiting, common-law *situationship* instead of making her his publicly recognized wife, a title that would have secured her legal status, social dignity, and proper standing. But verse 1 sets the tone: "In those days, Israel had no king." And when there's no king, it's every man and woman for themselves. Everyone did what was right in their own eyes. Everyone did as they saw fit. For the people of God, God had become, at best, an afterthought, a tool to advance their own fickle plans.

Our text makes it clear: the woman in Judges 19 steps out on the Levite. Her infidelity is meant to remind the reader of Israel's constant unfaithfulness to God—who, despite their mutinous disloyalty, continues to care for, protect, and provide for them, just as He does for us today. Given the lawlessness of the time—think "Wild West," minus the guns—where many people, including God's people and even their appointed leaders, lived like heathens, her betrayal was bold. In that cultural context, coupled with her vulnerability as a concubine, her act could have ended tragically—like a case from one of the *Forensic Files* or *Fatal Attraction* shows I've been known to watch. Overwhelmed by shame, frustration, or both, she fled to her father's house. Four months later, as verse 3 tells us, the Levite sets out—not to punish her, drag her before a magistrate, stone her, or shame her publicly—but to *persuade her to return*. Her father is ecstatic to see his son-in-law. Maybe she'd been eating him out of house and home. Maybe she was driving him crazy recording TikTok videos in her old room. Maybe the local gossip was wearing on him. Or maybe he was simply a genuinely hospitable man—or even heartbroken by his daughter's failure and concerned for how vulnerable she had become, should her husband decide to abandon her for good.

Whatever the reason, from verses 3 to 10, we watch an unlikely *bromance* unfold between the Levite and his concubine's father, while the woman herself remains a silent bystander. After five days of eating, drinking, sleeping, and repeated pleas from the father to stay just one more night, the Levite finally makes the decision to leave. He *meant* to leave on day four, but for reasons we aren't told, he waits until the afternoon of day five to begin the journey back to his home in the "remote hill country of Ephraim." If you haven't read ahead to the tragic conclusion—and calling it "tragic" is putting it mildly—the first part of Judges 19 might seem uneventful. They leave her father's house and stop to rest in Gibeah, a town in the territory of Benjamin. No big deal, right? Wrong. This wasn't a world where you could just "get your kicks on Route 66," cruising from place to place without concern. Travel was mostly on foot, sometimes with the help of pack animals. There were no GPS systems, cell phones, gas stations, hotels, or 24-hour stores. The terrain was harsh, and the roads were dangerous—not just because of the geography, but because of people: human traffickers, violent bandits, and all kinds of predators lurked along the way. Traveling at the right time—and knowing which places were safe—was a matter of life and death.

African Americans know something about this dynamic. After emancipation and into the Reconstruction era of the 1860s and beyond, Black Americans pursued citizenship, education, organized church life, housing, employment, and the ideals America claimed to uphold. But what met them in return were lynchings, harassment, false imprisonment, and discrimination. For more than a century in many parts of the country, Sundown Towns existed—places where Black people were explicitly or implicitly told they'd better be gone before dark or face the consequences. As retired sociology professor James W. Loewen documented in *Sundown Towns: A Hidden Dimension of American Racism*, nearly 450 such towns have been identified.[2] So, yes—*when* you travel, and *where* you stop, has always mattered deeply for those living under the threats of violence.

Back to the Levite. He and his party finally arrive in Gibeah, ignoring his servant's earlier suggestion to stop elsewhere. As the sun sets, verse 15 tells us, "They stopped there to spend the night. They went and sat in the city square, but no one took them in for the night." As the popular, medieval proverb goes, "Time and tide wait for no man." This is where the situation starts to feel chilling. Lawson Stone, in *Tyndale's Cornerstone Biblical Commentary, Volume 3*, page 452, writes: "The town square would be a perfectly legitimate place for strangers to camp, but in a tribal culture, an offer of hospitality would be expected. That none was forthcoming suggests something very wrong about this town."[3] How frightening. There's no 911 to call, no AAA or Geico roadside assistance. They are stuck in a strange place, in need of hospitality—but receive none. Ironically, they had earlier passed by the city of the Jebusites (verse 11), a pagan people known for idolatry and even child sacrifice—look at Genesis 15:16 and Deuteronomy 20:18. Yet it's here, in a supposedly *Israelite* town, where hospitality and protection *should* have been expected, that they are left vulnerable. There is no room at the inn. No one is willing to be inconvenienced. No one opens their door. And there is no recourse. If that makes the hairs on the back of your neck stand up, or triggers the sound effect "dun-dun-dun" in your mind, just wait until we finish the rest of chapter 19.

Lots of people know I'm not a diehard fan of any sports team. I realize that might be fighting words, but whether Michigan State or Michigan wins in football, for example, it doesn't really hold my attention—I simply don't have a dog in that fight. That said, I do occasionally watch a game, regardless of who's playing. And my biggest pet peeve is when players receive penalty flags that could've easily been avoided. Sure, stuff happens. *I get it.* An accidental jersey tug, a mistimed hit, a false start. I know. But not all penalties are created equal. What drives me crazy is when a player makes a big play and immediately launches into a full-blown

---

2. James W. Loewen, *Sundown Towns: A Hidden Dimension of American Racism*.
3. Philip W. Comfort, ed., *Joshua, Judges, Ruth (Cornerstone Biblical Commentary)*, 452.

performance—choreographed dances like they're The Temptations or Tina Turner. Backflips, elaborate handshakes, dramatic ball spikes, and everything else. I just want to jump through the TV, run onto the field, and tackle them! I can't stand it. In my opinion, celebrate during the game—absolutely. Enjoy the moment. But don't go overboard. That kind of celebration wastes time, energy, and focus that would be better directed toward the next play. And worse, it often results in a penalty that moves your team backward or gets you ejected from the game entirely.

That's the exact kind of flag I see in this text.

The Levite had reason to celebrate, just like we do in our lives. He did an honorable thing—he sought out his unfaithful wife, much like the prophet Hosea did with Gomer, and persuaded her to return. But for reasons we don't fully know, he let himself overindulge in celebration with his father-in-law. Maybe they got along really well. Maybe it felt good to have a reprieve from recent hardship. Whatever the case, he celebrated too long—five days of eating, drinking, and resting—and it endangered his life and the lives of those traveling with him.

Excessive celebration is the penalty flag in this passage. As far as we can tell, the Levite was a stand-up guy. He just lost focus. And you and I are no different. When things are going well, we're prone to lose focus, too. We start dancing like those football players—celebrating a little too long, a little too loudly, a little too boldly. Then the penalty flag gets thrown, and we throw up our hands in disbelief, when really, we have no one to blame but ourselves. The Holy Spirit can show you how this dynamic applies to your life—past, present, or future, but for the Maplewood Reformed Church family, hear this: Even if it doesn't always *feel* like we have much to celebrate, we *do*.

We have a budget that's being met. We have authentic fellowship. We have unity without uniformity as we seek God's will together. We have a facility that, while aging, is expansive, beautiful, and ready to receive whatever harvest the Lord brings. We have a congregation full of thinkers and doers—many who are both—and people who take the Word of God seriously. That, my friends, is no small thing. It is *worth* celebrating. But as God, in His perfect timing, opens doors we've been praying for—doors we've been asking, seeking, and knocking to find—we must celebrate without losing focus. We must resist the culture of excess *and* mediocrity. We must remain vigilant and ready: rising early to pray, to study, to listen, to serve, and yes—to leave on time—so that Maplewood is fully prepared to steward well all that God sends our way.

Wicked Men
Judges 19:16–30, July 28, 2024

IN A PAMPHLET PUBLISHED on April 23, 1770, criticizing the nepotism of King George III, the esteemed statesman Edmund Burke, who was born in Dublin, Ireland, wrote: "When bad men combine, the good must associate; else they will fall one by one, an unpitied sacrifice in a contemptible struggle."[1] Almost exactly a century later, the philosopher John Stuart Mill made a statement during a university lecture that has often been misattributed to Burke. While it's unclear whether Mill was directly influenced by Burke's writing, his remark echoes a similar sentiment:

> Let not any one pacify his conscience by the delusion that he can do no harm if he takes no part, and forms no opinion. Bad men need nothing more to compass their ends, than that good men should look in and do nothing. He is not a good man who, without a protest, allows wrong to be committed in his name, and with the means which he helps to supply, because he will not trouble himself to use his mind on the subject.[2]

In their own way, they argue that evil thrives when good is caught off guard, complacent, apathetic, weak-minded, afraid, or simply unfaithful to its duty of staying vigilant and protecting itself—and others—at all times. Although good may intervene with noble intentions, we know it doesn't always prevail. Evil, on the other hand, is marked by trophies, medals, and stolen property proudly displayed on the walls of its mancave. A persistent opportunist, sin is in it for the long haul. The wicked own homes, raise productive children, fight cancer, and invest in NASDAQ and S&P, just like anyone else. The wicked check out library books,

---

1. Edmund Burke, *Thoughts on the Cause of the Present Discontents*, 106.
2. John Stuart Mill, *Inaugural Address Delivered to the University of St. Andrews*, 36.

pinch pennies, burn toast, garden, go to the beach, and put on their leggings, jeggings, and jeans one leg at a time. The wicked do prosper, as the Bible tells us, but we also know that their troublemaking comes with an expiration date. Nevertheless, life is far less black and white, less predictable, and less equitable than many of us would like. At times, good shows up a day late and a dollar short, or so it seems, and there are moments when even its best efforts cannot fully protect or restore a beloved person, place, or thing. God's enemy has power here on earth—though limited—as he prowls around strategizing how to steal, kill, and destroy.

The decomposing body of 19-year-old Diana Medina was located near an eastbound exit ramp on I-66 in Northern Virginia on September 13, 1997, after she'd gone missing a few weeks prior, not long after their first meeting.[3] Not wanting to be late again for work at Ledo, a local pizza chain, and not having a vehicle, reluctantly, against her better judgment, she accepted a ride from Nathan Dante Young. With wanton disregard for her person, her hopes and dreams and precious value before God Almighty, he abducted her, raped her, and shot her 10 times with a Bersa .380 automatic pistol before dragging her body almost 40-feet behind a tree, near a fence. Vanida, Diana's older sister and my sister went to school together, just as Diana and I were classmates through most of our schooling, growing up around the corner from one another on the same Maryland military base. Due to evidentiary limitations, Fauquier County was forced to drop their charges, but since the cowardly episode crossed state lines—*of Maryland, Virginia, and DC*—which included him setting fire to his automobiles and disposing of the gun and ammunition, he was tried and convicted in federal court. For interstate kidnapping, interstate stalking, and two counts of causing the death of a person with a firearm during and in relation to a crime of violence, Young was sentenced to life in prison without the possibility of parole. In 2010, a Camden, New Jersey mother stabbed her two-year-old son, Zahre, whom she'd just regained custody of, and after decapitating him placed the head in the freezer.[4] Once she phoned the paramedics and confessed, before the police arrived suicide was next, as she stabbed herself in the neck; the PCP she was addicted to evidently playing a role. Her 911 call is chilling.

Earlier this summer, Kyrell Morgan, 21, was sentenced to 21 ½—43 years for killing his girlfriend's two-year-old daughter. Babysitting while

---

3. Brooke A. Masters, "Man Gets Life in 1997 Slaying," *The Washington Post*, 2000.

4. Lauren DiSanto and Dan Stamm, "Mother, Child Dead in Camden Murder-Suicide," *NBC Philadelphia*, 2012.

the mother was at work, Morgan wrote to her via text-message, "Brielle said I gave her boo-boos, and I squished her."[5] An autopsy found that the life, quite literally, had been squeezed out of her, to where the sheer concentrated pressure, they think, lacerated her pint-sized liver. The crime shows and movies we enjoy don't hold a candle to real life, because in real life the stakes matter. It's only there that real people die real deaths, often enough under horrible conditions, in the United States, with its law and order, and everywhere else around the world. Scripture is no stranger to this either, as Jesus, the Lamb of God and Lion of Judah, was, himself, subjected to assault, torture, and death on an old rugged cross, essentially, suffocating to death. Ever since Adam and Eve chose spiritual insurgency—*rejecting God's love, sinning in the Garden*—human beings have retained a thirst to spill blood and take life. Until such time, which is unknown to man, that in final judgment all debts are paid, life as we know it will be absent of nice, neat bows. Where humans are found, whether prosecution comes their way or not, a wake of carnage exists.

Today's passage is considered one of the most shocking and difficult stories in the Book of Judges—and one of the most troubling in the entire Bible. It is so controversial that—and I'm not exaggerating here—in some circles it is publicly redacted, devotionally avoided, criticized, and questioned as if it were non-canonical. In both biblically progressive and orthodox contexts, it is rarely preached on. Despite the dreadful nature of what lies before us, I find it hard to understand how a professing Christian can reconcile Paul's words to his apprentice Timothy: "All Scripture is God-breathed and is useful for teaching, rebuking, correcting, and training in righteousness." These 66 books of holy revelation were not given for likes, follows, or moral superiority, but "so that the servant of God may be thoroughly equipped for every good work."

The Levite, fresh from showing graceful restraint in seeking to rescue his wife from the shame of her adultery, was well taken care of by her father. However, he set out later than intended. Traveling through legitimate Israelite territory occupied by Benjamites, the Levite and his party find themselves stuck in the city square as daylight fades. They hope for, and expect, hospitality. It is then that "an old man," as he is described in verse 16, comes to their aid, inviting them to stay at his home. After all, they share a common origin in the hill country of Ephraim: it is where

---

5. Paula Reed Ward, "Stowe Man Gets at Least 21 Years in Prison for Killing 2-Year-Old Girl," *TribLIVE*, 2022.

the old man is from, and where the Levite is headed. At this point, they are depicted as upright, exemplary protagonists—having done the *right thing*, and their actions appear to be paying off...until they don't.

"Some of the wicked men of the city surrounded the house," verse 22. "Pounding on the door, they shouted to the old man who owned the house, "Bring out the man who came to your house so we can have sex with him."" It could easily fit into the *Book of Eli*, the post-apocalyptic, neo-Western action film from 2010 that starred Denzel Washington or Will Smith's 2007 blockbuster in the same genre, where his character, a military scientist, is in a knockdown-dragout, final battle for the survival of mankind. In one scene, a rapidly multiplying swarm of viral infected, mutated humans—*now monsters really*—are drooling, lurching, and banging violently on the thick, bulletproof but not impenetrable window of his temporary shelter.[6] Those inside this home that seconds ago was a place of peace are facing monsters of their own. Now the request that's made is horrific, yes, and oddly vile. It is surprising, especially that it comes from Israelite men, these Benjamites. It denotes a certain kind of ruinous perversion, for what I hope are obvious reasons to adults. It is psychopathic in nature, you might argue, but honestly, no more than the next set of actions.

Bidding to, in his mind, minimize the carnage and avoid the commission of homosexual rape, the Samaritan, who'd just saved the day, volunteered the Levite's concubine and his own "virgin daughter" to the men,[7] to do to them whatever they wished. This is lower than low, but wickedness knows no bounds. With the request landing on deaf ears, the Levite, who had yet directly engaged the situation, at least that we can see in the text; in verse 25, unsolicited, inserts himself: "He took his concubine (*his wife*) and sent her outside to them, and they raped her and abused her throughout the night, and at dawn they let her go." The way this all ends, whether the concubine lived through the night of carnal horror, or if "fallen in the doorway of the house, with her hands on the threshold," she didn't move because she was dead by then, or if she died on the donkey ride home, or something else, we do know for sure that once arriving home, the Levite, verse 29, dismembered her with a knife, "limb by limb, into twelve parts and sent them into all the areas of Israel," which sparked outrage among the tribes. Concerning this text, a lot of

---

6. *I Am Legend*, 2007.
7. Judg 19:24.

people can spend a lot of time struggling to make it say what it does not, sanitizing what it does say, or outright ignoring it. We're not doing any of that. It doesn't have to jive with our modern mind all the reasons why it is in the Bible, but we know that it's there, nonetheless, and therefore is important to God and should be important to us, as it is. It unquestionably illustrates this truth: "In those days there was no king in Israel. Everyone did what was right in his own eyes."

In a text like this—and maybe I'm the only one—I tend to personalize the biblical characters in ways that might be unfair, given my limited perspective shaped by a different time and place. This skews what I see and how I interpret it. For example, unlike the Levite and his elderly host, we have access to resources like guns from Walmart or Cabela's, doorbell cameras, emergency services, Wi-Fi, Crime Stoppers, pepper spray, cell phones, and more. This means we have options they simply didn't have. And while this doesn't guarantee criminals won't still act as criminals—because they will, which is why we lock our doors, stay vigilant, and avoid being easy targets—it's only fair to admit the privilege in the room. If I may say so, sadly, we've become, to some degree, a nation drenched in what Rob Henderson calls "luxury beliefs" in *Troubled: A Memoir of Foster Care, Family, and Social Class*. Henderson defines these as "an idea or opinion that confers status on members of the upper class at little cost, while inflicting costs on people in lower classes."[8] So, when some people say, "Defund the police," it's easy to say when they are disconnected from the harsh realities of why people call the police in the first place. It's also easy to say when the sting of injustice clouds your judgment. We want ethical, well-trained, well-supported, and well-supervised personnel to police us—held to the highest of standards—but throwing the baby out with the bathwater is nonsensical, in my view. The same goes for dismissive, know-it-all remedies to avoid war. You can burn your bra or protest Veteran's Day if you like, but your ability to do that is directly tied to the past, present, and future sacrifices of those who protect our way of life. None of this existed in the context of Judges 19:16–30.

Even with that in mind, the decisions made by these men were deeply wrong. I can't say the Levite and the homeowner should have run for it out the back door or made a last stand to fight for their lives against the mob, putting the women on a horse or donkey to escape if they could.

---

8. See Rob Henderson, *Troubled: A Memoir of Foster Care, Family, and Social Class*.

I just know that what they did was wrong. We're also not told that either of these men prayed once trouble started, which is a problem, since one was a follower of God and a Levite. This makes the Levite's actions, especially regarding the posthumous treatment of his wife—whom he worked hard to reconcile with—even more troubling. The thing about prayer is that you can pray while running away *or* while defending yourself. Prayer isn't always a stationary activity governed by silence. Only God knows what He might have done if they had asked for divine intervention. But they didn't. You and I are sometimes guilty of the same thing. We can learn from their mistakes.

I want us to be clear about one thing: this sinful episode is driven by God's people—the rogue Benjamites, but also aided by the Levite. Better than most, they knew God's Law. They knew that being inhospitable, sexually corrupt, or murderous, desecrating a corpse, or denying someone a proper burial (as the Levite did to his concubine) were strictly forbidden. But that didn't matter to them. These set-apart people, followers of the monotheistic God of Abraham, Isaac, and Jacob—who, absent any King James accent, said, "Be ye holy, for I am holy"—ignored His commands. It's a huge problem when God's people act like heathens, but you better believe it still happens today, and it will continue until Christ's triumphant return. We are sacred yet sullied people. Rather than trying to dress up our corruption in shiny, superficial ways, we should "tell the truth and shame the devil," and then pursue real, not fake community that fosters ongoing transformation and accountability. When we meet people who are hesitant to pray in public, keeping one eye open, maybe they've been hurt by those who claimed to be godly, but acted in ungodly ways. So, they're skittish for good reason. Maybe we should give them some space, relax, and show them love as best we can, while making sure to pray in ways these men didn't.

Most things in life can't be resolved with a Coke and a smile, and time doesn't heal all wounds. Evil lurks everywhere—in the hearts of the unrepentant, and sometimes even in the lives of the redeemed; next door, in our own homes, down the street, and far beyond. And yet, God is not dead. He is intimately at work in the thorns and thistles just as much as in the cake and ice cream—present in both the visible and the unseen. What we need are authentic, thoughtful, and meek Christians of deep conviction—those who believe that God makes all the difference. What we don't need are more petty, temperamental people speaking out of both sides of their mouths, swinging between love and hate. The Bible puts it this way: "Such a person is double-minded and unstable in all they do."[9] Or, "No one can serve two masters. Either you will hate the one and love the other, or you will be devoted to the one and despise the other."[10] At the start of this passage, the old man and the Levite appear righteous by all indications, but by the end, alongside a band of Benjamite rapists, they've both sold their souls down the river.

Despite the dreadful, foul, and unreliable nature of fallen men and women, God remains the perfect picture of reliability. Diana, Zahree, Brielle, and a nameless married woman who lived thousands of years ago—their suffering is not unique. So, watch the company you keep, and pray—as honestly as you can—like it matters. Like your life depends on it. Pray that God will use any means necessary to protect you from the kind of vicious cowardice and abuse we've read about. Gardner C. (Calvin) Taylor—affectionately known as the dean of Black preaching and the poet laureate of American Protestantism—pastored a church in Brooklyn, New York, for 42 years. He received the Presidential Medal of Freedom from President Bill Clinton in 2000. Taylor is remembered for saying:

> There are days when we can bring before God a deep and glad laughter of joy and gratitude. There will be other days when we can only muster a bitter, angry complaint. If it is honest, be confident that God will accept whatever it is we truly have to lift up before Him, and He will make it serve His purpose and our good.[11]

May the Lord our God bring beauty from ashes, as only He can, and graciously receive whatever hallelujahs, tears, or deep belly laughs we can offer—knowing that the wicked, the enemies of the Lord, will be consumed and vanish like smoke on the day of His choosing.

---

9. Jas 1:8.
10. Matt 6:24.
11. Gardner C. Taylor, *How to Preach a Sermon*, 2005.

When It Happens on Our Watch
Judges 20:1–23, August 4, 2024

UPON DISMEMBERING THE LIFELESS body of his unnamed wife—his concubine, with whom he had recently reconciled after her adultery—the once righteous Levite, now reprehensible, returns home and divides her remains into 12 parts, sending them to the representatives of all the tribes of Israel. This is the kind of outrage you could taste. From beginning to end, the ordeal was incredulous, unthinkable, unimaginable, abhorrent, scandalous, sinister, and sick. It caught the community completely off guard. Why a Levite, steeped in the Torah (the first five books of the Old Testament—Genesis, Exodus, Leviticus, Numbers, and Deuteronomy), would participate in such a loathsome deed is not explained, nor is his reasoning for desecrating his wife's corpse or nonchalantly sending the decomposing remains to his ancestral and spiritual kinfolk. At the very least, it seems that the conclusion of Judges 19 is meant to authenticate the violation. Each group must see and smell the aftermath for themselves, face the facts, hold court, and choose the next course of action. The power of self-perception is on display here, as it's easy to overestimate or underestimate ourselves. The Levite views himself as a heroic architect of unity and justice, all while showing no recognition of his sin.

How this morning's text concludes with verses 18–23 is notable. It may feel as though the Israelites were caught bringing a knife to a gunfight—that they misjudged their opponent, were out-strategized, or out-worked. While some of this may be true, what we know for certain, based on the text, is that they took an "L." They lost. Sometimes, we search for an intricate answer to explain life, but even with tutorials, coaches, supplements, cryptocurrency, and artificial intelligence, wins and losses remain part of the game. In a world where "living your best life" is so popular and showing up is assigned greater value than it deserves, we need to recognize that sometimes you just get whooped. It's okay for it to be that simple. It used to happen on the playground during recess, and it continues today in the Olympics, the stock market, elections, and on the battlefield. Emerging from Gibeah, 22,000 Israelite soldiers made the ultimate sacrifice, losing the first and, eventually, the second day's battles. We know this aligns with life because, even when you've given your best effort—whether at your job, in a job interview, in a court case, or at Monopoly—there are times you simply lose.

Another observation is that evil is not easily frightened. Look at the text. Verse 15 says that "at once," right away, the Benjamites amassed "twenty-six thousand swordsmen from their towns, in addition to seven hundred able young men from those living in Gibeah. Among all these soldiers there were seven hundred select troops who were left-handed, each of whom could sling a stone at a hair and not miss." The rest of Israel put together a formidable force of 400,000 for what we'd imagine conventional wisdom said would be a quick, decisive, landslide triumph. Someone once said, "If you're scared, say you're scared." Well, it doesn't seem like the Benjamites were, or maybe fear fueled them to be laser focused and tightly tethered to winning. Either way, the refusal to cooperate with the verdict from the nation's sentencing illustrates further how badly broken their hearts were. From verse 13, it seems that all they had to do was hand over "those wicked men of Gibeah," the rapists. And why? So that, Israel explained, "we may put them to death and purge the evil from Israel." The only thing is, the Benjamites weren't having it. They chose combat, for the sake of principle, lest they let this small group of their own be slaughtered, or because, as strange or scary as it sounds to us, they didn't see what happened as a big deal.

Not that we should be paranoid, but some of how we, Christians, in the West go wrong and specifically here on American soil, is that where evil is concerned, we act like nothing that insignificant is at stake. But that's not how evil rolls. It shows up as a well prepared, formidable foe, ready to *get down with the get down*. Evil is the bully of all bullies, with the bold plan show up at your front door, drag you outside and beat you down in front of your parents, your siblings, and your relatives who are visiting from out-of-town, and then confidently, with a smug face, say to them, "If you're feeling froggy, then leap. You can be next!" Evil doesn't waste time on low self-esteem, inadequate preparation or supplies, or what anybody will think of them. The focus is winning. *Period*. Granted, such a no-holds-barred mindset does not quite correspond with biblical faith at times, since Christ is our portion and in him final victory is conferred somehow in the past, present, and future; so, we want to be careful and wise. But none of this is essentially, by default, always at odds with the charge to "fight the good fight of faith," or to "seek peace and prosperity," or to "act justly and to love mercy and to walk humbly with your God," or to "take your stand against the devil's schemes." Christians have been given armor for a reason: the belt of truth, breastplate of righteousness, shoes of peace, the shield of faith, the helmet of salvation, the sword of the Spirit, "which is the word of God."

Last but not least, evil requires a response, and often a communal or collective one because, on some level no matter how you categorize it, some manners of immorality have a way of infringing on my life, and your life, and your neighbor's life, even if the scene of the incident is located on the other side of town, which we see in our passage. If the rest of Israel let this monumental disregard for human life—*a stain on the freshly laundered, white tablecloth of holy incarnation*—where would it end? Turning a blind eye would make them culpable. And to their credit, they made a good choice and then didn't give up when failure introduced itself. Anything worth having is worth fighting for or working for. Don't you let anyone tell you that tenacity, sticktoitiveness, and grit don't have a place in the Kingdom of God. We should notice, too, that although Israel's remaining tribes—*the non-Benjamites I mean*—were far from perfect since, "In those days there was no king in Israel. Everyone did what was right in his own eyes," they still did not commit the crime in question. They weren't there. They weren't involved. And they didn't condone or cover it up either. It was an independent action. Even so, it happened on their watch, and for the greatest good of everyone and unborn generations to come, and to honor God as best as they could understand, they couldn't sit around waxing poetic doing nothing. By a crazed mob of men with whom they shared strands of DNA, an abomination took place. What should never happen and certainly should never happen among God's people, did happen.

In the end, those who take by force, who cause chaos in their thirsty quest for power, and whose strongest allegiance is to themselves are cowards, and they are dangerous, just like these characters in Judges 19–20. They cannot be handled with kid gloves. According to Flannery

O'Connor, the celebrated Southern author and essayist, who died of complications from lupus in 1964 at the age of 39, said, "The truth doesn't change according to our ability to stomach it."[1] Our world is a mess, we know that. You'd hope that Christians could agree on that basic aspect of Original Sin, per Adam and Eve's fall and the consequences thereafter, that we all must wade through each day. What I find especially alarming nowadays, however, is that although the world is a mess, the Church is as well. And I don't mean individual churches—*as in the buildings, denominations, or programming*—so much as we, the people. Unfortunately, we, the people of God, commit evil in the name of God or we are privy to evil committed on our watch, and like cowards—however that might show up in our lives—we are nowhere to be found. Cowardice is found in all shapes and sizes, and presentations. The abrasive, overly aggressive individual, who likes to say that they are how they are on account of caring so deeply for people or the issues *and* the wallflower who has never been known to utter a terse, corrective, or critical word can both be cowards.

What I'm getting at is, although there's grace and mercy together with an understanding that we're all a bag of mixed marbles, in dire need of the Spirit's supervision, if we don't commit to first opposing evil when it shows itself within our own ranks, then our witness will diminish to nothing, to this waiting, watching, dying world that needs vocalization and demonstration of God's love. Atrocities of one kind or another are committed or sustained, partly because the truth we give lip service to is more conceptualized than actualized in a Person (Jesus), whom we have decided deserves everything from us because he gave everything to us. Thankfully, at least in this snapshot, the Israelites have shown us the way. Rebuking the world has its place, but it's comparatively easy. When we are reluctant to rebuke those in our spiritual family, we're on shaky ground. And the hotly contested and complicated political state we are in right now offers a ripe opportunity to be attentive to how, when, why, and with whom God might be calling us to reaffirm some truth. Of course, I'm not advocating waging war against a sister or brother in Christ, but everything is right about refuting attitudes or conduct that is obviously out of step with our family values.

---

1. Flannery O'Connor, *The Habit of Being: Letters of Flannery O'Connor*, 100.

But What Happens When?
Judges 20:24–48, August 11, 2024

"Not Like Us,"[1] is a trending Kendrick Lamar single, that actually, in a way, captures the events leading to the conclusion of Judges 20. A group of wicked men in Gibeah, who were Benjamites, banged on the front door of a home owned by an elderly man who had compassionately welcomed a small party of stranded out-of-towners to stay with him for the night. The chaotic commotion was followed by a demand that the male guest be sent out to these unwanted, malicious men so that they could assault him. To save himself, the man, a Levite, instead threw his own wife outside into the shocking mêlée, where she was subsequently abused and raped throughout the night. After succumbing to her injuries, he then dismembered her body. In sentencing these crooked, cowardly individuals to death, the larger assembly of Israel's remaining tribes sought to differentiate themselves, making it clear that when it comes to the Benjamites, they are not the same. They, understandably, want no association with them and their evil.

As we discussed last week, the Benjamites came to play—not merely to participate, qualify, or contend, but with their tribe's survival on the line; they came to win. They aimed to assert their dominance, to "kick butt and take names," to "go hard in the paint," and to tell their Israelite family members turned enemies that, in the words of Brand Nubian from 1993, "Punks Jump Up to Get Beat Down."[2] Benjamin defended the perverse actions of these rogue citizens while resisting any regulation by the Nation of Israel for mutual accountability. Like scenes from the 1980s movies *Back to the Future* and *Revenge of the Nerds*, attempted

---

1. Kendrick Lamar, "Not Like Us," 2024.
2. Brand Nubian, "Punks Jump Up to Get Beat Down," 1993.

bullying was occurring, leading them to feel justified in fighting to continue operating as they saw fit, regardless of the consequences. Whether physical or spiritual, and notwithstanding who initiated it, anyone at war holds core beliefs they are willing to die for. I wonder what those under the sound of my voice today are so thoroughly convinced of that you would not only endure ridicule or exclusion for, but also accept as a catalyst for losing what is irreplaceable, even up to your very life. Given the heinous crimes committed by their people, one might expect the Benjamites to agree to kill these men themselves or gladly hand them over to the Israelites. But not the Benjamites.

After two surprising defeats, victory finally arrives. In some traditions, this is where one might ask the rhetorical question, *"Won't He do it?"* In the aftermath of such an outcome, life feels sweetly vindicated. Thankfully, we have all experienced some versions of this. The bill was paid at the last minute. A breached or premature birth still resulted in a healthy baby. A relationship conflict was resolved after all. A terrifying health situation all of a sudden improved for you, your child, a co-worker, or a dear mentor. The promotion, contract, or loan was approved. The brewing nightmare was extinguished, even at the midnight hour, after which you can proclaim, "Victory is mine. Victory is mine. Victory today is mine. I told Satan to get thee behind. Victory today is mine." "Favor ain't fair," we might say. I agree; Christians should express gratitude when God fulfills the desires of their hearts. But what happens when we are bested?

It seems to me that one dirty little secret that must emerge from darkness into the marvelous light is that many Christians subscribe to a "name it and claim it" faith—a belief that God must come through in the manner and timing they desire, or He is not God at all. I hope I am not speaking out of turn, but this perspective is, in fact, not faith at all. These days, it is easy to view God as a gentle parent who speaks in soft, lullaby tones, negotiates pleasantly with His children to honor their unique expressions and independence, and always suggests or asks them to do something, lest their confidence be undermined by authoritarianism. Sadly, verses like Matthew 7:9 are often cited to justify this delusion, where Jesus asked:

> "Which of you, if your son asks for bread, will give him a stone? Or if he asks for a fish, will give him a snake? If you, then, though you are evil, know how to give good gifts to your children, how

much more will your Father in heaven give good gifts to those who ask him!"

Sure, they may stop short of claiming that during Jesus' earthly ministry, he was materially rich and lived a life of luxury, and therefore His disciples today are obligated to do the same, as some misguided individuals teach. Nevertheless, the underlying idea persists: a good God, our God, does not allow His children to experience anything less than victory, wealth, and happiness. When the Bible is read in this manner—believing that the Israelites and anyone who believes in the triune God are promised an undefeated record in life—a significant comprehension gap arises. The real issue, however, is a matter of the heart.

This may be controversial, but so be it—I recognize that there are parts of the Bible on which Christians can respectfully disagree, without one side being deemed right and the other labeled as the spawn of Satan. However, hear me when I say that if your takeaway from reading the Word of God is that, in this temporary, wounded experience of human life, you are supposed to win at everything by virtue of Jesus' spilled blood, *something is wrong*. Call the theological EMS. Sound the alarm. I don't want to say that you're not in the Book, but the Book may not be in you. There is a discrepancy or misunderstanding—a problem of epic proportions. It is commendable that the Israelites prayed about their situation, and we should do the same. This is a foundational component of what God's people do. However, prayer does not guarantee that life will change in the manner we desire. I know that the Israelites won, but what happens when they lose? *What about when you lose?*

"In those days there was no king in Israel. Everyone did as they saw fit." But in these days, with a New Covenant available, we simply cannot, should not lie to people. Preachers can't dumb down or distort the Gospel because either they, low-key don't really believe in it—*problem number one*—or they're afraid of how their sheep, their congregation, will respond. Congregations can't keep promoting easy, socially safe sayings about the Bible that the Bible doesn't say or that it does say, but doesn't mean what we keep saying that it means, just because the silent uneasiness in the room causes us more fear than dishonoring God does. The metaphor is imperfect, but faith is a bit like swimming. Aside from its recreation and the health benefits, swimming—*treading water and everything else*—is a life skill. I'm doing my best to join the club, as many of you know. I practice every day at the pool, even though learning to swim at the tender age of 45 presents a serious learning curve. But no level of familiarity or mastery of swimming means you can never drown. In a pool, in a lake, in the ocean, in a puddle, even the best swimmers can drown under the right conditions, like waves that overwhelm, exhaustion, a cardiac event, hypothermia, or an injured extremity that hampers one's ability to reach dry ground.

The story is told of how, in 2022, Anita Alvarez was rescued from drowning by her coach during a competition. Andrea Fuentes, the U.S. artistic swimming team coach, sprang into action, jumping into the pool when Alvarez fainted while still in the water[3]. A few days ago, the 27-year-old Alvarez and Team USA took silver in the Olympics. Last Thursday, at the CrossFit Games held in Fort Worth, Texas, during the swimming portion of an individual heat in a large lake, Lazar Dukic of Serbia, age 28, drowned.[4] In tethering yourself to God through Christ, eternal life—salvation—is promised. It is yours; freely given, freely received. However, Jesus said, "In this world you will have trouble,"[5] which means you will struggle in the water. Take all the flotation devices, watches that track your caloric output, fins, and kickboards you want. Take lessons. Practice. Improve your stroke and everything else that comes with it, as you should—just know that none of it guarantees you will not struggle in the water, just as we will all struggle in life. If you bow to Christ now, there will be only paradise upon your transition to being absent from the body and present with the Lord. However, bowing to Christ, although He readily helps and heals like no other, has never meant that everything is always hunky-dory. That's not the gospel.

I know that hearing from the book of Judges may have been challenging for some of us this past year, but the Bible, if we're reading it responsibly, is not about scoring the most points, instant gratification, or avoiding all scars, and scraps, and disappointments. Rather, anchored by Christ's witness, it teaches us how to be transformed, how to suffer well in facing the practical alongside the mysterious of life, seeing God's faithfulness in losses as much as wins. The shortest verse in all the Bible is

---

3. Sana Noor Haq, "Anita Alvarez: Coach Andrea Fuentes Dives into Pool to Save American Swimmer at World Championships," *CNN*, 2022.

4. Jamie Stengle and Josh Kelety, "CrossFit Games Competitor Lazar Dukic Dies During Swimming Event at Texas Lake," *Associated Press*, 2024.

5. John 16:33.

what? Yes, "Jesus wept" in John 11:35. He wept over the loss of his friend Lazarus. We weep over the loss of his own life on the cross, for our sake. And we wrestle with the losses we each face until he returns or calls us home. I imagine that part of why God allows earthly losses, I know at least speaking for me, is that there's no other way for me to trust him more and choose to taste and see, day after day, through pleasant and devastating experiences, that He is good.

In the case of the Israelite-Benjamin battle, evil was swallowed up in the end, which will indeed happen for us from time to time, actually many times in one form or another, just not all the time. Chatting with a friend several weeks ago one day, he mentioned that being alone and being lonely aren't the same. Obviously, it is natural for everyone to feel lonely at times, but a constant state of loneliness is harmful. Often enough, perhaps with caring intentions, we assume that anyone who is alone—*lives alone, is not boo'd up with a significant other, watches movies alone, gardens alone, vacations alone*—that, by default, they must be lonely. That's our issue, not theirs. Similarly, in the profoundest, I think, grand scheme of the word, someone who has lost is different than a quintessential loser. Every athlete, celebrity, or ordinary plain Jane or Joe who achieved anything of merit, didn't win at everything. Michael Jordan retired as a six-time NBA champion, with a 24–11 Finals record. He lost sometimes, but no one calls him a loser. The same with Tom Brady, Wayne Gretsky, or anyone else you can think of.

Those who follow Christ are not losers; far from it. But they will lose at times in life. Cancer or an aneurism. A hit-and-run or diabetes that's spiraling out of control. Divorce, or depression, or a home that goes up in flames, or imprisonment, or financial disaster. Tornados and Terrible Two's that never go away, or some spiritual malady, a "thorn in the flesh," that you've only told one other person about. Dementia, heartache, heartbreak, or a heart attack. None of this is easy to navigate. *Hurray for the Israelites.* I'm glad they won. But win, lose, or draw, if we put our trust in God our winning has already been confirmed for when it matters most. Jesus said, "And if I go and prepare a place for you, I will come back and take you to be with me that you also may be where I am."[6]

---

6. John 14:4.

When Even Good is Bad
Judges 21:25, August 18, 2024

IN WHAT USUALLY ENDS up being a contest between two parties, in the U.S. political system it is rare that the candidates and every ounce of their respective campaign agendas amount to a choice between *pure* good and *pure* evil. Without excusing dreadful behavior or, on the other hand, becoming sanctimonious, we must confess that neither angelic saints or boogeymen exist. Life is nuanced, complex, frustrating, and far more mysterious than linear categories permit. We'd love for the human experience, and our electoral process, to be neatly divvied into obvious opposites or extremes that, therefore, required little, if any, discernment, support, wisdom, or providential dependence. We prefer knowing that Mojo Jojo is bad and The Power Puff Girls are good; that The Joker, not Batman, is the irrefutable villain; that Peter Pan deserves our cheers while Captain Hook should be booed off the screen. At anything and everything, we want Hope to win and Calvin to lose.[1] We want it to be obvious that Austin Powers, G.I. Joe, Conan the Barbarian, T'Challa from *Black Panther*, Wonder Woman, and *Jurassic Park*'s Dr. Alan Grant are the good guys. If only it were that simple. Even so, please don't fall for the idea that right and wrong are unreliable relics no longer valid in our sophisticated world. Truth does exist, meaning that regardless of what a society or an individual says from generation to generation, or college to college, or nation to nation, or household to household, or candidate to candidate, absolutes endure that are objectively helpful or harmful, permissible or impermissible to God, the Creator-Father who knows best. According to

---

1. The Hope College football team worshipped with us this morning, to mark the end of their fall camp before the season begins. Each year as the season is about to get into full swing, the team attends an area church together and this time, given my connections with the head coach, they visited Maplewood. It was great!

the Bible's books, from Genesis to Revelation, abortion, racism, or, let's say, polygamy are just plain wrong, for example, and always will be, even if we think differently. As it has been said, "Wrong is wrong; and, there ain't no right way to do wrong." That's worth remembering!

This series has forced us to face topics like legacy and tradition, fear, prostitution, parenting, rape, revenge, marriage, idolatry, oppression and freedom, gender, and bullying. It has not been easy. We've examined instances of hand-to-hand combat that rivaled *John Wick*. And we have waded through shameful family values and disappointing leadership dynamics. Judges shines a light on what happened "in those days," way back when, but it's also a megaphone shouting for all of us to realize our present failings. This last verse in the last chapter contains a chorus that is scattered all around the book: "In those days Israel had no king; everyone did as they saw fit." In today's narrative, God's people, the Israelites, are foolishly thinking that two wrongs make a right, and they don't need God's guidance after all, they're basking in the glow of having laid the smackdown on one of their own.

What happened was, the Benjamites refused to allow a small segment of their tribe to face the death penalty, by the governing power structure for horrible, heinous crimes they'd committed. They chose war instead, and as clear underdogs, they actually *molly whopped*, I mean straight-up whooped the Israelites twice, like they stole something; although, thankfully, in the third and final battle, God gave the Israelites the "W."

In Judges 21, the "men of Israel," verse 1," make a solemn promise: "Not one of us will give his daughter in marriage to a Benjamite," the ancestral relatives they'd just beaten. And then in verse 5, they took a second oath that they saw as promoting unity *and* uniformity, making everyone toe the line, which they figured strengthened the whole nation as it rebuilt. But mind you, God didn't ask them for this. And had they asked, God likely would've told them *how* to proceed, but they did not ask and so in this instance they made fools of themselves. That happens sometimes when we act like we can make it on our own. In that sense, your age, or position, or statistics, or NIL deal, or major, or hometown don't matter. You've squared off against God, not grasping that your hands are too short to box with Him. Again, without any clearance from God, the Israelites' next big idea, in their feelings as they are about how depleted their brethren Benjamites were after the war, is to slaughter an entire town that had joined in the previous tribal conflict. There, all men, women, and children were put to the sword, except virgin women.

Having been decimated and lacking women to procreate with, the Benjamite clan would die out. So, to solve the problem, these virgins were given to them, only—*wouldn't you know it?*—there weren't enough to go around. Because of the first unsolicited and unnecessary promise to not give their own daughters in marriage to any Benjamite, they figured they'd let the remaining men kidnap young, unmarried ladies from nearby Shiloh. And so, equipped with insider information and permission, that's exactly what these dudes did. They hid in the bushes, and at the right time each one grabbed a new, unsuspecting wife, as if from a vending machine, returned to his home, settled down making a family, and acting like nothing sinister ever happened, as if God was pleased.

And these were supposed to be the "good guys." When even good turns out to be bad, we often feel at our wits end. Up a creek with no paddle. Perplexed. Unsure. Desperate and—*since late is better than never*—at last, the pump is primed for us to face the destruction caused by our own demons. This breakdown triggers us to look within and look up for help. Human beings need to be rescued. We need salvation. Some people know that they don't have it altogether. They accept that. They don't humble themselves before God Almighty and follow Him, but still, there's no fight in them to put on a performance of moral superiority. Another group of people, however, are sometimes harder to reach. They don't look like personified death and destruction. They may open doors and say things like, "Yes, sir" and "No, sir" or "Yes, ma'am" and "No, ma'am." Maybe they know the Bible pretty well, attended parochial school or from an early age found themselves plopped on the front row of some Baptist, COGIC, Wesleyan, or nondenominational church. They are, you might say in a conventional sense, *good people* who consistently do good people things, like the Israelites had in the preceding episode.

Your conduct matters, but so do your thoughts—most importantly, however, your internal devotion is what governs if God sees you as a "rival or disciple," someone who sees no need for Him *or* someone who has surrendered, as a student does to a teacher. This world, I'm saying, has no *good people*. We're all sick with sin, as a disease we're born with before it manifests in attitude or action. Throughout the Book of Judges, the Israelites whined, or took God for granted, denied Him, or defied Him because that's what fallen people do. Behavior matters and it matters a lot. My behavior matters to my congregation. Your behavior matters to your coaches, professors, and parents, as it should. And your behavior should matter to you. And should you one day cross over into the beautiful, burning, covenant-rooted sands of marriage, you will care about her behavior, and she will care about yours. It's just that there's more to it than the eyes can see. You can look, sound, and present yourself as God-fearing, but really be a talented actor on their way to hell. And I'd rather you hear the truth than *like me*, if I must choose, so you need to hear this. The Israelites weren't the Benjamites, but they were not innocent either, in both their own actions and their own decisions to usurp God's authority. "There is no one righteous, not one."[2]

At 20 years old, if God was real—*and I wasn't fully convinced then that He was*—my thing was, how in the world could He ever have any beef with me. I'd made it to college. I wasn't peddling dope. I hadn't killed anyone. In many respects, on the outside I was a stand-up, reliable young man, a *good dude*. But from where I was from—*my roots, my formative experiences*—I didn't know anything about Jesus. I wasn't in anybody's church or Bible study. No one was praying with me, and I wasn't praying myself either because that was not a core value of my family. But in my junior year at the University of Maryland, with my football days there already put to bed, I went to church and part of what the preacher said, which was what the Bible said, captured my attention: "all have sinned and fall short of the glory of God, and all are justified freely by his grace through the redemption that came by Christ Jesus. God presented Christ as a sacrifice of atonement, through the shedding of his blood—to be received by faith."

After that I was done. I said to myself, "If this is true—*and for whatever reason in that moment I was suddenly convinced that it was*—then 'all' means 'all', and that means I was included in it, that by default I am a sinner, separated from God, but that there's an offer on the table by which I can be saved from eternal punishment by grace through faith in Jesus Christ." That was it. It wasn't about being conventionally bad or good—*because remember, we're all bad anyways*—but having heard the truth, I knew I was on the hook for responding to it. It was my choice. I could disregard God if I wanted to and go back to life as I'd known it. It was my choice. But in the biggest ways, in an instant, obedience to God became my focal point. Would I surrender to Him or continue rebelling against Him, knowing

---

2. Rom 3:10.

that both paths have their own distinct outcomes? Nowadays, everyone still does what's right in their own eyes, but some people break free of the copycat culture, and make a godly investment that outlives them. Behavior modification comes later, as we learn God's character, study His Word, and are supported and challenged in Christ-centered community. Right now, what matter most is if you are being obedient or disobedient to knowing Christ as Savior. He can tackle your mistakes. He will work on your attitude and language. Over time, he will convict you of how to rehabilitate your lifestyle and way of thinking, but first, you must accept that he knows everything about you, having created you, and his desire is that you would not perish, but would surrender to him.

Bibliography

Agar, John. "Family Devastated by Apparent Random Killing by Neighbor." *MLive*, April 15, 2024. https://www.mlive.com/news/grand-rapids/2024/04/family-devastated-by-apparent-random-killing-by-neighbor.html
Ani, Marimba. *Let the Circle Be Unbroken: The Implications of African Spirituality in the New Diaspora*. Lawrenceville, NJ: Red Sea, 1992.
Augustine. *Confessions*, trans. by Edward B. Pusey. New York: Cosimo, 2007.
Barnes, M. Craig. *Hustling God: Why We Work So Hard for What God Wants to Give*. Grand Rapids, MI: Zondervan, 1999.
Beastie Boys, "(You Gotta) Fight for Your Right (To Party!)," track 7 on *Licensed to Ill*. New York: Def Jam, 1986.
Berman, Rabbi Dr. Ari. "To Ennoble and Enable: An Inaugural Vision," address delivered at Yeshiva University, New York, NY, September 10, 2017. https://www.yu.edu/news/to-ennoble-and-enable-an-inaugural-vision
Big Daddy, dir. by Dennis Dugan. Culver City, CA: Columbia Pictures, 1999.
Billy Ocean, "When the Going Gets Tough, the Tough Get Going," track 1 on *The Jewel of the Niles: Original Motion Picture Soundtrack*. New York, NY: Jive Records, 1985.
Bob Marley, "So Much Trouble in the World," track 1 on *Survival*. New York: Island Records, 1979.
Bobby Caldwell, "What You Won't Do for Love," track 7 on *Bobby Caldwell*. Hialeah, FL: TK Records, 1978.
Boyz n the Hood, dir. by John Singleton. Culver City, CA: Columbia Pictures, 1991.
Breakin', dir. by Joel Silberg. Los Angeles, CA: Cannon Films, 1984.
Brand Nubian, "Punks Jump Up to Get Beat Down," track 5 on *In God We Trust*. New York: Elektra, 1993.
Burke, Edmund. *Thoughts on the Cause of the Present Discontents*. London, England: J. Dodsley, 1770.
Cadence, dir. by Martin Sheen. Santa Monica, CA: Republic Pictures, 1990.
Carey, William. *An Enquiry into the Obligations of Christians to Use Means for the Conversion of the Heathens*. Leicester, England: Ann Ireland, 1792.
Carrie Underwood, "Jesus, Take the Wheel," track 4 on *Some Hearts*. Nashville, TN: Arista, 2005.
Cicero, Marcus Tullius. *De Amicitia* (On Friendship), trans. by Andrew P. Peabody. Boston, MA: Little, Brown, and Company, 1903.

Comfort, Philip W., ed., *Joshua, Judges, Ruth (Cornerstone Biblical Commentary)*. Carol Stream, IL: Tyndale, 2012.
Coming 2 America, directed by Craig Brewer (Culver City, CA: Amazon Studies, 2021).
Despicable Me, dir. by Pierre Coffin and Chris Renaud. Universal City, CA: Universal Pictures, 2010.
Dickens, Charles. *A Tale of Two Cities*. London, England: Chapman & Hall, 1859.
DiSanto, Lauren and Dan Stamm. "Mother, Child Dead in Camden Murder-Suicide." *NBC Philadelphia*, August 22, 2012. https://www.nbcphiladelphia.com/news/local/mother-child-dead-in-camden-murder-suicide/1938695
Don McLean, "American Pie," track 1 on *American Pie*. New York: United Artists Records, 1971.
Dr. Seuss, *The Cat In the Hat*. New York, NY: Random House, 1957.
Ellis III, James. *Tell the Truth, Shame the Devil: Stories about the Challenges of Young Pastors*. Macon, GA: Smyth & Helwys Publishing, 2015.
Elliot, Elisabeth. *A Lamp Unto My Feet: The Bible's Light For Your Daily Walk*. Grand Rapids, MI: Revell, 2004.
Family Matters, dir. by Richard Correll. New York: ABC/CBS, 1989–98.
Flint, Annie Johnson. *What God Hath Promised*. Addison, IL: Bible Truth Publishers, 1919.
Forrest Gump, dir. by Robert Zemeckis. Hollywood, CA: Paramount Pictures, 1994.
Frank Sinatra, "My Way," track 6 on *My Way*. Burbank, CA: Reprise Records, 1969.
Friedman, Edwin H. *A Failure of Nerve: Leadership in the Age of the Quick Fix*. New York: Church Publishing, Inc., 2017.
Frost, Robert. "A Hundred Collars," in *A Further Range*. New York: Henry Holt and Company, 1936.
Fuller, Thomas. *Good Thoughts in Bad Times and Other Papers*. London, England: George Bell and Sons, 1881.
Graham, Billy. *The Reason for My Hope: Salvation*. Nashville, TN: W Publishing Group, 2013.
Guy-Evans, Olivia. "Fight, Flight, Freeze, or Fawn: How We Respond to Threats." *Simply Psychology*, November 9, 2003. https://www.simplypsychology.org/fight-flight-freeze-fawn.html
Guy Ritchie's The Covenant, dir. by Guy Ritchie. Beverly Hills, CA: Metro-Goldwyn Pictures, 2023.
Haq, Sana Noor. "Anita Alvarez: Coach Andrea Fuentes Dives into Pool to Save American Swimmer at World Championships." *CNN*, June 23, 2022. https://www.cnn.com/2022/06/23/sport/anita-alvarez-swimmer-coach-spt-intl/index.html
Henderson, Rob. *Troubled: A Memoir of Foster Care, Family, and Social Class*. New York: St. Martin's, 2021.
Hewitt, Annie S. "I Need Thee Every Hour," in *The Hymnal of the Methodist Episcopal Church*. New York: Phillips & Hunt, 1872).
Ho, Rodney. "Acts with Georgia ties in Rolling Stone's latest 500 greatest songs of all time." *Atlanta Journal-Constitution*, September 15, 2021. https://www.ajc.com/life/radiotvtalk-blog/acts-with-georgia-ties-in-rolling-stones-latest-500-greatest-songs-of-all-time/BJBJ6QBBKRBJ3LN3DB76AL76PU
I Am Legend, dir. by Francis Lawrence. Los Angeles, CA: Warner Bros, 2007.
Jefferson, Thomas. *The Papers of Thomas Jefferson*, Vol. 11, 1 January–6 August 1787, ed. Julian P. Boyd. Princeton, NJ: Princeton University Press, 1955.

BIBLIOGRAPHY

Juvenile, "Ha," track 2 on *400 Degreez*. New Orleans, LA: Cash Money Records, 1998.

John Wick, dir. by Chad Stahelski. Santa Monica, CA: Lionsgate, 2014.

Kendrick Lamar, "LOYALTY," track 6 on *DAMN*, feat. Rihanna. Los Angeles: Top Dawg Entertainment, Aftermath, and Interscope Records, 2017.

Kendrick Lamar, "Not Like Us," single. Santa Monica, CA: Interscope Records, 2024.

Kingsolver, Barbara. *Demon Copperhead*. New York, NY: Harper, 2022.

Madigan, Tim *The Burning: Massacre, Destruction, and the Tulsa Race Riot of 1921*. New York: Thomas Dunne Books/St. Martin's Griffin, 2001.

Masters, Brooke A. "Man Gets Life in 1997 Slaying." *The Washington Post*, January 14, 2000.

Mathewes-Green, Frederica. "Whatever Happened to Repentance?" *Christianity Today*, February 4, 2002. https://www.christianitytoday.com/2002/02/whatever-happened-to-repentance.

Michael Jackson, "P.Y.T. (Pretty Young Thing)" track 9 on *Thriller*. New York: Epic Records, 1982.

Mike Tyson, interview by John Saraceno, *USA Today*, January 11, 2004.

Mill, John Stuart. *Inaugural Address Delivered to the University of St. Andrews*. London, England: Longmans, Green, Reader, and Dyer, 1867.

National Retail Federation. "Halloween Spending to Reach Record $12.2 Billion as Participation Exceeds Pre-Pandemic Levels," *National Retail Federation*, September 20, 2023. https://nrf.com/media-center/press-releases/halloween-spending-reach-record-122-billion-participation-exceeds-pre

Newton, John. "Amazing Grace," number 41 in *Olney Hymns*. London, England: W. Oliver, 1779.

Niebuhr, Reinhold. "The Serenity Prayer, 1943," in *The Essential Reinhold Niebuhr: Selected Essays and Addresses*, ed. Robert McAfee Brown. New Haven, CT: Yale University Press, 1986.

Nietzsche, Friedrich. *Beyond Good and Evil: Prelude to a Philosophy of the Future*, translated by Helen Zimmern. London, England: George Allen & Unwin, 1909.

Nina Simone, "Don't Let Me Be Misunderstood," track 1 on *Broadway-Blues-Ballads*. Memphis, TN: Phillips, 1964.

Lanier, Sidney. *The Poems of Sidney Lanier*. New York: Charles Scribner's Sons, 1884.

Leap of Faith, dir. by Richard Pearce. Hollywood, CA: Paramount Pictures, 1992.

Lin-Fisher, Betty. "Mother's Day Gift Budget: How to Celebrate Without Going Into Debt." *USA Today*, May 10, 2024. https://www.usatoday.com/story/money/shopping/2024/05/10/mothers-day-gift-budget-2024/73617893007

Lockley, Thomas and Geoffrey Giard. *African Samurai: The True Story of Yasuke, a Legendary Black Warrior in Feudal Japan*. New York: Hanover Square, 2019.

Loewen, James W. *Sundown Towns: A Hidden Dimension of American Racism*. New York: The New Press, 2005.

O'Connor, Flannery. *The Habit of Being: Letters of Flannery O'Connor*. New York: Farrar, Straus and Giroux, 1979.

OutKast, "Ms. Jackson," track 6 on *Stankonia*. Atlanta, GA: LaFace Records, 2000.

Palmer, Thomas H. *The Teacher's Manual*. Philadelphia: American Book Company, 1840.

Peterson, Eugene H. *A Long Obedience in the Same Direction: Discipleship in an Instant Society*. Downers Grove, IL: InterVarsity, 2024.

Prince, "Purple Rain," track 9 on *Purple Rain*. Burbank, CA: Warner Bros., 1984.

Redmoon, Ambrose. "No Peaceful Warriors!", *Gnosis: A Journal of the Western Inner Traditions*, no. 21 (Fall 1991): 11.

Roosevelt, Eleanor "It Is Not Fair to Ask of Others What You Are Not Willing to Do Yourself," *My Day*, June 15, 1946. https://www2.gwu.edu/~erpapers/myday/displaydoc.cfm?_y=1946&_f=md000366

Santayana, George. *The Life of Reason: Reason in Common Sense*. New York: Charles Scribner's Sons, 1905.

Sayers, Devon M. and Shawn Nottingham, and Emma Tucker. "4 Law Enforcement Officers Were Killed in Shooting at a Home in Charlotte, North Carolina." *CNN*, April 29, 2024. https://www.cnn.com/2024/04/29/us/officers-shot-charlotte-north-carolina/index.html

Segal, Erich. *Love Story*. New York: Harper Perennial, 2004.

Shaft, dir. by Gordon Parks. Beverly Hills: Metro-Goldwyn-Mayer, 1971.

Shari Lewis, "The Song That Doesn't End," track 2 on *Lamb Chop's Sing-Along, Play-Along*. Santa Monica, CA: A&M Records, 1992.

Slattery, Juli. *Rethinking Sexuality: God's Design and Why It Matters*. Multnomah Books, 2018.

Solzhenitsyn, Aleksandr. *The Gulag Archipelago: 1918–1956*, trans. by Thomas Whitney. New York: Harper & Row, 1973.

Spafford, Horatio G. "It Is Well with My Soul," 1873, in *The Baptist Hymnal*. Nashville: LifeWay Worship, 2008.

Stengle, Jamie and Josh Kelety. "CrossFit Games Competitor Lazar Dukic Dies During Swimming Event at Texas Lake." *Associated Press*, August 8, 2024. https://apnews.com/article/crossfit-competition-death-texas-lake-74b2aaac5962ce35dc40a3838a9a4076

Taylor, Gardner C. *How to Preach a Sermon*. Grand Rapids, MI: Zondervan, 2005.

Taylor Swift, "Anti-Hero", track 3 on *Midnights*. Santa Monica, CA: Republic Records, 2022.

The Buggles, "Video Killed the Radio Star," track 2 on *The Age of Plastic*. New York: Island Records, 1980.

The Clinton Affair, dir. by Blair Foster .New York: A&E, 2018.

The Commodores, "Brick House," on track 6 of *Commodores*. Detroit, MI: Motown, 1977.

The Cosby Show, season 1, episode 2, "Goodbye Mr. Fish," dir. by Jay Sandrich, aired September 27, 1984, on *NBC*.

The Equalizer, dir. by Antonie Fuqua. Culver City, CA: Columbia Pictures, 2014.

The Incredibles, dir. by Brad Bird. Burbank, CA: Walt Disney Home Entertainment, 2005.

The Mighty Mouse Playhouse, dir. by Connie Rasinski. Terrytoons/20th Century Fox Television, *CBS*, 1955–67.

The Shirelles, "Mama Said," track 3 on *20 Greatest Hits*. Nashville, TN: Scepter Records, 1961.

The Warriors, dir. by Walter Hill. Los Angeles, CA: Paramount, 1979.

Thomason, Kristen. "In Post-Christian Germany, Taylor Swift Music Brings People to Church." *Baptist News Global*, June 18, 2024. https://baptistnews.com/article/in-post-christian-germany-taylor-swift-music-brings-people-to-church

Twain, Mark. *Pudd'nhead Wilson and Other Tales*. New York, NY: Oxford University Pres, 1992.

Usher, "Good Good," track 1 on *Coming Home*. Mega/Gamma, 2024

Walker, Rob. "Don McLean on the Tragedy Behind 'American Pie': 'I Cried for Two Years.'" *The Guardian*, October 22, 2020. https://www.theguardian.com/music/2020/oct/22/don-mclean-american-pie-its-meaning-family-deaths-tragedy-60s

Ward, Paula Reed. "Stowe Man Gets at Least 21 Years in Prison for Killing 2-Year-Old Girl." *TribLIVE*, December 30, 2022. https://triblive.com/local/stowe-man-gets-at-least-21-years-in-prison-for-killing-2-year-old-girl

Wells-Wilbon, Rhonda and Nigel D. Jackson, and Jerome H. Schiele. "Lessons From the Maafa: Rethinking the Legacy of Slain Hip-Hop Icon Tupac Shakur." *Journal of Black Studies* 40, no. 4 (March 2010): 509–26.

Whodini, "Big Mouth," track on 4 *Escape*. New York: Jive Records, 1984.

Wilde, Oscar. "The Decay of Lying," *The Nineteenth Century* 25, no. 147 (January 1889): 36–56

Wu-Tang Clan, "C.R.E.A.M.," track 8 on *Enter the Wu-Tang (36 Chambers)*. New York, NY: Loud Records, 1993.

Xavier University of Louisiana. "Making the Impossible, Possible: Ne'Kiya Jackson, Who Submitted Proof of 'Impossible' Mathematical Equation, Will Be Attending Xavier University of Louisiana." *Xavier University of Louisiana*, August 15, 2023. https://www.xula.edu/news/2023/08/making-the-impossible-possible-nekiya-jackson-who-submitted-proof-of-impossible-mathematical-equation-will-be-attending-xavier-university-of-louisiana.html

"Annie Johnson Flint, Dead; Widely Known Poet: Bedridden for 30 Years," *The New York Times*, September 10, 1932.

"The Addams Family Goes to School," *The Addams Family*, season 1, dir. by Arthur Hiller. Aired September 18, 1964, on *ABC*.

www.ingramcontent.com/pod-product-compliance
Lightning Source LLC
Chambersburg PA
CBHW070742160426
43192CB00009B/1545